This school-based effort to cope more productively with certain problems in educational improvement is discussed in considerable detail. With the primary focus on staff development processes in and among schools, Dr. Bentzen and her associates not only describe DDAE (dialogue, decision making, action, and evaluation) but also show its relationship to other attributes of staff renewal.

As Dr. Goodlad, Director of the Research Division of |I|D|E|A|, put it, "If we come out of this having successfully changed some schools, but we don't know how, then we will have failed in this project. But if our attempts to change the schools succeed or fail, and we can explain pretty well how it happened, then the project will have been a success."

Dr. Mary M. Bentzen has been an elementary school teacher and administrator and conducted field research in education as a member of the staff at UCLA. At |I|D|E|A| she was coordinator of the Study of Educational Change and is presently participating in a new study of schooling in the United States. In collaboration with her husband, Dr. Bentzen also produces documentary films in education.

Jacket design by John L. Horton

McGRAW-HILL BOOK COMPANY
1221 Avenue of the Americas
New York, N.Y. 10020

CHANGING SCHOOLS:
THE MAGIC FEATHER PRINCIPLE

|I|D|E|A| REPORTS ON SCHOOLING
JOHN I. GOODLAD, *General Editor and Director*

EARLY SCHOOLING SERIES
Assisted by Jerrold M. Novotney

SERIES ON EDUCATIONAL CHANGE
Assisted by Kenneth A. Tye

CHANGING SCHOOLS: THE MAGIC FEATHER PRINCIPLE

Mary M. Bentzen
and Associates:
James J. Bishop
Gary J. Hoban
Ann Lieberman
Bette Overman
Alice Z. Seeman
David A. Shiman
Kenneth A. Sirotnik

Foreword by
Samuel G. Sava
Executive Director |I|D|E|A|

Introduction by
John I. Goodlad

A CHARLES F. KETTERING FOUNDATION PROGRAM

MCGRAW-HILL BOOK COMPANY
New York   St. Louis   San Francisco   Düsseldorf
London   Mexico   Sydney   Toronto

Library of Congress Cataloging in Publication Data

Bentzen, Mary M.
  Changing schools.

  (|I|D|E|A| reports on schooling. Early schooling series) (|I|D|E|A| reports on schooling. Series on educational change)
  "A Charles F. Kettering Foundation Program."
  1. School personnel management. 2. Decision-making in school management. 3. Individualized instruction.
  I. Bishop, James J. II. Title. III. Series: Institute for Development of Educational Activities. Early schooling series.

LB2831.5.B46   371.2   74-14527
ISBN 0-07-004821-5

CHANGING SCHOOLS:
The Magic Feather Principle

by Mary M. Bentzen

Everyone remembers the fable of Dumbo, the baby circus elephant. A little mouse convinced Dumbo to use his large ears as wings by giving him a feather, a magic feather, that would enable him to fly. Dumbo trusted his friend and so could fly, even without the feather, as he soon discovered. At last he had self-confidence.

This fable tells something important about principals and teachers as well, and it suggests a critical question for educational researchers. How can outside resources and stimulation be provided for schools which will encourage and enable them to try something different, to fly on their own? To answer this question, the authors decided to try the principle of the magic feather, to help schools to help themselves, to help them to realize that their success was due to their own efforts and abilities and not to outside expertise. This philosophy guided a five-year association with eighteen elementary and intermediate schools in the League of Cooperating Schools—the Study of Educational Change and School Improvement (SECSI).

"In writing this book, we have tried to give the reader a feeling for the process we went through—confronting questions that had to be answered in order to get on with the job, trying out answers which led to more questions, and so on. We were supposed to bring about change and to study what happened, and we were to accomplish these two tasks in a way that would add to our understanding of why and how schools do or do not change."

Development of Edu-
e of the Charles F.

onstructive change in
e primary operant for
ion.

ctive changes for the
lieves strongly in the
changes.

G. Chollar

t and
ecutive Officer
F. Kettering Foundation

This book is for the principals and teachers of the League of Cooperating Schools in commemoration of the new world we made together.

CONTENTS

FOREWORD

This volume is part of a series reporting on the five-year Study of Educational Change and School Improvement, conducted by the Institute for Development of Educational Activities, Inc. (|I|D|E|A|). This study's purpose has been to develop positive and workable ways to improve American education; its findings and conclusions have led, we believe, to one of the most promising efforts to help our schools help themselves.

Frustration was an all-too-common expression among educators during the 1960s as they tried to install one or more of the dozens of "innovations" promoted during the decade. Many had actually installed new curricula, new teaching techniques, and new modes of school organization. The frustrating factor was that so many of these innovations were abandoned, usually within two years or less after they had been introduced.

|I|D|E|A| was established by the Charles F. Kettering Foundation in 1965 as its educational affiliate and was given the specific mission of accelerating the pace of change in education. Rather than advocate yet another collection of "innovations" based on the best insights then available, we decided to begin by examining the total context in which change was to take place. Under the direction of Dr. John I. Goodlad, |I|D|E|A|'s Research Division selected eighteen schools from eighteen Southern California districts, the "League of Cooperating Schools," to participate in the design and testing of a new strategy for educational improvement. The volumes in this |I|D|E|A| series on change report on the variety of human and organizational influences that operated within this new social system of schools.

To highlight here the basic findings of this study would be premature. Each finding must be put in context before its significance can be appreciated. The point to be stressed here is that while a school must have the desire to change before it can do so, desire is not enough—it must also understand what Dr. Goodlad calls "the ecology of change," the complex of environmental factors that can defeat a school staff's most conscientious efforts to improve.

In view of continuing public criticism of the schools, our apparent inability to rescue many of our children from academic mediocrity or failure, and the widely felt need for more tested and proven innovations, this may be one of the most important studies of education ever undertaken. But pedagogic literature is littered with the corpses of past studies, many of them excellent, that failed to affect educational practice. Will this one make any difference?

We believe so. In addition to issuing results of the study, |I|D|E|A| has incorporated this change strategy into a school improvement program aimed at individualizing education, a new model of school organization necessary to permit the accommodation of individual differences, and an intensive, clinical training component for teachers and administrators. We call this the |I|D|E|A| Change Program for Individually Guided Education (IGE).

As this volume goes to press, more than 1,000 elementary and secondary schools in thirty-five states have adopted the IGE program, and the program has spread to American-sponsored schools in approximately two dozen other countries. It is clear that IGE, together with the research and developmental work on which it rests, already has had an influence on American education.

On behalf of |I|D|E|A| and the Charles F. Kettering Foundation, I wish to express gratitude to the school board officials, administrators, teachers, and parents whose cooperation made the Study of Change possible. They have advanced the day when change will become a way of life in education rather than a sporadic, temporary, and usually disappointing confrontation with forces that we have not previously understood.

Samuel G. Sava
Executive Director
|I|D|E|A|

INTRODUCTION

By the mid 1950s, educational reform in the United States was in high gear. The schools had been prodded and probed in every aspect and from every possible angle. There was nothing wrong, most reformers thought, that could not be corrected by new curriculum content, continuous progress plans, individualized instruction, or some other change. Never before had there been such a plethora of ideas, materials, gadgets, and innovative projects. Never before had there been such a supply of money for educational improvement.

But to many of us close to or involved in this reform of the schools, not everything looked rosy. Slippage from concept to implementation regarding such concepts as structure of the disciplines and inductive or discovery learning was monumental. There was a "gee whiz" superficiality about some of the hastily put together conferences; experts appeared full-blown overnight; there was an impatience with serious, questioning dialogue. The rhetoric frequently sounded like advertisements for real estate or airline travel. My associations with schools and their personnel suggested that the rhetoric and the reality of school improvement were far apart.

These associations and some of the studies of teacher education, school organization, and curriculum development in which I was involved raised questions in my mind. Why was the slippage from concept to classroom practice so great and so rapid? Why did visitors to our University Elementary School at UCLA perceive themselves to be incapable of bringing about change in their schools back home? Why do schools resist reforms which appear to have so much to commend them? I wanted some insights into such questions.

At about the time these queries were bouncing about in my reveries, I had what turned out to be a most consequential lunch with two vice-presidents of the Kettering Foundation, Edwin H. Vause and the late Charles F. Kettering II. They spoke about bringing into existence what became, in the following year, the Institute for Development of Educational Activities, Inc. (|I|D|E|A|). I spoke about my concerns for educational reform expressed above and the skeleton of a plan for simultaneously following up my queries and effecting productive change in schools. Our interests touched at several points. Subsequently, when the Kettering Foundation created |I|D|E|A|, it gave me a grant to put meat on the bones of my skeleton. A year later, my proposal became the major project of the newly formed Research Division of |I|D|E|A|.

As part of the proposal outlined for Mr. Vause and Mr. Kettering, I brought together some twenty-five superintendents of as many school districts in Southern California. The plan put before them was deliberately general. In essence, it called for them to designate one school—just one—in each of their respective districts to be a member of a proposed League of Cooperating Schools. Six months later, the League, consisting of eighteen schools, was in existence.

There was a *quid pro quo* in the proposed collaborative relationship. Each school, in seeking to improve itself, would permit us to observe and analyze the process. We, in turn, would provide certain mechanisms of support and, above all, would feed back the results of our inquiries into the ongoing process of change in the schools to the extent that teachers and principals saw such information as useful. We promoted no particular innovations, although we made no attempt to hide our biases. We gave no consultative help, in the sense of providing specialized, substantive, or technological assistance with instructional problems. We did provide bibliographies on problem areas identified by the schools, and we certainly supported the schools in their efforts to define and solve their problems.

This school-based effort to cope more productively with certain problems in educational improvement is discussed here in considerable detail. We referred to it as DDAE—dialogue, decision making, action, and evaluation. In this volume, Dr. Bentzen and her associates not only describe this process but also show its relationship to other attributes of staff renewal. Each school was supported in its efforts by the other schools making up the League and by the hub of this new social system—the offices from which we sought to maintain communication and provide encouragement. Some of this support was visible and tangible; but perhaps more important, we are beginning to realize, was the less tangible presence of people not belonging to any one school but concerned about what occurred in each and all—call it "tender loving care," if you will. Perhaps we constituted the equivalent of the mouse in the delightful tale of Dumbo from which the title of this book is derived.

The League of Cooperating Schools existed as a formally constituted entity for five years. Then, several of the schools became part of a consortium of schools brought together by the Graduate School of Education at UCLA largely for teacher education purposes. In several instances, individual schools joined with others nearby not previously in the League to form "Little Leagues." Even with the formal project terminated, we have maintained considerable communication with the League schools, frequently arranging for visitors to see the schools and occasionally involving former League schools in other projects. Many of the principals and teachers went on to posts of greater responsibility. Although these people left behind tangible evidence of school improvement, there is little doubt in our minds that what changed most were the hundreds of individuals involved.

What went on and what we learned about educational change is summarized in seven volumes and a series of documentary films, *The League.* One of these volumes was written by teachers in the schools and reports what they learned and did about individualizing instruction. The others, like this one, describe the general theory of the school improvement strategy, research procedures, techniques for leadership training, various conclusions from this cooperative endeavor, and so on. The present volume focuses primarily on staff development processes in and among schools.

Our central thesis from the beginning, albeit rather dimly perceived at the outset, was that the adults in schools ultimately must learn to help themselves. Nobody can or should do the job for them. This means that they must strive together, preferably with students and parents, to make their settings for daily work better places for human beings to spend a large portion of each day. This means that they must think together, plan together, decide together, and act together in dealing with the problems inevitably inherent in schools. This is not easy; in fact, it is extraordinarily difficult. Consequently, those seeking to so engage themselves need all the help they can get, and those who have not yet begun require encouragement. For schools to change, there must be an internal process and a structure to support and sustain it.

This process of continuing self-renewal is not being proposed here as a substitute for the several kinds of change efforts initiated and conducted outside of schools such as, for example, the research and development (R&D) model. We need more and better products in the form of curricula, evaluation procedures, instructional paradigms, and so on. But without a readiness for them and a desire to find better ways on the part of school staffs, even the very best of what enlightened R&D produces is rejected or ignored. What we envision as desirable is a school staff responding to its own problems and needs and then looking outside of itself for assistance from a wide array of available resources. Under these conditions, we believe, innovations will be selected and implemented; the fit between the rhetoric and the reality of change will improve.

Although assisted by many people, especially those listed as associates, Dr. Bentzen wrote what follows. She has managed to convey our probing, inquiring approach into the general strategy described and our experiences with the eighteen schools in a simple, almost homey style. She captures the spirit of mutuality accompanying our relationship with principals and teachers. She makes it clear that we began with the rudiments of a strategy—the bare bones of an approach proceeding first from inside each school—and gradually developed it to the point where its central elements are clear and firm enough to be transportable.

It is our conviction that the decade of the 1970s, unlike the 1960s, is a period of catching up on some of our previous, excellent ideas for improving schools. Our ideas, for a time, ran too far ahead of reality. This is a time for taking stock and for reconstructing. Our experiences with this process, extending over a period of six years, might be of some help to school staffs wishing to engage in the necessary tasks and to groups outside of schools wishing to help. What follows is a highly readable effort to share some of these experiences with you.

John I. Goodlad

ACKNOWLEDGMENTS

It was the task of those whose names are listed on the title page first to review the information collected by the staff of this project (themselves and others) over a period of five years, then to say what that information meant to them. We parceled out the work among us.

Bette Overman, Alice Seeman, Jim Bishop, and Ken Sirotnik dealt with the quantitative data. As data manager, Bette Overman prepared all the basic summaries of data with which we started, and at the end of the line designed the appendices. In between she was an invaluable member of our almost continual brainstorming sessions and, miraculously, never lost her patience on occasions past counting when one of us would suggest that maybe we might look at something in a slightly different way, if only the data could be reorganized just a little, you know—. Alice Seeman, who had borne the main responsibility for developing our measurements of the problem solving process in the schools, performed the fundamental analyses for and wrote the first drafts of the sections concerning that process and its relationships with personal characteristics of school staffs. Jim Bishop did intensive study of formal and informal organization within schools and wrote the first drafts of the material which deals with organizational patterns and teacher socialization. Ken Sirotnik served throughout as our mentor in measurement and data analysis. He has written all the technical information which appears on instruments and statistical procedures and is responsible for any success we may have had in staying within the boundaries of the simple descriptive measures which were appropriate to this study.

Gary Hoban, Ann Lieberman, and David Shiman worked on the non-quantitative data. Gary Hoban wrote the account of the initial reactions of school district personnel to the project. Ann Lieberman and David Shiman prepared preliminary summaries of field notes and other historical records and provided valuable fill-in data drawn from their extensive experience with teachers during the project.

Always with us as we went about making a book were the rest of our staff colleagues. Lillian Drag, director of our professional library, answered hundreds of questions for us, searching literature and library records, and assisted us in reconstructing a number of critical incidents in the project. Our editor, Judy Golub, quietly and firmly led us through the final stages of production, always encouraging in a job that we sometimes feared might never end. Carmen Culver time after time responded to requests for help, and her critical reading of several sections of the manuscript was extremely valuable. Kenneth Tye, our program officer, provided data from his work with the school principals and unfailing administrative understanding and support in the most trying delays and frustration that beset our efforts. To John Goodlad, of course, go our deepest thanks for the opportunity to speak our piece. His advice on the manuscript was always directed to helping us clarify our thinking. The reader should not assume that John agrees with all the interpretations which are offered in this book.

For the preparation of the successive drafts of the manuscript we were lucky to be able to draw upon the skills, the forbearance, and friendship of other members of the staff. In the early stages Joan Rydbeck made order out of the different versions of different parts by different people. Her great skills in manuscript production delighted the eye; her wide knowledge about the project was enormous practical help; and her confidence in the ultimate outcome of our efforts didn't hurt a bit. All the while Paula DeFusco managed ably and cheerfully to keep up with our demands for data tables, and Carol Mason was an unfailing back-up for the emergency jobs that became the rule. The production of the final manuscript we owe to the patient understanding of Masako Oshita, who somehow shepherded it through during a period of considerable pressure on the typing staff.

Some of the thinking that has gone into this book was stimulated by people who were not on our writing staff. Our perspective of our own project was broadened by the records left by former staff members and our recollection of conversations with them. In addition, although few specific references are noted in the text, we acknowledge the stimulation that came from reports on other studies of change processes, principally the work of Seymour Sarason, Matthew Miles, Ronald Havelock, and W. W. Charters and some of his colleagues at the Center for the Advanced Study of Educational Administration. Of course, the fact that these encounters with the thoughts of others on other projects were very valuable to us does not mean that we always agreed with them. Nor can we at all claim that our reading of the events in our own project will in all respects agree with interpretations that may be made by our former colleagues. An obvious point, but one that we want to make explicit: the reader should recognize that this story could have been cast in other molds.

Without all the people mentioned here this book could not have come into being, but the shape that it has finally taken is my responsibility. To my associates I feel a gratitude that I hope I can express in actions since I certainly cannot express it in words.

It is customary at this point to acknowledge the forbearance and assistance of one's spouse. In this case, my husband was totally involved in making a series of film reports about the same project that this book describes. Considering the agonies of both film-making and book-writing, we figure that we came out about even and both of us a bit ahead of where each of us would have been alone.

Mary M. Bentzen

ONE

THE INTERVENTION STRATEGY

CHAPTER 1

THE STUDY OF CHANGE

When we were a year and a half or so down the road on our project to study change processes in a group of elementary schools, someone pointed out that the way in which we were beginning to think and talk about our work was reminiscent of the modern fable of Dumbo, the baby circus elephant.* The aptness of the remark brought into focus for us the image that had been flickering throughout our confrontation with our task. We proceeded thereafter with a greater understanding of what we might be about.

You will recall that Dumbo had a marvelous natural gift. He could fly. In the beginning, however, he didn't know that he could fly. His ability was due to his large ears, which could serve as wings; but since such big ears were not the usual case among elephants, Dumbo was for some time ridiculed by all the other elephants. This continual putdown was devastating to Dumbo's self-concept. He considered himself a failure as an elephant, unti he was befriended by a mouse who spotted Dumbo's true talent. But because Dumbo was afraid to try much of anything on his own, the mouse first had to convince him to use his ears as wings. So the mouse gave Dumbo a feather, a magic feather, he said, that would enable Dumbo to fly. Dumbo trusted his friend and so believed in the feather. With the feather he began to fly and win great praise from all who watched him. One day, to his horror, Dumbo dropped the feather in midflight. As he fell he heard his friend call out, "You don't need the feather! You can fly!" Dumbo tried, and he flew. At last he believed in himself.

The fable, we think, tells something important about principals and teachers in our schools. We will not try to trace all the possible

---

* The person who noted the similarity (at a cocktail party which occurred during the official social life of the project) was on the central staff of one of the school districts associated with the study. It is unfortunate that I did not know his name, for I would like to thank the gentleman publicly for his contribution. M. B.

points of similarity, but the Dumbo story represents our approach in the project that will be reported on in this volume. We, the researchers, thought that school staffs could do more than they believed they could do. We believed that they were capable of daily marvels.

This belief guided our five-year association with eighteen elementary and intermediate schools. To explain how it did so will take most of this book. We will begin by describing the project in which the association took place.

THE SECSI PROJECT

The project was called the Study of Educational Change and School Improvement At first we didn't notice the obvious acronym, but after it was brought to our attention, we happily referred to ourselves as the SECSI project and the SECSI staff. We, the SECSI staff, were members of the research staff of the Institute for Development of Educational Activities (|I|D|E|A|).[1]

The initial aim of the SECSI project was to study what happened when schools tried to change. What sorts of problems did principals and teachers see facing them? How did they cope with their problems? Why was it so difficult to effect change in schools? That it was difficult seemed pretty obvious. By the time our project began, the notion that innovations were needed in schools had been around for some years, and quite a bit of money and effort had already gone into trying to change schools. The success of these programs had been spectacularly small. A good many different reasons were offered for the lack of success, but in the accumulating reports about innovations that had been attempted, one deficiency was clear. There simply did not exist adequate descriptions of the daily events that occurred in the schools which were the targets of would-be change programs.[2] It was primarily to draw a rudimentary sketch of how pressure to change looked in the everyday garb of school life that John I. Goodlad, Director of the |I|D|E|A| Research Division, initiated the SECSI project and brought the SECSI staff together.

Several possibilities were open to Goodlad for a study of the ordinary events in schools which were relevant to attempts at innovation. Our project could select at random a group of schools and simply observe if, what, and how they tried to change or whether they resisted change. Or, we could study some group of schools that were participants in a specific innovative program. Or, we could ourselves intervene in a group of schools to try to bring about change and, at the same time, study what happened to those schools. Goodlad chose the last course for the SECSI project to follow.

From the start, then, we were committed to two tasks: *to effect change and to study change*. This course seemed to offer a distinct advantage. By grappling ourselves with problems of how to change schools we would surely become more sensitive to those features of school life which stood in our way and those which could be called on for support. Insofar as this greater awareness would help us lay bare certain regularities of schools under pressure to change, the task of trying to effect change should contribute to the task of studying change. But in the proposed course of action lay, too, an obvious danger. It's easy to get caught up in trying to make something work; we could become so involved in trying to bring about change that we might neglect to pay careful attention to what was happening in the schools. What *we* hoped to learn, however, was to be the paramount aim. As Goodlad often put it, "If we come out of this having successfully changed some schools, but we don't know how, then we will have failed in this project. But if our attempts to change the schools succeed *or fail*, and we can explain pretty well how it happened, then the project will have been a success." We had cause to remember this admonition on several occasions.

In addition to our commitment to the twin tasks of effecting and studying change, there was a third characteristic of the SECSI project which is crucial for the reader to understand. Our intervention in the schools was directed only at the interactions of principals and teachers and was evaluated only in terms of those interactions. We defined our task as trying to bring about and study change processes as they appeared in the adult life of the schools. We did not work with pupils and we did not systematically describe or measure teachers' work with children. The decision to limit the project to an investigation of the behavior of the school staffs rested on a position which has been presented elsewhere by Goodlad. In that presentation Goodlad summarizes the need for a broader range of subject matter in studies of schooling.

> Goals for education and schooling tend to be stated in the form of some desired changes or accomplishments for students: citizenship, work habits, understanding selected concepts, and the like. Consequently, efforts to improve tend to focus on specific pedagogical procedures and the measurement of pupil outcomes, with some accom-

panying feedback designed to provide information for revision. This effort to refine ends and means and the relationship between them is exceedingly important but insufficient. It fails to account for other factors which may be of considerable importance. . . .

The ultimate criterion for judging school programs is, indeed, what happens to students in them. Unfortunately, however, exclusive preoccupation with this criterion often has led to short-term experiments and premature rejection or endorsement of this or that technique. Meanwhile, the general context of schooling within which the experiments are conducted, which probably has a great deal to do with what is happening to the students, remains unchanged. We often merely tinker when more fundamental examination and rehabilitation of the organism is called for.

Current concern and a growing body of evidence regarding the functioning of schools suggest that, in addition to precise ends-means relationships of goals and instructional procedures, we must devote attention to the major variables making up the character of schools.[3]

It seemed to us that the ways in which school staffs live their professional lives is a legitimate subject for an inquiry into the problems of changing schools. Without denying that the ultimate proof of whatever pudding we offer will have to come from demonstrations which relate it to desirable pupil outcomes, we simply state that we have used the resources of one project to get a clearer picture of part of the crucial background and conditions of those outcomes.

The SECSI project was first conceived as a cooperative effort of |I|D|E|A| Research, a group of eighteen schools, and the Graduate School of Education of the University of California at Los Angeles. As it turned out, the UCLA School of Education was able to play only an initiating role in the project, so our report will focus on the two chief actors in the story, the schools and the SECSI staff.

THE LEAGUE OF COOPERATING SCHOOLS

In 1966, at the beginning of the study, the group of schools that participated in the SECSI project was christened the League of Cooperating Schools. The League members were eighteen elementary and intermediate schools that lay within a 150-mile radius of the |I|D|E|A| office.[4] Each school belonged to a different school district, and the eighteen districts were spread over nine counties in Southern California. Schools were chosen to participate in the League so that the group would represent, as nearly as possible, a microcosm of American public schooling. Goodlad and his staff negotiated with the districts before the start of the project to select schools that would give us this microcosm.

The League Districts

The first step in forming the League was taken by Goodlad and Howard Wilson, then dean of UCLA's Graduate School of Education, who held a dinner meeting at a local hotel for representatives, mostly superintendents, from the central administrative offices of the various districts which had been selected to participate in the League. At this dinner meeting, Goodlad explained to the guest administrators the thinking behind the League of Cooperating Schools concept as well as the advantages involved in joining such a consortium. Essentially this meeting was a persuasion session in which the different school districts, through their superintendents or their representatives, were asked to join the League and to support, in a variety of ways, its objectives.

At first this meeting, in which representatives of a number of divergent school districts met to discuss a collaborative grouping among themselves, was a novelty. But the intent, obviously, was to do more than provide a pleasant business dinner for administrators. While virtually all the administrators in attendance readily subscribed to the high ideals involved in working with other districts to bring about positive innovation in a school within each of their districts, the real test of their commitment came after the meeting. To join the League and to accept its high-sounding objectives meant more than the good wishes expressed after dinner; it meant support of a district office for educational change within the framework of a new intervention strategy. District support would have to include whatever financial aid was necessary, for Goodlad made it clear that |I|D|E|A| would provide no funds to League schools.

The initial enthusiasm expressed by administrators from the districts which ultimately joined the League was quite heartening. All the district administrators were eager to become associated with a project which had the blessings of the UCLA Graduate School of Education and which had the support of the Kettering Foundation's |I|D|E|A|. Thus, the League project, at the beginning, started with a close relationship between the |I|D|E|A| research staff and the eighteen district offices.

There were, however, a few superintendents who at first expressed a cautious reserve about joining the League. One superintendent, for example, made a point of communicating his belief that educational research and research institutions generally deal with issues that are irrelevant to individual schools. This reservation was typical of the caution of several other superintendents who were uneasy about their status relationships to the |I|D|E|A| and UCLA staffs which were to coordinate the League activities. However, once reassurances had been given, even these few hesitant superintendents quickly decided to commit their districts to participation in the League. For the most part, judging from the favorable publicity given to the project in each of the participating districts, the desire of the various central administrations to gain prestige from their affiliation with |I|D|E|A|, Goodlad, and UCLA as well as to effect change in their districts was strong.

After these superintendents agreed that they would have a school in their district participate in our project, before any public acknowledgment of their desired involvement with the League could be made, they had to secure the official approval of their respective boards of education. Formal board approval of the project involved the acceptance of the League Agreement which specified that the district office would:

1 Designate, for the duration of the project, one school as its representative unit for innovation and research
2 Establish community support and understanding of the district's participation in the League of Cooperating Schools
3 Allow the individual school to deviate, where desirable and feasible, from general school district policies
4 Promote harmony among other schools in the district toward the League school
5 Provide released time to principals and teachers for League activities
6 Provide funds for
   a Travel expenditures for principals
   b Substitute time
   c Additional secretarial help
   d Additional educational resources

In all the districts selected, the League Agreement was accepted, and by the spring of 1966 the League of Cooperating Schools officially came into being. The various superintendents, with other members of the district office, next had to select the school within their district which was to participate in the project as well as determine how much support should be given to these individual schools.

It was the intention of the |I|D|E|A| staff that the various district offices would designate the individual schools which were to participate in the League and that once the necessary district support had been given and special provisions had been made, the chief interaction which was to ensue would be between the |I|D|E|A| interventionists and the local school staff. This is not to say that we at |I|D|E|A| wished to minimize the role of the district in the project; however, it does show that a certain flexible, less traditional authoritarian role of the central office was perceived to be a desirable prerequisite before meaningful intervention for change could begin to take place in the schools.

This desired flexible attitude on the part of the district offices was present in most cases but not all. Those offices which demonstrated a lack of flexibility first encountered difficulty in their method of selecting a school in the district to participate in the League. While most of the district offices consulted with the faculty, or at least with the principal of their League-designated school, several did not. Instead, several of the central administrations arbitrarily told a school it was to join the League of Cooperating Schools. One school so designated, which was to become a highly innovative member, originally balked at joining the League because of the superintendent's arbitrary decision that it participate in the project. In fact, this particular staff first learned of its involvement by reading a story about it in the local newspaper. This lack of consultation created initial hostility toward both the superintendent and |I|D|E|A|; indeed, most of the staff believed that the superintendent became involved in the project only to better his own image as an innovator. Later, however, the hostility in this particular case subsided as did less open demonstrations of a lack of desire to join the League in other schools.

Once the individual schools within each of the districts that were to participate had been identified, it became the task of the respective central offices not only to inform their communities of participation in the League but also to establish some degree of community support for each of these schools. Communication of the basic information about the League was not a difficult task for any of the district offices; all the central administrations were eager, at the outset of the project, to provide news releases to their local newspapers which presented them and the district in a favorable light. These newspaper stories did provide the positive public relations effect which many of the districts desired.

Establishing community support for the League schools, however, was a more complex matter and became the task of the individual school itself. While none of the district offices, to our knowledge, ever publicly denigrated participation in the League, none of these offices directly attempted beyond the initial press release to involve the community in the project.

It would appear safe to conclude that, up to this point, district involvement in the League, with the few exceptions noted above, was virtually the same in all the participating districts. The level of support not only on policy but also in matters of special financial and personnel help given by the central offices, however, did differ from district to district. This difference, to some degree, should have shown up in the ways the various League schools demonstrated their commitment and ability to innovate as well as their success or lack of success with the change process. Whether or not this turned out to be the case, of course, was of interest to us and will be discussed later.

The League Schools

Most of the varied conditions found in elementary schools throughout the United States were indeed found in the League. One of the League schools, for example, came from a district serving only 1,200 children, while another was in one of the largest school districts in the nation, providing for the education of more than 650,000 pupils. Other districts were found at almost every level within this broad range. The range of individual school sizes represented within the League was also broad. At the beginning of the five-year project the smallest League schools had student populations of little more than 200, while the largest consisted of 1,000 or more. Again, the League schools as a whole were spread throughout this range.

But size is not the only dimension on which schools differed in the League or, for that matter, elsewhere. The problems of teaching and of effective planning and decision making in schools may be aided or inhibited by the school plant itself. Among the League schools, the same diversity of physical working conditions as is found virtually everywhere in the country was represented. A third of the League schools were built during the period from 1925 to 1945. Others came into existence only in the last decade, and one League school building was completed in 1967, a year after the League project began. Among these eighteen schools could be found both the most traditional and the most modern of educational plants and facilities. Some were organized exclusively in terms of the traditional self-contained classroom unit; others had been designed to facilitate flexibility in the instructional enterprise. Some of the latter schools were constructed in the form of teaching "pods"; others had movable walls, learning centers, laboratories, and so on. Still other League schools had to operate with a large number of temporary structures, portable classrooms, and the like.

Another kind of diversity was found in the geographical regions and ethnic populations which the schools of the League served. One of the League schools, for example, was in an area with a large concentration of Mexican-American agricultural workers, and most of the children taught in this school were of Mexican-American descent. In other League schools, from one-fifth to one-third of the school population was black. A number of League schools had all-white student bodies. The geographic areas in which League schools were located included rural regions, centers of urban concentration, and rapidly growing suburban areas and "bedroom" communities surrounding Los Angeles and other Southern California cities.

The League teachers and principals themselves represented a broad range of personal characteristics. Most of the teachers were women, and most of the principals were men, as is true of elementary schools in general. But, for example, the average teacher age might be twenty-seven years at one League school and over forty-five years at another. Many League teachers started their careers in the League while many others had full teaching careers behind them. The wide range of experience represented by League teachers was apparent not only within the League as a whole but in individual schools as well. In a few schools the variation in teaching experience among faculty members was small, but in most it was relatively large. The principals also represented different levels of professional experience. A few were in their first jobs as principal; others had been administrators for more than fifteen years.

Finally, the League schools represented a variety of beliefs about what constituted good educational practice. Even though a major purpose of the SECSI project was to foster educational change in the single school, the League schools were not chosen for participation because they were considered innovative. A few League schools welcomed the opportunity to be in a group which was to try new ideas; many more League schools had little, if any, initial interest in such a venture. It is fair to say that the educational programs in League schools in 1966 were a reasonably good representation of the patterns of childhood schooling which could be found in this country at that time.

The League as a group provided a wide variety of settings in which we could both encourage and observe the processes of change. In order to illustrate these processes, we will refer to individual schools at times throughout this book. The reader will need background information about each school if he is to get a feeling for the situations in which our examples occurred. To this end we have provided a thumbnail description of each League school and have placed these descriptions in alphabetical order by name of school in Appendix A. We suggest that the reader can, with this arrangement, quickly find information about any school which is used to illustrate a point in the text. In addition, for quick reference, the table on pages 14 and 15 presents basic information about each of the schools.

The descriptions in Appendix A include more than pictures of the schools as they were in 1966. Over any five-year period most organizations will undergo change, planned or unplanned. In the League schools there were changes quite apart from anything that our intervention might have intended. We note three major changes of this sort in the description of individual schools. First, principals and teachers came and went for a variety of personal reasons, more in some schools than in others. Second, the communities served by some schools changed in terms of size and socioeconomic and racial characteristics. Third, district offices made changes in the physical plant or in the organization of some of the League schools. Later in this book, we will talk about how these changes may have affected the kind of innovation which we wanted to bring about and how our intervention might have, after all, had something to do with those changes which we did not intend.

In addition to the League schools, two other groups of schools consented to provide us with information gathered from a number of questionnaires and a few interviews. The first of these groups is the Comparison schools. The Comparison schools consisted of one other school in each of the eighteen League districts. Each Comparison school was randomly selected from those schools in the district which were of comparable grade level and roughly the same size as the League school. (In two districts, where the League school was the only intermediate school, the Comparison school was selected from the elementary schools in the district.) The Comparison schools gave us data in the spring of 1970 and the spring of 1971. The second group of schools is the Out-of-State schools. These were thirteen elementary schools from four states other than California which volunteered to complete questionnaires for us in the spring of 1971. The Out-of-State schools represented several different kinds of school setting. Appendix B gives demographic information on Out-of-State schools. We are truly grateful to both of these groups of schools for their assistance in this study.

THE SECSI STAFF

Over the five years of the project, approximately forty persons were at one time or other members of the SECSI staff as senior staff members, research assistants, secretaries, and consultants. A few were associated for only short periods; a few were staff members from start to finish; most worked on the project for two to three years. In the world of American public schools the League approximated a microcosm; in the world of educational inquiry the SECSI staff represented most of the backgrounds and skills and most of the orientation toward research commonly found in the spectrum of projects which attempt to study and to improve schools. Our ranks encompassed "researchers" and "practitioners" and several divisions within each of these camps—researchers who favored designs for hard data and those who were inclined to softer methodologies; practitioners who had differing conceptions of the roles of principals and teachers and the role of change agent. Before we were through, our staff also included members outside the field of education. During the first two years, most of the staff members were people with experience in elementary school teaching and/or administration, and practitioners outnumbered researchers. Thereafter, a number of new staff members with research backgrounds were drawn from other areas, chiefly sociology, psychology, and business administration.

This change in the composition of the SECSI staff reflected the two main phases of the League study. The effort in the early years was to become familiar with the schools, to get to know the principals and teachers, to see what they saw as problems. In the early years, also,

THE LEAGUE SCHOOLS

Name	Principal	Approximate No. of Teachers		Approximate No. of Pupils		Grades		Approximate Percent Minority*		Urb./Sub./Rural	School Plant
		1966	1971	1966	1971	1966	1971	1966	1971		
Antigua	Steve M., 1966–71	20	20	470	470	K–6	K–6	20	20	Urban	Old†
Bell St.	Amanda Q., 1966–67 Peter M., 1967–71	20	20	450	450	K–6	K–6	60	60	Urban	Old
Country	Andy S., 1966–71	30	30	700	700	K–6	K–6	10	30	Suburban	New‡
Dewey Ave.	Stan M., 1966–68 Edith B., 1968–70 Stan M., 1970–71	30	35	1100	1100	K–6	K–6	10	10	Urban	Old
Fairfield	Ben U., 1966–71	45	45	1300	1300	K–8	K–8	95	95	Rural	Middle§
Frontier	Jason R., 1966–68 Tim M., 1968–69 Carl C., 1969–71	15	15	250	250	7–8	7–8	5	5	Rural	Middle
Hacienda	Jeff H., 1966–March '67 Chris M., March '67–71	15	30	450	760	K–8	K–8	5	5	Suburban	New
Independence	Duncan D., 1966–67 Arnold Z., 1967–71	30	30	900	900	K–6	K–3	20	60	Urban	Old
Indian Flat	Chet O., 1966–71	25	25	750	750	K–6	K–6	5	5	Suburban	New

School	Teacher(s)										Location	Plant
James	Joe A., 1966–71	20	20	650	650	3–6	3–6	15	15		Urban	Old
Mar Villa	Adam S., 1966–71	20	20	480	480	K–6	K–6	10	40		Urban	Old-Renovated
Middleton	Florence P., 1966–71	25	25	700	700	K–5	K–5	10	10		Suburban	Middle
Peace Valley	Everett W., 1966–68 Mike D., 1968–70 Roy R., 1970–71	30	50	800	1000	6–8	7–8	10	10		Suburban	New
Rainbow Hill	Gene G., 1966–71	20	20	430	430	K–6	K–6	5	5		Rural—Military base	New
Seastar	Dave W., 1966–Jan. '71 Paul S., Jan.–June 1971	25	25	800	800	K–6	K–6	20	20		Urban	Middle
Shadyside	Russ D., 1966–67 Lucy K., 1967–69 Brad C., 1969–71	20	20	500	500	K–6	K–3	10	60		Urban	Old
South	Alex R., 1966–70 Harry L., 1970–71	25	25	670	670	K–6	K–6	10	10		Urban	Middle
Woodacres	Jerry W., 1966–67 Leonard B., 1967–71	10	25	250	750	K–6	K–6	5	5		Suburban	New

* Black, Mexican-American, Oriental
† School plant is more than 15 years old
‡ School plant is 1–4 years old
§ School plant is 5–15 years old

the foundation had to be laid for the intervention strategy. These jobs seemed to require a staff with considerable practical experience in schooling. The majority of staff members during this period worked part-time and were graduate students in doctoral programs in UCLA's School of Education. All these research assistants, twelve men and one woman, had had teaching experience. They and several full-time staff members who came from the fields of educational administration and supervision carried out most of the work involving contacts with principals and teachers. At the same time a few full-time research specialists and part-time consultants worked on the development of research tactics.

The second phase of the project evolved as concepts were clarified about the new intervention strategy and about basic change-related processes which were being identified in the schools. During the last two years the SECSI staff was much smaller and included, as well as educators, members whose professional training was in sociology and psychology. In these last years, the two major tasks—intervention and research—did not so clearly divide the staff into two groups. All staff members during that time were involved both in contacts with schools and in designing and carrying out the study of what happened.

ORGANIZATION OF THIS BOOK

In writing this book, we have tried to give the reader a feeling for the process that we went through—confronting questions that had to be answered in order to get on with the job, trying out answers which led to more questions, and so on. We were supposed to try to bring about change and to study what happened, and we were to accomplish these two tasks in a way that would add to our understanding of why and how schools do or do not change. Our two tasks raised all sorts of questions, and we continually prepared tentative answers and tried to second-guess the next questions. Some answers held up, some failed; some anticipated questions never materialized. Other questions caught us off guard, and we had to decide whether or not we could afford to try to answer them. Finally, there were questions and answers that we didn't even recognize until the project was over.

The process of confronting questions and trying out answers, of course, occurs in many kinds of human activity; it is simply formalized in research projects. Most reports of research projects, however, convey very little of this process beyond the careful presentation of a set of questions and the findings related to those questions. Researchers who read such reports are often able to guess, on the basis of their own experience, what might have happened that was not reported, but in the eyes of nonresearchers, research projects and researchers have become austerely divorced from the daily muddle of problem solving with which they are familiar. We think that this popular image of research is unfortunate as well as inaccurate. In this book we have tried to inform the reader about our experiences in the SECSI project in addition to reporting our findings.

From the outset, the SECSI project was conceived as one which would change to some extent as it went along. John Goodlad expected ideas to be born and grow, some to live and some to die in the course of the five years of the study. Our major tasks were clear and did not change. How we went about them did change as we tackled or chose to ignore questions that faced us at every step. There have been research projects neater looking than this one, in the sense that they dealt only (in reports, anyway) with a set of questions and procedures which were carefully spelled out at the beginning. We expect to be faulted in some quarters for not having set our scientific blinders more firmly in place at the start, so that we could create for ourselves the illusion of a distinct path along which we would proceed with few distractions and a carefully arranged body of data. For our part, however, we do not believe that the SECSI project was unique or even unusual as an example of a long-term effort to keep a clear head in the face of the hard-core untidiness of the school world. Nor do we believe that the common practice of sweeping any mess under the rug before opening a project to public view will ultimately serve to increase understanding of how human beings can obtain useful information by studying other human beings.

The first series of questions that plagued and intrigued us arose when we faced the task of intervening in schools. We were to try to bring about change. But how? A number of intervention strategies had been developed by other organizations, but none of these strategies had offered a satisfactory solution to what seemed to us the fundamental problem for anyone who wanted to effect widespread change in schools.[5] *How can outside resources and stimulation which will encourage and enable a school to try something different be provided for all schools?*

The problem, as we saw it, posed a basic dilemma. On the one hand, a close association between an outside expert and a school might bring about a change in the school as the expert tailored his services to meet conditions in that school. A number of intervention programs had used this strategy. The usual long-range result, however, had been for the school to revert to its old ways after the expert left. Another drawback is that it is simply not reasonable to suppose that there would ever be enough experts to provide continuous consultant services for every school. On the other hand, a greater number of schools could be reached by some form of packaging of the knowledge and services of experts. Intervention programs offering new curriculum materials are a well-known example of this kind of strategy. Very little change has resulted from these efforts, however, since impersonal packages can rarely deal effectively with the specific problems encountered by individual schools. In brief, it seemed to us that in order to be effective an intervention strategy had to reach all schools *and* take into account conditions which varied from school to school; yet, in order to be feasible, the strategy had to accept the inevitably limited availability of outside experts who could serve individual school needs.

To meet these requirements for an intervention strategy that would be both feasible and effective we decided to try the principle of the magic feather. We would help schools help themselves. Our contribution would be the magic feather to get them started. We would help them realize that their success was due to their own efforts and abilities, not to outside expertise. Chapters 2 and 3 describe how the new strategy took shape around these questions:

What is the basis for thinking that the new strategy might change behavior in schools?

Why should the strategy be feasible?

How does the strategy require that we, the interventionists, behave?

What happened? How did we behave toward the schools? How did the schools behave toward us and with one another?

Our second task was to get some kind of handle on what the process of change looked like in the project schools. Decisions about specific innovations we would leave up to each school; we would try to bring about in every school staff only one change—an increased willingness to look more closely at what they were doing, to consider alternative things to do and alternative ways of doing them all.

What we wanted to study then was essentially a school staff's receptivity or lack of receptivity to change. On what should we base our description of such receptivity? Others had approached the receptivity question by settling on a specific educational innovation, then assessing the degree to which that innovation was adopted in several schools. In keeping with our belief that needs for specific changes varied from school to school, however, we had renounced advocating across the board any particular innovation in curriculum, instruction, or school organization. Nor did it sit well with our understanding of *responsible* receptivity to base our description on a counting up of all the innovations that we might spot or a school might claim during the course of the study.

We believed that *responsible receptivity to change* actually involved a whole host of factors—more characteristics of school staff life than we could realistically hope to study. Still, we wanted to talk about it in terms that would make sense no matter what the relevant conditions were in a given school. Was there any set of behaviors common to all schools that might prove to be an indicator of the large set of conditions relevant to receptivity? An obvious candidate for such a key description was the process by which a school staff copes with whatever comes its way, including proposals for change.

We occupied ourselves with trying to identify the behaviors that make up this process, and Chapter 4 tells how we arrived at the basic process of *dialogue, decision making, action, and evaluation,* which we soon called DDAE, as the set of behaviors by which all staffs carry out the business of the school—the process by which they consider change or reject it. We were able to check out to some extent how well the quality of the DDAE process served as an indicator of other school conditions that we thought were involved in responsible receptivity to change, and Chapter 5 describes what we found. Together these chapters address two questions:

> How can we describe DDAE as the basic process by which a school staff indicates its responsible receptivity to change?
>
> How do certain characteristics of principals, teachers, and the school organization seem to relate to the DDAE process?

Chapters 6, 7, and 8 describe how our concept of the DDAE process was integrated with our new intervention strategy. As we became convinced that the extent of a school's openness to change was reflected in the basic process of DDAE, we tried to use our strategy to focus the schools' attention on how this process was being carried out, to think about how they would like to carry it out, and to consider what changes might be necessary. In order to learn about what went on in the schools, we were guided by a principle commonly used in field studies—for a given set of events, get as many different kinds of descriptions from as many different points of view as you can. By studying the differences and similarities of the resulting descriptions we were able to get a feeling for the complexity of "simple" daily happenings in schools. Our sources of information included informal conversations with principals and teachers; tapes and written observations of meetings; reports of visits to schools; records of phone calls and letters; interviews with principals, teachers, and school district personnel; monthly reports from principals and selected teachers in each school; and a battery of questionnaires given at the end of each school year. In addition to these a film record was made of the activities in the project, for we believed that certain aspects of the look of change could not be captured in words.[6]

We have used all these sources of information in telling the story in Chapters 6, 7, and 8 that arose from our concern with these questions:

> What implications did attention to the DDAE process have for our intervention activities?
>
> How did the schools respond to what we tried to do?

We drew upon all our data also as we tried finally to assess what kinds of information can be assembled to describe the four types of schools which we identified in the project: those that maintained relatively high receptivity to change, those that failed ever to reach a high level of receptivity, those that moved from a lower level to a higher level, and those that slipped back from a high to a low level.

At the end of the project we returned to the general questions with which we had begun. Chapter 10 describes our new understandings as we faced our original queries:

> What are the fundamental requirements for an intervention strategy that will help schools maintain openness to new possibilities in schooling?
>
> Can we describe certain basic components in the daily life of school staffs which will increase our understanding of how this openness is won or lost?

We have organized our thinking around three major topics. First, we discuss the progress we made in clarifying and beginning to operationalize the concept of responsible receptivity to change as it relates to self-renewing schools—what is required of staff relationships and the climate of the school. Second, we present our case for the magic feather principle as an intervention strategy which is founded on the schools' ability to change themselves and suggest that the socialization of schools as organizations as well as the socialization of individuals is involved in maintaining openness to change. Finally, we raise some questions which our experience has caused us to ask about how research in schools can be most fruitfully conducted.

NOTES

1 The Institute for Development of Educational Activities, Inc., is an affiliate of the Charles F. Kettering Foundation. |I|D|E|A| has sought both to maintain a program focused on certain immediate highly visible needs and to come to grips with long-term issues of educational improvement.

2 A thought-provoking exposé of the little knowledge we have about ordinary school life and its implications for change efforts is found in Seymour B. Sarason, *The Culture of the School and the Problem of Change*, Allyn and Bacon, Boston, 1971. The staying power of entrenched practices in schools is documented in John I. Goodlad, M. Frances Klein, and Associates, *Looking Behind the Classroom Door*, rev. ed., Charles A. Jones, Worthington, Ohio, 1974.

3 John I. Goodlad, "Staff Development: The League Model," *Theory into Practice*, vol. 11, no. 4, October 1972, pp. 207–208.

4 A nineteenth school originally planned to be in the project but within the first year found it impossible to participate. No information about that school is included in this report.

5 A comprehensive description of the change strategies which have been most often used appears in Ronald G. Havelock, *Planning for Innovation Through Dissemination and Utilization of Knowledge*, The University of Michigan, CRUSK, Ann Arbor, 1971. A critique of change strategies is offered in Mary M. Bentzen and Kenneth A. Tye, "Change: Problems and Prospects," in *The Elementary School in the United States*, 72nd Yearbook of the National Society for the Study of Education, University of Chicago Press, Chicago, 1973, pp. 350–379.

6 These films have become a documentary series, *The League: Film Reports on |I|D|E|A|'s Study of Change*, Information and Services, |I|D|E|A|, Melbourne, Florida, 1972.

CHAPTER 2

THE LEAGUE AS A
SOCIAL SYSTEM

A history of any series of interactions among people is necessarily a construction which reflects the writer's choices in the selection of both the events which are described and the explanations which are offered to connect those events. This is no less true for accounts of interactions that occurred in research projects than it is for accounts that appear in news items, memoirs, and history texts. And only insofar as the reader has information about the choices that have been made can he gauge the relationship of the account at hand to other accounts that might be given.

The writer who describes a field study such as ours may select events in at least three ways. He may choose from records, left routinely or voluntarily by other people, of a history in which he did not participate. He may recount what he himself remembers of events in which he did participate. Or, the writer may use information about events which he obtains by asking particular questions of participants. In putting together our history of the interactions among the SECSI staff and the League schools, we have made use of all these sources. Our story includes some events that we did not see, presented as they were described and interpreted, both in free accounts and in response to specific questions, by principals and teachers or by staff members other than ourselves. This history includes, too, our own reconstructions of happenings at which we were present and about which we made notes and have memories.

The ways which are available to the field study reporter for interrelating the events that he has selected parallel the options which he has for the selection of those events. Thus, he may simply report several explanations that are given by those who experienced the events, or he may choose one explanation from among several. Another alternative is to offer his own interpretation of events which he himself

23

experienced. Or, finally, he may build his explanation by viewing events only as they relate to a notion which he has in mind about how they could fit together. Our choices were ordered primarily by the last option. As we wrote, we tended to see events and explanations as fitting or not fitting the cluster of ideas which came to generate the League intervention strategy.

It is, of course, a hallmark of experimental research, compared with many other kinds of question-answering ventures, that it does select, organize, and interpret the events which it observes in relation to an explicitly stated, preconceived explanatory framework. We cannot claim quite this purity of thought, since the concept of our intervention strategy did not exist full-blown at the start of the project and so did not systematically direct all of our observations during the project. As we noted earlier, our study of change in schools was itself an example of change in an organization engaged in a long-term research project. We were, as a staff, committed to a common task; yet we could not long ignore our various perceptions of that task as we tried to fashion productive day-to-day encounters among ourselves and with the schools. In the course of these encounters we—along with the schools—tested, revised, discarded, and invented ways of behaving and notions of what we were about. We cannot hope to trace every step in the pathways that crisscrossed among people, beliefs, and actions, within and between the schools and the SECSI staff. We think it an integral part of our story, however, to recognize the existence of that web and to tease out whatever strands we can catch hold of as we reconstruct what happened among people with different perceptions and changing ideas in purposeful contacts with one another.

THE BEGINNING OF A NEW INTERVENTION STRATEGY

We began the task of developing and testing a new approach to intervention in schools with a basic belief and two basic questions which that belief immediately raised. Our belief was that the single school is the most appropriate target for a change strategy. John Goodlad presented the case for this approach several years before the SECSI project was initiated:

> The individual school has a body politic made up of parents and pupils; a professional team of teachers with a designated leader; the necessary accouterments such as buildings, equipment, and materials. These are the essential ingredients for establishing a tradition . . . a past

against which to appraise the present and plan for the future. These are the essential ingredients, too, for creating an institutional personality. . . .[1]

We believed that much of the failure of intervention strategies to effect change had resulted from their failure to take advantage of what Goodlad called the "organismic wholeness" of the single school. We wanted a strategy that would work primarily with the entire professional team—principal and teachers—in each school to plan and implement changes that were meaningful in the individual school situation. Yet a strategy that would intervene in one school at a time seemed to have two glaring weaknesses. The first weakness came to mind when we thought of what it was like for one school alone to try something different. Just the uncertainty of the outcome of any innovation was enough to slow up a timid staff. Add to this uncertainty the distrust, ridicule, and hostility that are often directed toward a school that dares to be different, and we could see that the resolve of even a courageous staff might not hold up if it saw itself pretty much alone in a definitely unfriendly environment.

The second apparent weakness of the single school approach lay in the large variety of resources that would have to be made available to many school staffs with many different problems. We knew that the usual manner in which change strategies had provided specialized assistance had been to assign one or more expert consultants to a school, and we knew that the changes made with this kind of strategy tended to last only slightly longer than the period of consultant help. Even if we could learn how to make changes stick in a school after the experts left, it seemed utterly impractical to consider a strategy which required the interventionists to supply special consultant help to every school. We might with really hard work be able to bring it off in eighteen schools, but there would not likely ever be enough interventionist-consultants to make this a feasible avenue to widespread change in schools.

Thus, our first commitment—that we would focus our intervention strategy on the single school as a unit—had led to our first two big questions. How could we devise a strategy which would stimulate each school to cut a new path through its own particular woods, yet leave no school with the feeling of hacking it alone? And how could we, with limited resources, devise a strategy that would furnish a variety of resources to a number of schools with many different problems? We began in keeping with our belief in the single school as the target for change. We designed the League of Cooperating Schools as a group of *individual schools,* not of districts or of persons. Then, with eighteen single schools, we started work on the two questions we had put to ourselves. Our first move was to try to make each school feel that it was in the company of others like itself, all engaged in an exploration of ways to improve the schooling that went on within their walls.

FORGING LINKS AMONG PRINCIPALS

The first year of the League began in September 1966, but twice in the summer of 1966 the principals of the League schools were brought together by the research staff in three-day conferences to learn about the SECSI project. Throughout these discussions, we emphasized the theme of innovation, recognized the problems faced by a single school in attempting change, and began to create the image of the League as a group which could overcome these problems. We explained our commitment to the idea of the single school as the most effective unit for change and our assumption that the principal, as chief administrative officer of the school, was the key agent of change. Each principal was asked to plan with his staff a project that would allow them to work on changes that would be meaningful in their specific school situation. We made it clear, however, that we had no money to give the schools for these projects.

During the first year the League principals and the research staff established the pattern of joint meetings that was to be maintained throughout the project—an all-day meeting once each month at the research staff offices, and two- or three-day conferences near the beginning, middle, and end of each school year in one or the other of the several areas in which League schools were clustered. At most of the meetings during the first year the principals listened. They listened to encouragement to plan a new role as League principals, to explore new ideas with their staffs, to work on ways to communicate their ideas to other schools in their districts. As publicity about the League project appeared in local newspapers or professional journals, the research staff brought it to their attention. At almost every meeting the principals heard a speaker present an aspect of recent thinking about innovation in education, and the principals were asked to communicate these ideas to their staffs. They were encouraged to begin to work on appropriate projects for change and not get bogged down in day-to-day problems.

The principals also had some time to listen to one another. In several meetings there were scheduled opportunities to share information about specific school programs and problems, and socializing on the fringes of the time limits of meetings increased as the group met month after month. By the end of the year, we felt that they were identifying themselves as League principals. We solicited their opinions in interviews held with each principal at the end of the year and in the evaluations and recommendations which they offered in the course of their meetings. We found that while two-thirds of the principals were less than satisfied with the progress their schools had made toward planning innovative projects, every one of the eighteen stated that it was very important that they meet together. Several recommendations were made to increase communication among principals and to provide more opportunities for them to offer one another suggestions for working out problems in the individual schools. The principals had recognized the motivating power of the new group. They expressed their recognition variously.

What would you say is the most important thing you have done in the League?

"Going to League principals' meetings. At first I was not overly impressed with the group of League principals, but this has changed. Now I feel they are extremely capable. Of course, part of this is due to the fact that they have changed." (Adam S., Mar Villa)

How important do you think it is to hold LCS meetings?

"Contact must be maintained. I would like more sharing among the principals. Problems should be discussed and hashed out." (Dave N., Seastar)

"Very important. When we meet together, there is a lot of fellowship, there is an opportunity to talk with others, and it does a lot for my morale. Just being a member of the League is a morale factor in itself. But, I think there should be a time for business and a time for pleasure in League meetings. Sometimes more important things go on in the informal part of the meeting than in the business part of the meeting." (Chris M., Hacienda)

"Very important. This is the only thing that pulls us up out of the little holes that we were in before. It gives us an outside contact that we need to stimulate some new ideas, and it gives us a feeling of belonging to a new group—a group that is different from the ones we have been in before. It pulls us up out of the little holes." (Alex R., South)

How do you feel about the LCS principals' meetings?

"There seems like a lot of minutes that nothing really happens. I expect more interaction and we're not getting it. I enjoy, I look forward as much to luncheons where we can sit down and kick around ideas. We still are not a group. I want to get to know the other principals." (Gene G., Rainbow Hill)

"I continue to find out that there is a world beyond that of the district." (Joe A., James School)

In the spring of 1967 no League principal felt alone in the world of trying to change schools. We saw that we had made some headway on one of the questions that had been raised at the start of our first year. More important was our clearer vision of the power of the group we had created. The League had been formed as a group because we had believed that it was too much to ask a single school to risk the loneliness of being different. Now we saw principals actually taking heart in being together. It was not simply a matter of clinging together for comfort. They could and were encouraging one another to adventure. They themselves were doing part of what had been the job of the SECSI staff. We had begun by telling the principals that they were to be an innovative group. Now, the principals were telling this to one another.

SOCIALIZATION AS AN INTERVENTION STRATEGY

We thought more about what we, as interventionists, were trying to do. What, fundamentally, is involved in trying to get schools to change? First, the school staff must usually perform new behaviors or new combinations of old behaviors. They may be asked, for example, to use different instructional techniques, to organize themselves in different ways, to adopt different subject matter, to approach problems in a different manner, to establish different kinds of communication patterns. We know that people in any group usually acquire new behaviors through some kind of socialization process. That is, they learn to do what is expected of them by another person or persons in the group. Usually, we think of socialization in connection with the child who learns how to behave by meeting the expectations of his parents. We recognize, however, that adults, too, must undergo socialization, since it is clear that the socialization of the child cannot prepare him for all the roles he will have to play in his adult life. Thus, new behaviors are required of and learned by most adults who enter professions, marriage, and senior citizenship—to name but a few of the settings in which adult socialization occurs.

What if we tried to cast the problem of intervention in schools as, first of all, a problem in the resocialization of school staffs? Viewed this way, the first task of an intervention strategy is to identify an appropriate socialization agent and to use that agent to encourage the desired new behavior. *Socialization agents* are defined as people whose expectations matter to the person(s) to be socialized and, consequently, whose influence is apt to bring about the new behavior. When we look at examples of socialization situations, two types of relationships stand out between the socialization agent and the person(s) to be socialized. First, the agent may be perceived as superordinate in some respect; the basic example of this type of relationship is the parent who acts as socialization agent for his child. Second, the agent may be perceived as a peer; the socialization of adolescents by their peer group is a dramatic example of this kind of relationship.

It seemed to us that traditional interventions with school staffs had been drawn from the parental model of the socialization agent. As an expert consultant, the traditional interventionist commanded attention because of his superior knowledge and influenced behavior by rewarding conformity to his advice. Our analysis of these interventions, however, had suggested that the parentlike model of socialization agent might not be the best choice. As pointed out earlier, in the first place there would never be enough expert consultants to carry out the parentlike model in all schools. Furthermore, the typical consultant intervention, although it had often been powerful in initiating new behavior in a school staff, had shown little success in maintaining the new behavior after the consultant had left the scene.

Given these serious shortcomings of the parentlike model for intervention, we thought it reasonable to consider, as an alternative, an intervention strategy based upon a peer group model of socialization. In theory, an intervention strategy which relied upon a peer group to resocialize school staffs would require the existence of a group of schools which members identified as a group and in which the members encouraged one another to perform certain new behaviors. If one of the encouraged behaviors (i.e., group norms) was "to be receptive to change," a school staff in this group would try out innovative ideas, not in order to win approval from an outside expert but because the staff saw its school as a member of a group in which this kind of behavior was expected. Conceivably then, close contact between an expert consultant and each school would not be required. A school would receive approval from other member schools if it behaved according to expectations for the group and would be made aware of disapproval from other members if it did not behave as expected. The power to reward and punish, instead of being concentrated in a small number of outside experts, would be shared among many member schools. If the power to reinforce the expected behavior were indeed to lie in the group, the new behavior might be maintained indefinitely, since the schools would remain and could retain this power after interventionists had left. We saw, in short, the possibility of building a peer group of schools which could enforce its own group norms for innovative behavior.

So we began to think of the League as a peer group of schools. Time after time we drew on the chalkboard a circle of symbols representing the eighteen schools, and we drew lines that connected them. We talked about what the lines, which tied the symbols together on the chalkboard, might consist of in school life. What, in reality, might bind the schools together in ways that would make them want to see themselves as members of the League? The question could not be ignored because if a peer group is to be effective in getting its members to behave in certain ways, then the members have to care about belonging to the group. They must, that is, be susceptible to the influence of the rewards which the group offers to "good" members. But why should the schools value belonging to the League and therefore try to behave as a League school "should behave?" Part of the answer we had learned from the principals. They valued the group for the intellectual stimulation and moral support it provided. So far, so good. One ingredient of the connecting lines might be a feeling of togetherness in confronting the unfamiliar.

PROVIDING RESOURCES TO THE SCHOOLS

Yet we were concerned about finding other ingredients that would make those interschool ties stronger. And there remained the other basic problem which we had posed for any intervention strategy that started with the single school: How can useful resources be provided to individual schools with a variety of individual problems? We had asked each school to identify and work on changes appropriate to its situation. What help would they need and where would help come from? The first year brought us daily evidence that the question was, indeed, critical.

The Research Assistant's Role

At the beginning of the first year, each of the research assistants on the SECSI staff was assigned to one or two League schools. The initial job, as we saw it, was to get acquainted with the schools and particularly to learn about the principals' leadership styles and about ways in which we could assist schools in identifying meaningful projects to work on. With these objectives in mind, each research assistant introduced himself to the principal of his assigned school, offered to work with the school in whatever way the principal thought best to help the staff get started in assessing needed change, and began a yearlong series of regular visits to the school. While the amount of time spent by research assistants in schools varied, each school was visited, on the average, about twice each month.

The League principals responded in various ways to the presence of the research assistants and to the opportunity to define a role for the assistant in their school. Their responses seemed to take one of three general forms: acceptance, resistance, or escape. Of course, some principals gave evidence of more than one of these forms of reaction, but considering only the dominant form in each case, the principals divided (equally as it happened) into three groups.

A third of the principals were immediately accepting of the new resource offered to the school in the person of the research assistant. The principals of Hacienda, Woodacres, and Dewey Avenue moved quickly to incorporate the research assistant as an additional resource to implement plans for change which they already had in mind. These principals knew what they wanted the research assistant to do, and while the role varied somewhat among the three schools, it included in all cases a considerable amount of time spent in interacting with teachers for purposes made clear by the principal. This active acceptance was perhaps most pronounced at Hacienda and was described by the research assistant in his year-end summary:

"They have asked me for some very specific suggestions, but for the most part their questions have been: Do you approve or not? Whenever

I have made suggestions, these have been put into effect almost immediately. At the first conference, I suggested to the principal that teachers in each unit should have some released time for group planning. He asked how this could be done, and I made two or three suggestions. We stayed up until 3:00 A.M. working out the specifics. The plan was put into effect the following week."

The principals of Peace Valley, Fairfield, and Shadyside also welcomed help for their schools, but they had not formed plans for using it. While none of these principals tried to abdicate his position as formal leader of his school in the exploration of change, each one did lean on the research assistant for information and direction as to what changes should be attempted. Much of this dependence came from their admitted feelings of limited competence in certain areas—limitations that now loomed larger to them, faced as they were with expectations to move outside of familiar routines. There was also, on the part of these three principals, a strong but unfocused desire to make full use somehow of what they saw as a storehouse of knowledge suddenly made accessible to them. For example, Ben U. at Fairfield time and again expressed his joy and wonderment that his out-of-the-way school now could draw help from people who were up on the latest thinking in the field of education. He was more than happy for the research assistant to be in frequent contact with the teachers, but the pattern and content of the interaction was left largely up to the research assistant to work out.

A third of the principals showed resistance to the offers of the research assistants. During the first year all these resisters limited and structured to some extent the research assistants' interaction with teachers. The principals at Bell Street and Independence indicated that they had no need for the research assistants and maintained only cursory relationships with them. (At the end of the year, however, the Bell Street principal retired and the Independence principal moved to another district. The principals who followed them were more receptive to the League.) Florence P. at Middleton decided to move very slowly in her school in determining changes to be made and politely but firmly resisted most suggestions from the research assistant as to how she might further involve her staff in planning.

Three other principals who manifested initial resistance were behaving differently before the first year was over. The research assistant assigned to James School tried for more than three months before he succeeded in establishing a working relationship with the principal, Joe A. In his year-end report the research assistant stated:

"I think there are some plausible reasons for it taking this long. Joe A. was new to the school. During this time he was not only faced with the additional burden of his League participation, but he was also attempting to establish a positive rapport with his staff. As a result of some of the input received at the principals' conferences and meetings, Joe was also developing a new manner of working with his staff. Unknown to any member of the research staff, Joe was attempting to change his own administrative behavior pattern from that of satisfying the expectations of the district to that of involving teachers in decision making and taking into consideration the needs and interests of both youngsters and teachers in making these decisions. This understanding and partial explanation did not become clear until the principal was interviewed at the close of the second year."

If Joe A. could be described as a secret learner, Steve M. at Antigua and Dave W. at Seastar, probably the two most vocal of the initial resisters, might be described as learners-in-spite-of-themselves. Innumerable times during the year Steve M. accused the SECSI project of being "too philosophical" and scorned research as having little practical value. Nevertheless, his school had been assigned to the League, and Steve, as befitted an experienced principal, went about his new duty to start an innovative project in a businesslike way. In the course of his dutiful performance, he made increasing use of the research assistant as a procurer of informational reading materials for the staff and as a personal consultant to the principal. By late spring he asked the research assistant to enter some staff discussions at the school, and, when interviewed, Steve admitted that his original feeling that what was being asked of him was impossible had been altered to a feeling that it was only half impossible. He said frankly that he thought he had learned more in the past year than he had learned in the previous sixteen years.

The other vocal resister, Dave W. at Seastar, was sure that John Goodlad and the research staff had something up their sleeves that he didn't know about, and he made his anger known about such secrecy. Since he was caught in the situation, however, he felt obliged to try to repeat to his teachers whatever he heard from the speakers at the principals' meetings. Within a few months he realized that his tactic of repeating lectures was only making his staff as suspicious of him as he was of the research staff. At this point he turned to the research assistant for help in working out the problem, and the rest of the year was spent in trying to get the generally hostile staff of teachers to look more closely at what they were doing.

Finally, a third of the principals seemed to be concerned primarily with personal escape from their school situations. At Country, Indian Flat, and Mar Villa, the principals frankly felt inadequate to perform for their own staffs the new role of change agent, which they realized was necessary. They turned to the research assistants to take over much of this role.

> "Teachers began identifying the types of activities they would like to try for the next year. They looked to Adam for help in pursuing their interests, but Adam felt unable to assist them. In discussing this problem, we agreed I would become directly involved with the Mar Villa faculty. This opened a discussion about the principal's role. During the discussion, Adam seemed embarrassed to identify the role functions he now performs. He recognized the importance of interaction and effective communication between a principal and his staff yet felt very inadequate in this regard. He recognized the need for a principal to supervise, initiate, and implement but said he doesn't really know how to perform these functions. There is a tremendous gap between his conception of the proper role to play and how he actually performs the role." (Research assistant, Mar Villa)

> "Andy S. said he was a poor discussion leader and I could do it much better. The pattern was as follows. I would come to the school. Andy and I would talk for about a half hour. Then there would be a meeting. I kept trying to make him leader, but he kept abdicating. He felt he would implement the ideas but wasn't good at getting teachers to talk about ideas. Many times he said he was learning himself." (Research assistant, Country School)

> "Chet was new to the district and new as a principal. He was scared to death to be a 'League principal.' He tried to withdraw from the League several times but was encouraged to stay." (Research assistant, Indian Flat)

A less obvious form of escape occurred with the principals of Frontier, South, and Rainbow Hill. Each of these principals had shown some degree of disenchantment with his profession before the start of the League and had perceived the opportunity to be in the League largely as personal salvation. Alex R. (South School) described the feeling:

"I was hoping to break out of the rut of the same people, the same ideas being mulled over and over. You know this business can be deadening. We did exactly the same thing every year. I always knew what was going to happen at every meeting. And I was sick of seeing the same people and hearing them say the same things. At our meetings, whenever a question came up, I knew what everybody would say. And when somebody started to talk, you wouldn't even have to listen because you knew what they were saying. I told you that I was going to be a butcher. I thought that chopping meat all day would be more exciting than this humdrum business. Being in the League has really gotten me out of the rut."

To these principals the research assistants were yet another welcome source of stimulation, but in one way or another they avoided coming to grips with how new ideas could be implemented in their own schools. This is not to say that these principals did not make plans for innovative school projects. Each of them did and discussed the plans with the research assistant. Yet the plans were, to some extent, dream worlds which did not take into account the resources available to the single school. For example, Alex and his staff proposed to meet the problem of fatigue in children by radically changing the schedule of the school day. Of course, changes in dismissal time would necessarily involve districtwide action. In addition, each of these principals had serious communication problems with his staff, but any discussion of these problems had to be initiated by the research assistants, and then the discussion was generally with the principal only, since in these schools the research assistant's contacts with teachers consisted primarily of observing meetings.

Innovative Projects in the Schools

As far as most of the principals were concerned, the focus for the relationship with the research assistants and the rest of the research staff—whatever form it took—lay in the expectation that each League school would come up with a project, i.e., clear plans for some kind of innovative activities in the school. In interviews at the end of the year the principals revealed how they perceived this expectation and how they felt about it. The first perception had more or less been that they were to come up right away with a "significant project" and that they would receive a lot of direction in doing so. Although most principals expressed some kind of pleasure with what they saw as their prestigious association with leaders in education, the dawning realization of their own obligations, as Alex R. (South) told it, had not always been joyful.

> ". . . There were lots of principals who were worried about this project. I was scared to death. After you've been in the same old rut in this business for a few years, you wonder if you have anything to offer. I know we were all scared to death at the first conference. They started out too fast. I felt like some kind of nut. But things have smoothed out."

The smoothing out occurred as the principals came to understand that they were not expected to change their schools overnight and as they became accustomed to the idea that each school staff was to decide for itself what changes might make sense for it. There was, however, much less smoothing out of teachers' fears, anxieties, and frustrations during the year. First of all, the teachers had less understanding than the principals of what was expected of the League schools. In interviews with a sample of teachers at the end of the year, over half expressed uncertainty about their obligations, and another third saw only a vague requirement "to experiment." Secondly, many teachers had started with the mistaken belief that they would receive special provisions of some sort, and they were anxious about their ability to do anything different without such resources. The going was often rough when principals began to discuss with their staffs how they might develop a League project for the school. In the words of Ben U. at Fairfield:

> "At some of our first meetings the teachers were as confused as I was, not knowing for sure what was going to happen. And, of course, a lot of people aren't particularly ready to make changes in the first place. We went through some troubled waters. The teachers asked me, 'What do you want?' and the principals asked the research staff, 'What do *you* want?' "

But, one way or another, the League school staffs kept on trying to talk about new ideas. Teachers reacted to invitations to try various changes in much the same ways as had principals; some accepted the opportunity, some resisted, some tried to avoid the whole thing. A staff was not necessarily all of a piece in its form of reaction; often acceptors, resisters, and would-be escapees taught in the same school. Nor was the dominant staff reaction always the same as the principal's reaction.

By the end of the year only about a third of the schools had a specific change project in operation or detailed plans for such a project. In a number of cases, principals who had made plans had to discard them because the projects required more funding than the school could get or because they were too elaborate to be manageable in the actual school situation. Yet in all League schools the amount of discussion and exploration of ideas had increased enormously. The input which had been provided through speakers and consultants during the year was oriented generally to the broad concept of individualization of instruction but had not promoted any specific how-to-do-it. School staffs had to decide how the concepts which had been introduced might apply to their situations. The range of topics that resulted was broad indeed. Staffs asked themselves how they could better cope with fatigue in children, what kind of team teaching might be helpful, what steps they could take toward nongrading, how they could devise better ways to report to parents, what would make better reading and math programs, how they could improve attitudes toward school among disadvantaged pupils.

The discussions went on between schools as well as within schools. The research staff had encouraged teachers and principals to visit one another's schools, and at least a few teachers from every school had made visits before the first year was over. There was almost total agreement among the teachers and principals that the visiting was desirable and important. Even principals who were described earlier as resisters allowed their teachers to visit other schools. The chief reasons given for favoring interschool visits was that visiting was the best way for teachers to get "new ideas." Almost as frequent were expressions of the value of moral support and the need for teacher-to-teacher information:

". . . another thing, it gives us confidence when we can see what other schools are doing. Sometimes it gives you support for what you are trying. And sometimes you find out you aren't doing too bad as it is." (Teacher, South)

"Visiting gives a chance for teachers to pool ideas and information and to critically evaluate some new ideas being put into practice. It also helps the principal to get the teacher's viewpoint. I visited a League school earlier in the year and learned many new things which we are now discussing for use in our plant. Also, we noticed some pitfalls that perhaps we can work around." (Teacher, Middleton)

"Visiting lets teachers know that they aren't the only ones having difficulty. It gives them a chance to exchange ideas at the teacher level, not the administrative level." (Teacher, Indian Flat)

"It is important to see projects going on that might help to find answers to problems you have been trying to solve—ideas for your group. If teachers talk together and exchange comments about things that haven't been successful, they may keep others from trying things that haven't worked." (Teacher, Mar Villa)

"Visiting cuts down the time needed to find solutions." (Teacher, Dewey Avenue)

The interviews at the end of the year indicated that almost all teachers wanted more League activities that would bring together teachers from different schools. They wanted teacher discussion groups, more visiting, some sort of publication that would tell what was going on in the schools. They wanted to talk with other teachers about "how to deal with the particular types of children that I am teaching." They wanted to be able to get follow-up information on ideas they had borrowed from other schools:

"I am trying what they are doing at Hacienda, but I would like to see one of their master planning sheets and how they do it. It is not working to suit me yet." (Teacher, Bell Street)

They saw improved communication among teachers as essential to what a school would be able to do:

"We need more chance to know what's going on. The principals are free to go to meetings, and they can spend a whole day getting new ideas. But then we're expected to find out everything in one hour, and it just can't be done. We never even hear about most of the things that are going on. Yet the teachers are the ones who are expected to make the changes." (Teacher, South)

Most of the principals supported the teachers' desire for more involvement in the League. Chris M. (Hacienda) noted that greater involvement would, he thought, help break down teacher resistance to change. Dave W. of Seastar agreed that visiting had opened the minds of his teachers, and a research assistant reported that the visits on which Dave had accompanied his teachers "made a dramatic change in Dave's own attitude—he really was fantastically enthused by what he saw." Dave himself reported,

"I think I am more aware that League intervention is helping us do something. I thought the research staff did have some hidden ideas beforehand, but I see now that they really wanted us to develop ideas."

The realization that school staffs were truly expected to identify their own needs for change brought mixed reactions. In the first place, it was very difficult for many principals and teachers simply to come to this realization. Later on in the course of the project, Steve M. (Antigua) reminisced,

> "We sat around and waited for John Goodlad and his staff to tell us what they wanted done—just tell us and we'll do it. It didn't happen. Believe me, it didn't happen."

Hard as it was for principals, it was even harder for teachers. And for good reason:

> "The biggest problem facing the staff is that never before have they been asked for their opinions. They have either been told or have been asked to read about how to do things. Now they are called upon to search for themselves and are treated as if they really mattered. For most of them this, along with the changes that have taken place, has proved to be truly a traumatic experience." (Teacher, Antigua)

Very often the initial trauma was followed by excitement and daring:

> "His ideas have changed considerably. He realizes that now he is not going to get any particular packages, but that he has been given the chance to initiate his own program, a chance to use initiative in working with other teachers. What he now sees to be in operation in the school is the teachers are beginning to be able to make some decisions of their own. He remarked that he has tried many things this year, some that worked and some that didn't work. The most important thing that he has seen in his membership in the League of Cooperating Schools is the opportunity to experiment—the opportunity to visit other schools and see what others are doing." (Report of interview with teacher, James School)

> "I am very satisfied because, as I say, the fact that I have had the freedom to do anything I wanted to do has given me the courage, and I needed courage. I think that is the main thing. It has given me the courage to try things that I would never have tried before." (Teacher, Fairfield)

More often, however, school staffs turned, with caution or panic, to those people who were supposed to know. Time and again research assistants reported that school staffs were requesting "recipes" for innovative programs. Some teachers longed for the security of expert judgment:

> "The research staff should be planning how to go about carrying out change. They should be evaluating whether such change is good or bad." (Teacher, Antigua)

"If we do something wrong, I don't care—tell us. I would like to have someone come in and help me. If something I do could be done better, show me, and I would be glad to take the help." (Teacher, Fairfield)

Our second anticipated problem had appeared—more resources than we could offer were needed. Whether their reaction had been exhilaration or dismay, the great majority of teachers and principals by the end of the year were saying that they wanted more of something that was usually called "concrete ideas." They often related this to a desire for a different kind of consultant help from the research staff. The words of one teacher express a response that was heard from many teachers:

"The consultants that came up here didn't give us new ideas and methods to make them work so that we could bite into them and put them into action in the classrooms. Practically every meeting that we had was more or less bringing out the ideas of the teachers. Maybe that was the purpose of it, I don't know. But, what the teachers were really expecting were some concrete ideas that they could digest—and put into action." (Teacher, Fairfield)

Yet the same teacher, like many others, made it clear that he did not mean that teachers should simply be told what to do. In speaking of a few changes that had been made in his school as a result of additional funds which the school had received from a compensatory education project, he explained:

"Everything that was put into the program was more or less from outside specialists, which I think is a good idea. I think we got a lot out of it, but I believe that the teachers would have become more involved if they could have done more of this themselves."

In a similar vein, a substantial number of principals were expressing a desire to participate in planning the group's activities. In sum, the year-end interviews revealed that while teachers and principals were divided into those who preferred direction by experts and those who were eager or willing to experiment, there was great agreement on the identification of two major problems. First, they wanted to become much more involved in League activities. Second, in the words of a Dewey Avenue teacher, "The biggest problem is getting more direct help at the teacher level in solving practical problems."

NOTES

1   John I. Goodlad, "The Individual School and Its Principal: Key Setting and Key Person," *Educational Leadership*, 13, October 1955.

CHAPTER 3

A PEER GROUP OF SCHOOLS

It seemed, to some extent anyway, that the schools had bought the notion of being members of the League. At least by the end of the first year none of them had asked to get out. Although there was a fair amount of confusion, uncertainty, and skepticism among the school staffs, the resistance reaction, as far as we could tell, was no longer dominant in any school. Furthermore, we saw the beginning of a generally held expectation for what the behavior of a League school should be, for now there seemed to exist among the school staffs an image of the League as a group committed to exploring new ideas in schooling. The image was certainly fuzzy around the edges, and in some quarters inspired only "we'll just see if it works" rather than "let's get on with it." But the image did exist.

Perhaps we had going for us an incipient group norm in the League which placed value on a school's attempts at innovative behavior. To nourish such a norm was certainly our intent, for the norm lay at the base of our hope for a peer group of schools which would encourage each of its members to assess its own situation candidly and to be open to possibilities for change. We rejoiced in the evidence that many teachers, as well as principals, now felt reassurance from being in a group of schools which was exploring change. It was terribly important that the League develop common understandings and mutual supports which would increase willingness to take risks, and perhaps the most important of these understandings was that failure in one attempt did not mean permanent disaster. In fact, equanimity in the face of possible failure seemed to be increasing in League schools.

Our joy, though, was somewhat watered down by the simultaneous confirmation of our strong hunch that when the schools defined their own needs for change, their requests for help would be as various as the teaching situations represented throughout the League.

How could this help be provided? There was no doubt about the gap that existed between the assistance that school staffs looked for and the resources that were easily available to them. We began to see more clearly certain characteristics of the typical setting of the elementary school which are inimical to the development of self-renewing behavior, which, as we said in Chapter 1, was our goal for the schools. The concept of self-renewing schools conjures up an image of each school doing its own thing with resources ready at hand, but the truth of the matter seemed to be that a school was hard put to get the resources it needed to stray on a path of its own. District offices allocated services to all their schools from a central pool, according to schemes which usually allowed little flexibility for the school staffs who used them. Districts, furthermore, typically offered few appropriate resources for a school that might be toying with ideas outside of the current district pattern of schooling. Thus, even though League schools had been formally granted the freedom to deviate from district norms, the organization of district resources tended, in general, to conserve the status quo so that League schools could find little district assistance in making their freedom a reality.

We noted, too, that even if a school received resources from specially funded programs outside of the district, it gained little in the way of greater control over a wider range of resources, for the services offered by special programs were usually focused and distributed to reach only a few specific program objectives. When League schools faced the need, then, for resources for individual school projects, they turned for help to us, partly because they saw nowhere else to turn.

Partly too, of course, they turned to us as the instigators of the new expectations and (therefore) as the experts who were supposed to know how the new expectations should be met. Both those who were looking for surefire recipes and those who were seeking ways to stretch their own thinking viewed the SECSI staff as the people with the answers.

We had hoped to encourage the League schools to decide for themselves what changes they needed to make, but we realized now that in spite of our high purpose we had slipped into the usual expert-client relationship with the schools. And we began to see that this relationship itself is another characteristic of the typical elementary school setting which stands in the way of a school's becoming self-renewing, for it is the expert-client model which usually sets the tone for the interaction between a school and all of its outside resources.

The model defines the school staff as the client in need of the higher-level information possessed by the outsider. This definition is so taken for granted by all parties that the consequences of such a relationship are rarely inspected.

But there are consequences. We had already seen the extent of what we were beginning to call the "tell-me-what-to-do" syndrome. This dependency reaction is not surprising when one realizes that a school staff's whole experience with outside resources has probably been perceived by teachers and administrators alike as getting the benefit of all the expert knowledge that they can. And the traditional definition of the situation persists, even though the outside consultant may try sincerely to convince the staff to determine for itself what kind of additional information it needs.

Perhaps one reason for the persistence of the traditional definition lies in the general practice of having outside experts evaluate a school staff's efforts at innovation. The evaluation may be a formal requirement of a project for which the school receives extra funds; it may be routine inspection by district personnel; it may occur as informal comments by a consultant. Expectations of outside evaluation, we discovered, come automatically as part of a school staff's association with outside experts, even if the outsiders intend to leave evaluation up to the school. So it seems only logical for a school staff to look to the expert for the answer that will ultimately earn for the school the pat on the head that really counts.

On the other hand, we had noted that an acknowledged "expert" in the eyes of teachers and principals was not, paradoxically, often credited with knowing much about actual school problems. There was certainly skepticism among school staffs about advice that they received from those who did not have to face the same kind of Monday morning. The upshot seemed to be that outside help was construed as being expert all right but not necessarily as being immediately helpful.

The typical relationship, then, between an elementary school and its outside resources pictures a world in which all the worthwhile knowledge for a school staff at work on school improvement is produced, distributed, and evaluated by nonschool people, "nonschool" in the sense that they are people who are not members of school staffs comparable to those to whom they are dispensing information. True, many expert consultants have had experience in elementary school teaching and administration, but it is recognized that, as specialists or researchers, they have moved to a "higher" level. In this definition of the situation, the school staffs must look to people unlike themselves for guidance and critical judgments about the process of improving schools. Without seriously questioning this basic definition, school people react with varying degrees of uneasiness, which we saw reflected in the League schools' persistent quest for more help in solving practical problems. The salient consequence of casting all the schools' relationships with outside assistance in the expert-client mold is, it seemed to us, an ambivalence in school staffs toward their resources and toward their own capabilities, which stands in the way of a school staff seeing itself as a group reasonably able to define and work on its problems. Yet a staff must see itself as this kind of a group if it is to develop a self-renewing school.

FINDING NEW RESOURCES FOR SCHOOLS

Could we somehow break out of the expert-client mold and still come up with the practical help that the League schools wanted? What they were asking for did make sense. Although League principals and teachers did, for the most part, seem to be motivated to try out new behaviors in schooling, they needed to know more about what new behaviors looked like, and they needed to develop skills in performing in new ways. We had succeeded in providing the first spark; we had caught the interest of the schools. We had further succeeded in providing, through speakers at meetings and visits to schools, enough information to titillate or annoy school staffs. (Both reactions opened discussions on the possibilities for change.) But we had not gone very far in providing help for teachers who were trying to find the daily shape of new practices. We still were faced with the fact that even apart from the questionable value of the expert-client relationship, with the resources of the SECSI staff and the limited number of temporary consultants that we could afford, we would never be able to provide the extent of assistance that the League staffs were requesting. Yet we had raised a lot of expectations which had to be met somehow if the League was to become a group with the power to keep its members involved in finding more effective ways to solve school problems.

We took another look at our role as interventionists. It was almost certain that our initial success in arousing the interest of League schools had been due largely to what they saw as prestigious association with a nationwide organization and with "names" in education. Since then we had apparently moved toward developing school-to-school interaction itself as a source of rewards for school staffs, but the SECSI staff was still seen as the place to turn for advice and help. Obviously, we could not hope to go much further in building strong peer group bonds among the schools as long as we were the sole possessors of the resources that they needed to meet new expectations. Even the group ties which had been formed would start to deteriorate as soon as the schools began to compete for our limited services. Our approval would become all that counted; the group would be a group only in those symbols which we drew so hopefully on our chalkboard.

To make the peer group a reality we had to get rid of the critical power that we held, and we thought we saw a way to do it. Out there in those eighteen schools were a great many teachers and principals who had come up with creative solutions to the everyday problems which arose when schools tried to change their ways. It was true that the schools were asking for more help, but they had not been standing still while they waited for help to come. In every school there were people who regularly worked on their own to develop new skills through attending in-service classes and reading professional literature. A few schools had access to materials and consultants provided by specially funded projects. Futhermore, the schools were not all working on the same thing. For most of the problems that were brought up, we could find League schools in various stages of solution. Individualizing instruction in reading, reporting pupil progress to parents, grouping children flexibly—in these and a good many more areas there were schools that were just beginning to work and schools with more experience. To this range of skills and needs which we knew existed in the League we could add our evidence of the power of teachers' interschool visits and the teachers' requests for more involvement in League activities. The pattern that these pieces suggested, all put together, seemed pretty clear.

League school staffs could act as resources for one another in developing new skills and new solutions to meet new expectations. With school people helping one another, the total number of available resources would be increased far beyond what we or any intervention team could ever provide. Teacher-to-teacher, principal-to-principal information, furthermore, would be perceived as highly relevant to the problems encountered in making what looked good on paper look good in a classroom. To cap it all, the sharing of resources within the group should strengthen mightily the interschool ties that we were trying to build. Membership in the group would become important not only for the moral support but also for the professional assistance that it provided. We could, in short, divest ourselves of unwanted power and at the same time increase the effectiveness of the League as a self-propelling milieu in which schools learned to value and to practice receptivity to change.

And so we came to the principle of the magic feather in bringing about change in schools. The rationale went something like this:

1 Within the League group of schools there was a great pool of resources which could be used by the schools to help one another solve many of the problems that they needed to solve in order to explore paths to improvement. These resources included the moral support that schools could offer one another, the stimulation that could come from the exchange of ideas, and the practical information that could be shared as fresh ideas were translated into daily schoolkeeping. With these resources, in fact, the group could become a social system strong enough to do most of the job of maintaining itself while identifying and working on appropriate changes.

2 The League schools were not really aware of this capability they had as a group. They were accustomed to being directed by nonschool people.

3 If we were to activate the group's ability for self-directed change, we had to find ways to prove to the schools what they could do. We had to devise a magic feather—an intervention that would allay fears while the group consolidated and learned to exercise its real power, but an intervention that created no dependency upon us which would undercut that power.

How were we to make this rationale come alive in our activities with the schools? During the next two years we looked for tactics. A few guideposts were visible at the start. For one thing, we would certainly encourage more interaction among League teachers so that problems and solutions could be shared. We realized that, in addition to this exchange of knowledge, there would still be occasional need for information which could not yet be provided by any League people. We could probably get hold of specialists for this kind of limited assistance all right, but we would have to beware of allowing the schools to fall back into total reliance upon outside experts.

Another action that seemed indicated was reconsideration of our request that each school come up with a specific change project. Even though we had made it clear that the schools, not we, were to decide on the changes to be attempted, the projects were irrevocably tabbed as our requirement, and we were perceived as the eventual evaluators of their success. To continue this situation could scarcely encourage the schools to look away from us for advice and help. We had noticed, too, another phenomenon that seemed to call for rethinking the formal project notion. Although most League staffs had spent some time trying to work out the requested change projects, whenever principals or teachers got together at League affairs, their discussion concerned many smaller headaches which had arisen as staffs became involved in trying to assess where they were and how they might better do what they were trying to do. Perhaps "projects," as such, should be de-emphasized and schools should be urged simply to get to know themselves better.

Finally, it seemed that we should take League principals and teachers up on their requests to plan their own activities. In part, this was indicated as another way for us to bow out of the role of running the whole show, but we thought this should also build commitment to the League as an arbiter of standards of behavior, for there is a great deal of evidence that when group members actually engage in making decisions about what the group should do they are more apt to perform that behavior.

With these thoughts in mind, we began to try to change our role in relation to the League schools and watch for problems, which we were sure would accompany such an attempt.

INCREASING TEACHER PARTICIPATION

The word around the SECSI staff was now to "build the social system of the League," and the phrase soon became almost synonymous with increasing teacher involvement in League activities. Over the next two years five major types of interaction settings were developed by the SECSI staff to promote further teacher participation. First, interschool visiting was strongly encouraged. During the first year, the research assistants had come to know pretty well the programs and problems of most of the League schools. Now they were alert to every opportunity to suggest to the principal or teachers of school A that a visit to school B might afford useful information on a mutual interest or problem. Before long principals and teachers were often taking the initiative in arranging visits and in exchanging materials. (For example, a number of League schools developed ways to report pupil progress to parents that got away from grades on report cards, and there was much informal sharing of materials on these new ways of reporting.) We did not learn about some of these visits until after they had occurred, and it is certain that visits took place which never were recorded in the research files. As teachers became more experienced in the use of one another as resources, the pattern of the visits became more sophisticated. Visitors went with specific questions in mind; the host teachers arranged time to discuss with their visitors what had been observed in classrooms; the visitors followed up their experience with discussions back at their own school.[1]

A second kind of teacher interaction occurred in what were called "area meetings." Although the League schools were spread over nine counties in Southern California, it was possible to group the schools in three or four geographic clusters. We arranged for as many principals and teachers as possible in each of these clusters to meet together in one of the schools once or twice a year. The area meetings consisted of small and large group discussions of topics in which the schools had indicated interest and included some form of social activity (coffee, lunch, or tea, depending on the time of day).

Also drawn from the expressed interests of League staffs were the topics around which we devised another kind of teacher participation. Consultants, often from outside the project, led special sessions on specific topics three or four times a year. Principals were asked to bring two or three teachers with them to these seminarlike meetings.

Closely related to this kind of activity was the use of the League curriculum library. This collection of professional literature was housed in the SECSI offices and was directed by a member of the SECSI staff. Teachers and principals were encouraged to draw materials from this library and to consult with the library director about additional sources of information. The library director also regularly prepared and circulated to the schools bibliographies on areas of wide interest.[2] League principals and teachers used the library extensively. Meetings which were held in the SECSI offices took place in this library, and after every meeting most attending principals and teachers stayed to select material to take back to their schools. Numerous special visits were paid to the library as school staffs tackled new problems.

Most dramatic of the League events was the All-League Conference which was held once a year. An all-day Saturday affair at a Los Angeles hotel, each conference was attended by the League principals and about half of the teachers in the League schools. The format called for an opening address by a well-known figure in education, relating aspects of innovation in education to the opportunities that the League afforded its members. Various combinations of discussion groups then grappled with translating into school practice the message of the speaker, and people got to know one another better at coffee breaks and lunch.

Finally, the SECSI staff tried to supplement face-to-face encounters with a League newsletter. Three times during the first year League principals had received copies of a publication which was referred to as a League newsletter but which was more nearly a vehicle for providing the League schools with additional information about the thinking of innovative educators who were then well known on the national scene. In the second year the principals and teachers began to insist upon a newsletter that was truly about what went on in the League schools. The format of the newsletter was changed to feature information and pictures which highlighted school programs and League activities, and copies of the newsletter were sent to teachers as well as to principals. The production of the newsletter, however, was still entirely in the hands of the SECSI staff.

In the course of all the League activities which now brought together different segments of League school staffs in conversations about the nitty-gritty of changing schools, the talk of specifically designed school "projects" gradually faded away. Teachers had no time to spend on showpieces in innovation. Familiar patterns of daily behaviors were coming unglued in League schools as staffs asked themselves and one another if what they were doing made sense in terms of what they hoped to accomplish. Enormous effort was turned to finding new ways to fit together old behaviors and to learning new behaviors to fill just-discovered gaps.

At every opportunity, League teachers sought advice and suggestions from one another. Teacher meetings of all kinds were studded with sharing of concrete examples of how-to-do-it, watch-out, this-might-work—the fallout from daily coping with the unsettling ideas and questions which now roamed the professional lives of League school staffs. Many teacher discussion groups were led by teachers. Throughout these sessions an emphasis upon individualization of instruction was clear and was to be expected since the bulk of the input we had provided in the first year had favored discussion of this concept, but the resulting problems and tentative solutions reflected the various school settings rather than one formula.

With every encounter the teachers asked for more. The most common reaction expressed by teachers at meetings or on visits to schools was that there had not been enough time that day for all the sharing that they had wanted to do and that the opportunities for them to come together were too infrequent. From informal conversations, interviews, observations of meetings, and teachers' responses on meeting-evaluation forms, the SECSI staff tried to learn why there was such enthusiasm for interaction among League teachers. It was clear that teacher-to-teacher communication was perceived as a way of getting practical assistance, but far and away the most powerful reward offered by teacher interaction seemed, on the face of it, to be simply the continuing confirmation of togetherness in a risky but virtuous struggle.

Closer inspection of the material which produced this impression revealed that the expressions of enthusiasm were composed of several distinct strands of feelings. First, an important function of teacher participation in League activities had simply been to decrease teacher ignorance about the League organization itself. After the first All-League Conference, a teacher commented, "I feel more involved—like now I know what it's all about!" That League teachers were, on the whole, very vague about what they were into had become apparent at the end of the first year. While many teachers had accepted this as just another manifestation of the teacher's lot not to know, the opportunities to learn firsthand about the League—ideas and people —clearly raised a lot of spirits.

An almost immediate outgrowth of their new knowledge about what was going on became another reason for enthusiasm. Once the League was understood as an effort to push out the boundaries of what might be attempted in the search for improved schools, school staffs saw themselves as members of a select group.

> "This conference did much to make me feel a part of the League as a force for the improvement of instruction."

> "There's pride in knowing that education methods are no longer at a standstill."

At first, comments like these tended to come only from schools that had been relatively enthusiastic about the League project to begin with, but as time (and meetings) went on, expressions of professional pride in being associated with an avant-garde group appeared in schools where initial reaction to the League had been cool.

The reason which most frequently seemed to underlie teachers' enthusiasm about communication with other teachers was, however, the relief that the communication offered from the aloneness and dullness they had come to know in teaching.

> "It used to be that we always knew what was going to happen when. We all taught in unison—the same social studies units and the same everything at the same grades, you know. And now we try different things in different ways. You can't be sure just what is going on where. It's a lot more work, but it's very exciting." (Teacher, Dewey Avenue)

> "It was just great! Very stimulating!!" (Teacher, Rainbow Hill)

Often awkwardly put, often naïve, these expressions which appeared in conversations and questionnaires grew, in their sheer redundancy, to an eloquent statement of the bleakness of the ordinary life of teacher-in-a-classroom.

Another strand of thought could be detected early in the teachers' praises of League school interaction. Many comments indicated awareness of the staff of each school as a working group. In a few cases, teachers seemed to perceive contacts with other staffs as reinforcing their beliefs that their own staffs were doing better than most. More frequently, teachers spoke of their own staffs profiting from exposure to others:

> "I feel a part of a bigger group now and desire to try ideas more freely. Others have made mistakes but have tried."

> "I found that, in my belief, we have changed at Fairfield, and that thinking and planning there seem to go on more so than in some other schools."

> "As a staff we felt discouragement and a certain sense of futility before the conference. Now we recognize that the struggle to reach goals is shared by all League schools."

> "There was a little more unity and a feeling of 'we want to try something' in our faculty after the League meeting." (Comments after first All-League Conference)

The habit of speaking as a member of a staff group became pronounced as the League experience continued, and while there were at any one point a few schools which felt they were far ahead of the pack, these schools were not always the same ones, and they were always outnumbered by the schools which saw their contacts with other League staffs as boosters of staff morale and spurs to further group effort.

As League school people began to make evaluative statements about their own staffs, they wanted to involve more teachers in participation in League activities. Their reasoning was that there was a better chance for follow-up in a school if all (or most) of its teachers who faced a particular problem or held a particular interest could seek information and support through visits to other schools and discussions at League meetings. Efforts to broaden League participation within each school staff, however, brought the schools up against a major problem that from the start plagued teacher activities in the League. Could teachers be freed from classrooms to meet with one another? In order to visit the classrooms of other teachers in other schools such freedom was required, and although full-day conferences were held on Saturdays, area conferences and seminars were best scheduled for periods that overlapped with a few hours of the regular teaching schedule. Simply to tack teachers' meetings on the end of a full workday compromised their professional importance and suggested an invidious comparison with League meetings for principals, which routinely occurred during standard working hours.

How to free teachers to discuss problems and possible solutions with other teachers became, and remained, a constant headache for most League schools. Requests to their districts for released time for teachers to attend League activities brought positive responses to little more than half of the League schools. For those schools, the released time came in the form of a certain number of days per year on which teacher substitutes would be provided and/or a certain number of minimum teaching days per year. (Minimum days are days on which pupils leave school an hour or so earlier. The time lost to pupils on minimum days is made up in other ways, if necessary, to meet state requirements.) The released time allowances fluctuated over the years of the League, but while they certainly helped the school staffs who received them, they were never large enough to eliminate completely the problem of finding ways for more teacher participation in League affairs. The problem was, of course, compounded for the schools farthest away from the SECSI offices where many meetings were held and where the League curriculum library was housed. But, one way or another, all League schools did find ways. The ingenuity displayed by school staffs was considerable. They reorganized classes so that teachers could cover for one another; they used single teachers to supervise noncredentialed but competent personnel; they arranged for the principal to teach for the day. With these and other solutions, League activities for teachers were made possible, but never as extensively as the teachers or we would have liked.

The League was conveying more than reassurance to individuals and escape from the humdrum. School staffs were seeing themselves as *groups* coping with problems. Comments from principals and teachers revealed a clearer focus for the image of what "a League school" should be. A League school wasn't sure that it was doing the kind of job that it wanted to do, it tried new ideas, and it made mistakes—often. The image stuck, even though it didn't win praise in all quarters. From the time a principal first reported in a League meeting that his school was known as "the funny farm" in his district, that label was claimed by all League schools and came to be a badge of difference worn with considerable pride.

OTHER SCHOOLS AS A RESOURCE

A second major problem arose within a short time after the thrust to promote teacher interaction began. We brought it on ourselves, for we had slipped into encouraging a disproportionately high percentage of visits to a few schools only. At the start of the League it was obvious that Hacienda was the only League school which was already deeply involved in innovative practices. Time and again teachers from other schools were urged to see for themselves what could be done by visiting Hacienda. During the next two years Dewey Avenue, Shadyside, and Woodacres attempted highly visible "innovative" programs and joined Hacienda as the most-visited schools.

Somewhat belatedly we became aware of the dangers that we were courting by inadvertently creating a "star" system in the League. Veiled complaints and open gibes from principals evidenced the beginning of an unwanted competition among the members of the group. Nor were the overvisited schools always content with their one-sided role; Hacienda teachers, for example, were elated with the new ideas that they got on their first visit to another school, which did not occur until late in the second year. We could not see as certain, furthermore, that the logic of having teachers who were somehow "farther behind" (as innovators, in this case) observe those who were "farther ahead" was widely effective. While many teachers were indeed excited by what they saw in the very different-appearing schools, others chalked off such observations as essentially irrelevant to their own situations. One teacher spoke for many when she described Hacienda as "meant for another planet." Even though this particular teacher admitted that after their Hacienda visit she and her colleagues "changed the seating arrangement of desks and have never gone back to rows," the perceived gap between the two schools was too great to trigger much further exploration in the visitors' own school. This kind of reaction, of course, deprived visiting of its "reality" power with teachers, and to avoid it, we began to try to arrange more visits that might allow teachers to discover new ideas in relatively familiar-looking surroundings.

Our larger goal of decreasing dependence upon the SECSI staff, however, seemed to require that schools be able to arrange visits, as well as other communications, by themselves. To do this they needed more information than they had about the resources to be found in each League school. During the first year the close association of research assistants with the schools had, in a sense, created a central pool of information in our offices; we could use this information or pass it on to schools, as requested. In the second year our intervention staff was smaller, and in keeping with the plan to avoid encouraging the schools' tendency to lean on outsiders, they visited the schools much less frequently and only in answer to specific requests. In the third year the intervention staff was reduced to three people, and their visits to schools were still fewer. Although this progressive withdrawal did counteract the view of the interventionist as the prime mover in the school, it at the same time diminished the store of information about the schools which was available in any one spot. In order to recover a central pool of descriptions of League resources under the new intervention conditions, during the third year we requested each school to provide us with information about its own resources. Written descriptions of the resources in each school were then provided in a packet to each principal. This compilation was called the Needs/Resources Bank, and our hope was to find a way for the schools to update the information periodically.

REACTIONS TO THE NEW INTERVENTION STRATEGY

The fundamental problem, however, that was revealed by our effort to consolidate the strength of the League schools as a group was the staggering difficulty rooted both in the expectations of teachers and principals and in the beliefs of our staff members. There did truly seem to be almost universal agreement among League teachers about the value of their contacts with one another, and many teachers were content with the prospect of solving problems together:

> "It was great to have Dr. X. come out to our school, but I think visiting other schools is a better way to spend our time and money." (From a teacher report, Indian Flat School)

Many other teachers, though, were not willing to lose consultants from our staff. They wanted both SECSI consultants and teacher communication for various reasons. First, there always existed a contingent of teachers who demanded the security of getting approval from outside experts who knew the answers. Second, there were teachers who relied continually upon recognized experts for initial stimulation to seek new paths in familiar fields. Neither of these kinds of teachers quarreled with the new role for League teachers as consultants to one another; that was OK for certain practical advice and equally practical moral support (like, "I need to know I'm not the only one crazy enough to try this"), but the final approval or the original stimulus, they felt, must come from a nonteacher. All these teachers, furthermore, had expected the SECSI intervention staff to provide the kind of assistance that they wanted, and with the loose, exploratory intervention plan of the first year, most teachers had found some behavior in our staff which reinforced their expectations. Consequently, they were to some degree disappointed with our efforts to de-emphasize our consultant role and to play up the teachers' capabilities to provide mutual help. Compounding the problem was the fact that the large group of teachers who were not dismayed with diminished consultant services from SECSI, teachers whose appetite was whetted to get on with developing new ways in which they could help one another, were all too often frustrated by the limitations imposed by the shortage of time available to teachers for such activities.

In the first confusion of the attempted shift in the interventionist's role, the principals' reactions were distinctly, but somewhat curiously, different from those of the teachers. The principals were almost unanimous in objecting to the curtailment of visits by our staff to their teachers. Teachers, they maintained, needed this prestigious inspiration along with increased contact with other teachers. On the other hand, principals welcomed the prospect of our withdrawal from complete control over their own League activities. From the first year, a number of principals had persistently suggested that they plan their meetings themselves, and, as time passed, they increasingly voiced the observation that we might be providing them with too much input. The principals made no bones about wanting more time for informal interaction in order to find out in their own way more about one another and the League schools.

In response to the principals' reactions and in keeping with the plan to shift responsibility to the schools, we adopted the formal position of trying to pass the reins to the principals for the planning of League activities. The principals willingly discussed possible activities among themselves and with teachers and suggested topics for meetings. They were less willing to execute their suggestions, claiming that they lacked the time and dissemination facilities. This follow-through they left up to us and, on occasion, they noted that this relationship with the SECSI staff was the way the League should be. That is, the principals and teacher representatives should indicate what they wanted in League activities and leave it to the SECSI staff to produce appropriate results.

Our formal plan, then, to relinquish most of our control over the content and process of League activities did not quite come to pass, nor did the reasons lie entirely in the League principals' resistance to dealing with details. For part of our staff the effort to change our role was, at best, halfhearted. There had been no objection to the notion of strengthening the peer group bonds of the League, but different understandings of just what this notion meant surfaced quickly as the conventional role of consultant-interventionist was threatened by proposals of new intervention tactics. The new tactics required the interventionist to act only as a facilitator in bringing together League resources and League problems. The neutral qualities of such a role revealed two basic themes which divided the several conceptions of the interventionist role held by our staff members. One split occurred around the belief that the judgment of the intervention staff should ultimately prevail whenever it was necessary to assess, for any purpose, the work of the schools. This position had been reflected in the near creation of a star system among the schools. The second division centered on an acquired need for dependent clients, which seems at times to accompany commitment to the traditional interventionist role. One of our intervention staff members later described this need:

"It is so gratifying to go to schools and have people tell you how great you are. It is much more difficult to constantly work to do yourself out of the consultant role—to say, 'I can't help you with this, but Miss So-and-So from such-and-such school can.' We were asked not only to stop taking rewards which are comfortable, but to shift them to teachers or others within the system who can do the job as well or better."

While agreeing on the need to develop new ways of helping schools cope with change, when the chips were down our entire staff could not agree to restrict themselves to a strategy which would have interventionists forego the practice and pleasures of a superordinate position with respect to the League schools. The upshot was a potpourri of intervention tactics, some of which clarified the self-help abilities of the schools and others which nurtured continued dependency on the SECSI staff.

By the end of the third year a new set of problems was apparent. We had caught a glimpse of a long way down a road that led to schools bringing about change for themselves, but getting to that place seemed chancy at best for it would require, in a sense, flying in the face of our own history. We had started with a deliberately vague role vis-à-vis the League schools, in an effort to leave freedom for all parties to explore fruitful relationships. Each of the League school people had, of course, defined the SECSI role to suit his own preferred expectations, and on the SECSI staff we, too, had fashioned roles that met our several needs and beliefs. When the concept of the League as a self-directing and largely self-supporting innovative system had taken hold of our thinking, we had shifted some of our total intervention effort to allow or to inveigle the schools to use their own capabilities. As a whole, however, our intervention strategy was now a patchwork of internal inconsistencies, for it still accommodated tactics which kept alive the traditional expert-client relationship between the intervention staff and the League schools.

If we were to find out whether or not we could create a magic feather intervention and whether or not that kind of intervention would actually work, we had to relinquish the intervention tactics which were very likely to keep the schools dependent upon us. We had to mount an intervention strategy which was consistent with the magic feather principle. The new strategy might fail, but if it were not all of a piece, we could never tell much about why. We remembered our early cautions to ourselves not to get so caught up in trying to improve the League schools one way or another that we forgot our major goal of trying to learn more about why and how schools do or do not change.

And so the decision was made to spend the last two years of the project in an effort to test, as best we could, the intervention strategy that was implied by the magic feather principle. The decision led to a reorganization of the SECSI staff and the loss of some staff members. The decision would also lead, we were sure, to trouble with those League school people whose expectations for us would not be fulfilled. Nonetheless, we entered the last two years with new clarity about our two tasks. We would restrict our intervention to the magic feather strategy, and we would continue to develop a concept of the process that lay at the roots of change in schools. We had been building a picture of this process at the same time that we were discovering the power of the peer group in schools. It is to that story that we now turn.

NOTES

1 An example of this sequence of visiting activities is shown in the League film *Try It Sometime*, Part III of the film series *The League*, Institute for Development of Educational Activities, Melbourne, Florida, 1971.

2 Typical, though more extensive, examples of these bibliographies are "A Bibliography on the Process of Change" by Lillian K. Drag in Carmen M. Culver and Gary J. Hoban (eds.), *The Power to Change: Issues for the Innovative Educator*, McGraw-Hill, New York, 1973, pp. 245–277; and Lillian K. Drag, "A Selected Bibliography on Individualizing Instruction," in David A. Shiman, Carmen M. Culver, and Ann Lieberman (eds.), *Teachers on Individualization: The Way We Do It*, McGraw-Hill, New York, 1974, pp. 175–212.

TWO

STUDYING THE
CHANGE PROCESS

CHAPTER 4

THE SELF-RENEWING
SCHOOL

At the start of the League we had focused almost exclusively on the principal as the person in the school whose behavior either did or did not usher in change. The research assistants had been asked to observe each principal's leadership style in his school, and we tended for a while to speak among ourselves of a school's capacity to change only in terms of its principal's proclivities and skills.

We changed our way of talking, however, before the first year was out. We saw principals try hard to do what they felt they should do. Some succeeded, others failed.

"From the beginning, the first principal, Jerry W., was seen as a dynamo with great ideas. However, when it came to implementation, he assumed the SECSI staff would do it. When Leonard B. became assistant principal, he began to see all the 'people problems' that got in the way of these ideas. It wasn't until Leonard became principal that the school really got on its feet. Leonard's style is far more relaxed than Jerry's and, although not nearly as flashy, he spent great amounts of time (e.g., evening meetings) welding the staff together to work on its program." (Research assistant's summary report, Woodacres School)

"The faculty meeting each Wednesday was supposed to promote League activities. These weekly meetings became the jousting grounds between the principal and the staff. At each meeting, an informal agenda was announced by the principal, and then this agenda was subverted by the teachers. It became a game to see how successfully the agenda could be destroyed. Some of the League topics came last, least, or failed to come up at all. The principal resisted this game with varying degrees of success but usually lost. A typical encounter went something like this:

Principal: 'Today, we need to talk about just what it is that Frontier Junior High School wants to do as a League project. We need to get down to some specific objectives, a closer look at what it is that we feel is important.'

Teacher: 'Excuse me, Jason, but I think you ought to know that Cathy H. really tore up my fifth grade today. When I took her out in the hall and tried to write a detention slip on her, she told me to "shove it up my ---." Now, what are we going to do about this?'

Principal: 'Well! I'm certainly not going to tolerate that, etc., etc., etc.'

Several other teachers then joined the 'one upmanship' game to promote a long discussion on discipline. Forty-five minutes later, Jason tried again to focus on the burning problems of education, only to have Mrs. X arise and announce that she had to go pick up her baby from the babysitter. She was followed by Mr. Z who had to make a phone call— and so ended another faculty meeting.

There were times when the staff was trapped into talking together on League matters, but usually when the thinking of a few people began to reach a profound stage, you could count on one or two teachers to counterattack with charges of 'ivory tower,' 'nice-but impossible,' etc. This usually killed the creative contributions effectively.

As a consequence, the principal undertook one more strategy. He introduced the 'projects' himself. His enthusiasm met with reserved, polite silence. If this did not stop him, the staff had one more defense— to make counterproposals, apparently off the top of their heads.

At one point, one of the teachers suggested that field trips were extremely important to children and most appropriate for junior high school children and went on at great length to describe what he considered might be a worthwhile project for the League—supplying busses and field trips for the students." (Research assistant's report, first year, Frontier School)

The importance and individuality of the whole school staff in the success of the change effort emerged over and over again. The principal, as the administrative authority, had indeed the formal power to insist upon or to outlaw a potential change. Only in some situations, however, did the principal's actions forecast accurately what happened in the school. In other situations the principal's actions, by themselves, were not a very good predictor of what followed. For a principal's blessing on a given change to pass into action, the teachers had to be willing or able or both; and for a principal's ban of a potential change to be effective, teachers had to agree or be powerless or intimidated.

The more we saw out there in the League, the harder it was to talk or even think of "schools" in any simple way. We could not avoid, nonetheless, our task of finding ways to describe how the schools coped with pressure to change. Since we were supposed to initiate the pressure, we had to come at the description by first asking ourselves just what we were trying to accomplish with our intervention in the League schools. At the end of the first year, the SECSI staff agonized through weeks of what seemed almost endless meetings, confronting (or at least trying not to run away from) this question. The fruits of our labor—the welter of hopeful phrases, intense arguments, uncertain compromises, and fleeting pronouncements—can be reduced to the following paragraphs only by virture of their distance in time.

Before too long we reached agreement about not wanting to advocate any single, specific change in curriculum, instruction, or school organization; each school must do what was appropriate to its situation. We also agreed that we did want each school to be sensitive to changing school needs and to be capable of adjusting to a changing environment. The term "self-renewing school" was then much in use, and we interpreted it as congenial with our hope for the League. We wanted to help the League schools become self-renewing schools.

This was a big order—probably too big to execute and certainly too big to document. Even assuming that we could spell out what we meant by self-renewing (and at one point we actually attempted to), it just didn't seem likely that we could try to affect, much less keep tabs on, all the pieces of school life that would be part of such a definition. So, we began the process of settling for less than the whole thing at once. What chunk of the constellation of factors that we meant by a school's potential for self-renewal might we start to work on? What part was closest to the heart of the matter?

Primarily, we felt that self-renewal implied a receptivity to change. However, we did not envision a self-renewing school leaning with every passing wind of innovation. To us the self-renewal syndrome took account of the individuality of schools and tied a staff's choice of changes to its assessment of individual school circumstances. The attitude toward change that we looked for could best be called *responsible receptivity to change*, and our image of it was a school in which the staff regularly faced up to who they were, what they had, and what they wanted, and, in figuring out how to get from here to there, would seriously consider paths that they had never traveled as well as paths they knew. That was the line we would take. We would try to nourish in League staffs a responsible receptivity to change.

For our task of describing what was going on in schools that were trying to change, however, "responsible receptivity to change" was still too large a chunk to deal with even though it did appear less awesome than "self-renewal." We had to cut down still further and settle on some aspect of this receptivity which would meet several criteria. First, we wanted the aspect that we chose to be visible in everyday school life, for our basic task was to tease out the ordinary look of change. Second, we wanted to be able to build around it intervention activities that would consider the school staff as a unit. Third, we wanted it to be present in some form in all schools, whatever their degree of receptivity and whatever their other differences, and fourth, we wanted to see some clear hypothetical connections between it and other aspects of staff receptivity so that it might direct our intervention and description to a coherent cluster of factors.

To us, these criteria added up to looking for a process common to all school staffs through which any staff considers, accomplishes, or blocks any change. Such a process, we thought, might be described as simultaneously serving two functions. It acts as the daily arena in which all the school conditions that can combine to produce responsible receptivity to change interact and, as it were, continually negotiate the pattern that they will form together. At the same time, the process is being carried out according to whatever the current school pattern is; the process, in other words, is expressing the current degree of the staff's responsible receptivity to change. We reflected upon what we had observed as the principals and teachers coped with new expectations. In spite of the differences among schools, we thought that we could identify at least four kinds of behavior that all staffs engaged in to carry out their daily business—and any proposition for change becomes part of the daily business. In all schools there occurred some kind of *dialogue* about what was to be done—maybe only among a few people, maybe fragmented, but there was dialogue. In some way *decision making* took place—by the principal alone, in a few splinter groups, or with staff consensus. Some form of *action* was evident—individual or group, reasoned or intuitive. And somehow *evaluation* was accomplished—in private or public, planned or afterthought. Then dialogue again took up, consciously or unconsciously, the results of the evaluation.

This cyclical process might do to organize our thoughts about responsible receptivity to change. It seemed to satisfy our criteria of visibility and inclusion of the entire staff as a unit. We could look at the different forms the process might take in any school, no matter the degree of responsible receptivity to change, and look for other facets of school life that seemed to be related to the process. To start with, what would the process look like in a staff that possessed such receptivity? Early in the second year of the project we produced our first sketch of the kind of dialogue, decision making, action, and evaluation which we thought occurred in staffs that were responsibly receptive to change:

DIALOGUE which

1 Involves interaction between principal and teachers, teachers and teachers.

2 Is continuing; i.e., is the chosen means for dealing with concerns, issues, problems.

3 Is pervasive; occurs formally and informally—i.e., planned meetings are not the only place dialogue originates, and dialogue does not terminate there.

4 Involves the entire staff; everyone listens to everyone else; all points of view receive consideration; people are not afraid of each other.

5 Is substantive; concerned with instruction, curriculum, and school organization. However, we recognize the process is *not* deficient because the dialogue may deal from time to time with other concerns.

6 Involves the staff in the processes of evaluation and inquiry.[1]

  a Evaluation

    (1) Principals and teachers are comfortable with the concepts of objectives, evaluation, and research.

    (2) Principals and teachers discuss what kind of people they want their students to become.

    (3) The staff identifies the role the school should play in producing these kinds of boys and girls.

    (4) Attention is given to ways of assessing how well the school is carrying out its role and selecting criteria against which results can be judged.

    (5) Attention is given to the program in the school to ascertain how the role might better be carried out through comparisons between the end products and the criteria.

  b Inquiry

    (1) Staff looks at many sources of data—their own points

of view, the relevant situation, current practices, research findings.

(2) Staff formulates and examines the assumptions necessary to their educational decisions.

(3) The staff faces openly and makes explicit what they accept and what they reject.

DECISION MAKING based on
1 Staff involvement in dialogue.
2 Consideration of alternatives.
3 Weighing of evidence.
4 Selections made from among the alternatives.

ACTION through which
1 Decisions are implemented.
2 More dialogue occurs, thus renewing the entire process.

With this description as a touchstone for observation and intervention, we set out to gather more information about variations in what we now called DDAE—the obvious solution to the tedium of saying "dialogue, decision making, action, evaluation." At the same time, we would get the schools to help us think about DDAE.

Although League activities for teachers increased after the first year, the monthly meetings of the principals remained the backbone of the contact between the SECSI staff and the League schools. It was therefore in the regular meetings of the League principals that we made most of our early efforts to call attention to the emerging concept of the DDAE process. Through dozens of informal conversations and several formal statements, the words "dialogue, decision making, action, and evaluation" became familiar to the group, and although the details of the DDAE process were not as yet clear, its general import came through.

A NEW ROLE FOR THE PRINCIPAL

The principals were not much concerned with our quest for greater conceptual clarity about DDAE, but they were greatly concerned with what a school's responsible receptivity to change implied for the role of the principal. At the start of the second year, the principals began what turned out to be a sustained effort to redefine their role in the League schools. By the end of the project, this effort had encompassed many kinds of activities and had contributed substantially to an understanding of the DDAE process. It began, however, with about half of the League principals setting to work with a SECSI staff member on a rather vaguely defined task of looking at what a principal ran into when he tried to be a change agent.

The early outpourings of the principals in this volunteer task force testified to what they had learned in one year about how change is or is not accomplished in a school.

"Last year I took the material on change that I received from |I|D|E|A| and the ideas that I got from |I|D|E|A| and told the staff about them. We made almost no progress. Finally, when I became desperate, I decided to get the staff involved in school problems, and they went like a house afire. They really go when they are able to identify problems and to solve problems.

The key was their perception of me as a principal. The teachers could see right through me. I was controlling things. The test came when I let them go ahead with a reading program that I did not support. They were always telling me before, you say one thing and do another.

This process involves trust. I mean, the teachers came to me and said, 'So you really do trust us.'

The extent to which change has occurred is the extent to which the teachers feel free. I had to change, not them.

Of course, we can't just let teachers go. There are some political realities.

Now I go into their classrooms and ask questions. I say why are you doing this? Why are you doing that? Why! Why! Why!

Until teachers get involved there is no hope." (From minutes of volunteer committee meeting, second year)

Against this background, our staff member who was meeting with the group focused their efforts on producing a description of a role for the principal that would free a school's potential for continual self-renewal. During the year the volunteer task force worked out a proposal that the principal should act as a monitor of the basic processes that occur in the school. At the end of the year they presented their ideas to the whole group of League principals for discussion and informal adoption.

The case for the role of principal-as-monitor began with the proposition that teachers should make all instructional decisions in the school:

"We operate on the basic assumption that teachers can learn to make valid instructional decisions if allowed to make mistakes and learn from them. We believe, furthermore, that teachers will not change unless they are deeply involved in defining and assessing the school's goals and the methods of achieving those goals. Innovative instructional decisions passed down from upper administrative echelons will, in the main, be subverted for many reasons, not the least of which is the fact that teachers must be emotionally involved and committed to a decision before it is effectively implemented." (Report from principals' volunteer task force, second year)

The committee's report then asked, "If teachers make all instructional decisions, what does the principal do?" and went on to answer the question:

"The *first* role for the principal is that of decision-making monitor . . . to insure that teachers engage in systematic or rational decision making. He does not make the decision; he insists that they make the decision using what are considered appropriate steps or procedures in problem solving. . . .

The principal's *second* role is to act as group-process monitor. The principal needs to be well informed about group dynamics. He needs to see the weaknesses in using parliamentary practices, he needs to find ways to insure that influential blocks of teachers do not control all decisions and stifle minority views. . . .

A *third* role involves the principal as a resource person. The principal need not be an authority on all educational practices, but he should know where authoritative information can be found. . . .

We believe the position taken in this paper offers a promising way of improving instructional decisions and of developing truly professional principals and teachers." (Report from principals' task force, second year)

The role proposed for the principal was a dramatic shift from the actual behavior that most of the principals had exhibited at the start of the League. Time after time, one or another principal had explained that he had built his success on a reputation for running a tight ship, for straight-from-the-shoulder decision making. Nor had this style been associated only with "safe" decisions in schools that shunned new ideas; the same kind of no-nonsense leadership had also marked some openly innovative efforts. An example is the situation at Dewey Avenue School which had quickly moved to make several changes:

"Principal Stan M. called a meeting of his school staff and announced that the school had become a member of the League. He explained that many changes would occur next year. He added that anyone who would not be comfortable in this type of setting should ask for a transfer. Some did just that. The rest waited with some apprehension and uncertainty for what would come.

At a subsequent staff meeting, Stan asked the staff to write down their ideas concerning current problems in education. Few of the staff identified team teaching or nongrading as a means of solving any of the ailments of American education, but Stan was interested in nongrading and team teaching as approaches providing for differences in children's abilities. He felt that the League could provide an opportunity for him to bring these ideas to fruition.

To help convince his staff that nongrading and team teaching are effective ways of organizing the school, Stan arranged a summer meeting for his staff with an expert in team teaching. Attendance was voluntary, but everyone came. They might have attended because of interest, or it might be that they felt they had better find out about team teaching if that is what they would be doing next year.

The principal gave me the impression that he made all of the substantive decisions in his school. For example, he made all of the class groupings for the entire school (1,200 children) each year. He made decisions about placement of teachers, organization of bookrooms, playgrounds, lunchrooms, etc." (Report, first year, Dewey Avenue School)

Nonetheless, the notion of a different kind of principal behavior came to be of critical importance in the history of the League and in the growth of the concept of DDAE as the process which reflected a school's receptivity to change. The idea of the principal as a monitor of staff processes, indeed the very label "principal-as-monitor," was gradually but surely picked up by the League schools, though not always easily, for some principals were not eager at first to look at themselves. (One principal, during an early meeting of the volunteer task force, noted that he had come to discuss change in the school, but as far as his own behavior was concerned, he could see no problem.) The meaning of the monitor role was steadily built up in the group as individual experiences and thoughts were shared in all sorts of discussions. The principal as a monitor of staff processes became, quite explicitly, *the way that a League principal was supposed to be.*

FOCUSING ON DDAE

During the third year of the project we pulled together anew our observations and our assumptions about the DDAE process in schools. Watching and listening as the principals and their staffs worked out the monitoring role had given us more data on how the daily enactment of the DDAE process looked in different school situations. We could see that the process varied in appearance, but we certainly couldn't hope to document every difference. Still, to use DDAE as an organizing concept in describing responsible receptivity to change, we had to be able to talk about variations in the way the process was carried out.

So again we looked for a smaller bite to take. Could we identify a few key characteristics of the DDAE process that would give us a brief description of how receptive it was to change, no matter what the particular situation in which it occurred? We began to devise a series of questions that went through several stages of development. We clarified our own ideas about what might be important aspects of DDAE and tried these ideas out in questions which we put to teachers and principals. Their responses and comments led to several revisions in the questions. Finally, we settled on questions that asked about four characteristics of the DDAE process. These four characteristics, we felt, would lead us to a reasonably good *first* description of the DDAE process as the way in which a school staff arrived at and expressed its degree of responsible receptivity to change.

The first characteristic, the first thing we wanted to know about DDAE in each school, was the *scope* of the process among the staff members. Our fundamental question here was how many people participated in the several stages of the process—in the dialogue, in the decision making, etc. The proportion of staff members who were typically involved in the process, we said, should give us an idea of how much chance there was for varied points of view to influence ways of dealing with school business. We must emphasize this reasoning. Our interest in the scope of the process did not have to do primarily with concern for "democratic" DDAE or wide representation as a value in itself, but with concern for the larger number of sources which wider representation made available for different ways of looking at problems and for different orientations and skills in devising and carrying out potential solutions. In schools where the principal alone or the principal and a few teachers usually carried out most of the DDAE process in handling school affairs, there would be less chance of breaking out of the established order—however enlightened that order seemed to be at any given time—than there would be in schools with a wider base of participation.

The second characteristic of the DDAE process that we wanted to know about was the *importance* of the deliberations of which it consisted. Did a school staff see itself spending time just going through the motions, or were its dialogues, decisions, actions, and evaluations meaningful to the staff's professional life? We assumed that the degree of perceived importance of DDAE was related to responsible receptivity to change because a staff whose DDAE process was, in its own view, largely an exercise in fluff would rarely be dealing seriously with new possibilities in the practices of schooling.

The third characteristic about which we wanted each school staff to give us information was the *relevance* that the conduct of their DDAE process had to the ongoing operation of the school. Did the DDAE process consist of bits and pieces of discussions, decisions, actions, and evaluations which were triggered only by the vagaries of individual concerns and sudden crises, or did the process reflect an integrated, continuing staff deliberation of the issues it must face in the daily operation of the school? The extent to which the DDAE process was seen as relevant to the total school enterprise should, we felt, signal the school's capacity for identifying and executing appropriate alternatives to the status quo.

Finally, the fourth characteristic of the DDAE process which concerned us was the *flexibility* which the process exhibited. Were decisions, for example, the last word on the subject, or were they recognized as tentative? To what extent were actions seen as experimental? In the degree of flexibility of the parts of the DDAE process we thought we might see reflected a school's tendency to keep a number of options open as it coped with the problems that came its way.

These four characteristics of the DDAE process—its *scope, importance, relevance,* and *flexibility*—became, then, the basis for the questions that we asked about DDAE. Our questions took several different forms. One set appeared on a questionnaire which was filled out by everyone on a school staff.[2] (This questionnaire is the first instrument in Appendix C.) Other questions were asked during interviews with a sample of teachers from each school. Still another form that the questions took came on a rating sheet which was used by observers at school staff meetings, and the questions also determined the way we analyzed written reports which we received from certain teachers. Though the form varied, however, the questions always asked about those characteristics of the DDAE process which we had settled on as our basic indicators of its quality in relation to a staff's responsible receptivity to the change. The table on page 72 summarizes the ground that our description covered. On the left side are listed the

DIMENSIONS OF RECEPTIVITY TO CHANGE WHICH WERE USED
FOR MEASUREMENT OF THE DDAE PROCESS

	Dialogue	Decision	Action
Scope	How open is it?	How concensual is it?	How extensive is it?
Importance	How meaningful is it?	How substantive is it?	How significant is it?
Relevance	How sustained is it?	How consistent is it?	How patterned is it?
Flexibility	How inquiring is it?	How flexible is it?	How modifiable is it?

four characteristics of DDAE which we chose to consider. For each
characteristic there is the general question that we had in mind when
we observed or inquired about that characteristic as it applied to
dialogue, decision making, and action. Evaluation was not treated as
a separate element until the last year, and then we asked only about
the degree to which the staff planned for evaluation. There is no reason to suppose, however, that evaluation could not be described in
terms of the same four characteristics that were used for the other elements of the DDAE process.

In using these questions to gather information about the DDAE
process, we took account of one particular aspect of school organization. We recognized that a staff works sometimes as a total group,
sometimes in smaller groups—teaching teams, grade groups, special
committees. A typical pattern is a continual interaction between the
total group and various subgroups, with the total staff group dele-
gating responsibilities to subgroups and subgroups bringing ideas and
problems before the whole staff. Therefore, when we asked our questions about DDAE, we asked the school staff to answer them twice—
once as they applied to the DDAE process in situations where the
whole staff was working together and again as they applied to the
DDAE which was carried out in subgroups. Since we suspected that
the quality of the DDAE process within a single school might not be
the same for the total school staff and for various subgroups, it
seemed better to describe the DDAE process separately for total staff
and for subgroups before we ventured a composite picture of the
school.

We need to emphasize two limitations of our measurement of
DDAE (and of course there are more than two). First, we are not at all
suggesting that these four characteristics which we chose to describe
the DDAE process tell us all we should know about how that process

acts to encourage or inhibit change in a school. We are saying that these four traits seemed to be reasonable pegs—judging from our observation and talks with teachers and principals—on which we might begin to hang descriptions of the DDAE process as it related to responsible receptivity to change. Second, our conception of the DDAE process and the features of that process which we chose to describe are concerned with the quality of the process, not with its quantity. We did not, that is, think of one school as having *more* DDAE than another school and therefore being more receptive to change, but of schools having different *kinds* of DDAE processes which indicate more or less receptivity to change. This is not to deny that the question of the quantity, or the frequency, of the DDAE process in the school organization is an important question. Indeed it may be, but we simply did not deal with it systematically in this study.

NOTES

1   In this first attempt to describe the process, we talked of "evaluation" as part of "dialogue," though eventually we treated "evaluation" as a separate element. For the convenience of the reader we have used only our final division of four separate elements throughout the text.

2   The questionnaire asked that each person think of a particular problem or change or plan that the staff had worked on and then answer the questions in terms of what had happened in that instance. It usually reduces the tendency to express only general likes or dislikes if a person tries to describe a single specific occurrence; and since everyone on a staff chose his own example, we hoped that a variety of choices would give us a reasonably good picture of the quality of the DDAE process as a whole.

CHAPTER 5

SCHOOL CHARACTERISTICS AND DDAE

Even after we had determined what characteristics of DDAE we were going to focus on and had decided to consider both the total staff and subgroups of teachers, we were still not without problems in gathering descriptions of the DDAE process. One difficulty arose from the fact that we were encouraging attention to the DDAE process in the League schools while studying it at the same time. This mixture of intervention and research has the advantages and disadvantages of much action research. The special disadvantage is that as the intervention focused on the DDAE process, one could argue that it would be difficult to discriminate between the "real" quality of DDAE in League schools and mere testwise responses about DDAE.

In this respect, it mattered little whether the DDAE measurement was done via questionnaire, interview, or even observation. Enlisting the subjects as partners in a research enterprise inevitably teaches what the "correct" response is—which meant, in our case, teaching League staffs something of the presumed significance of the DDAE process. That was exactly what we wanted to do, but it does not make for an elegantly controlled research investigation of the DDAE process. We simply chose to risk this possible contamination of League data. Happily, as we will report later, the data suggest that the League in general reacted to our questions by thinking carefully when they were asked to describe DDAE in their schools.

We were not on the same tricky ground when we collected DDAE data from non-League schools, but here another limitation faced us, for we had to rely most heavily on our Basic DDAE Questionnaire in order to gather descriptions of the DDAE process from a large number of schools. As mentioned earlier, we did get other information about DDAE in League schools through interviews with teachers and by observing staff meetings. But since we were primarily interested in looking at DDAE in as wide a range of school conditions as possible, the only practical way to get comparable information from all the schools who cooperated in the study was to collect data via questionnaires.[1] We realized that no questionnaire was apt to give us more than a superficial glimpse of a process as complicated as our vision of DDAE, but we could make a start by learning what we could from the questionnaire that asked about our four hypothesized characteristics of the DDAE process.

From the answers to this Basic DDAE Questionnaire (Q1),[2] we checked our reasoning on several of the assumptions that we were making about the DDAE process. First, the questionnaire data revealed that though there were indeed differences in some schools between the quality of DDAE as it occurred in the total staff and the DDAE that went on in subgroups in the same school, the overall patterns of the two kinds of DDAE were similar enough that we could legitimately combine them to make a composite DDAE score for a school.

Although our data did indicate that the DDAE concept (as defined by the Basic DDAE Questionnaire) was not a unidimensional phenomenon, we were able to demonstrate sufficiently high and positive interrelationships among the questionnaire items so as to render a single, total score on the instrument which would be a meaningful index of the level of school DDAE as perceived by the school staff (T5.1).[3] The data from the Basic DDAE Questionnaire showed, furthermore, that dialogue, decision making, action, and evaluation did appear to be pretty much a cumulative process; that is, they tended to occur in sequence with any given topic (T5.2). Of course, we do not believe that dialogue, decision making, action, and evaluation are always neatly and tidily separated and proceed step by step in a routine fashion. The most cursory observations in schools reveal feedback loops from decision making back to dialogue or jumps from dialogue to action. But, in general, our data suggest a rudimentary ordering from the first D to the E. We were also able to check on whether teachers' answers about DDAE seemed to be greatly influenced by their age, their years of experience, or by certain attitudes that they held toward the world in general. It was comforting to learn from our data that this did not seem to be the case because if it had been, we could not have been sure to what extent the descriptions of DDAE were just roundabout descriptions of a variety of personal traits (T5.3).

When we inspected teachers' responses on the Basic DDAE Questionnaire with a statistical technique called factor analysis, we discovered that the responses could be said to describe two qualities of the DDAE process as a whole (T5.4): how *salient* it was and how *open* it was. These two qualities—salience and openness—looked like reasonable indicators of the amount of responsible receptivity to change that a DDAE process itself might possess.

Our questionnaire, limited though it was, made a certain amount of internal sense. Now we had one more important question to face: How well would our abbreviated description of the DDAE process work as an indicator of a larger set of school conditions which theoretically favored or opposed responsible receptivity to change? The evidence which spoke to this question came from data showing how our assessments of DDAE quality related to scores from other questionnaires about a variety of aspects of school staff life. At the end of the project all our questionnaires were given to League schools and to two other sets of schools. The first set consisted of one randomly selected elementary school from each of the eighteen League districts. Each school was about the same size as the League school in its district. The second set was composed of thirteen elementary schools scattered over several states other than California.[4] With the responses to the questionnaires we could make certain comparisons among the schools. We could compare League schools with non-League schools, and we could compare schools which scored high on DDAE quality with schools which scored low on DDAE quality (League and non-League schools combined). Later chapters take up some of the comparisons of League and non-League schools. Right now we jump ahead of our story long enough to present data on how the quality of the DDAE process, as we measured it, was related to other school conditions.

CHARACTERISTICS OF HIGH AND LOW DDAE SCHOOLS

Using all the DDAE information that we had (including observation and interview data where they were available), we developed a composite or summary DDAE score for each school and ranked all 49 schools (18 League schools and 31 non-League schools) on their scores. The Basic DDAE Questionnaire score received the largest weight in forming the composite rank. We then called the top one-third high-level DDAE schools; the next third, middle; and the bottom third, low (T5.5). Now we could look at various data for each of these three groups and see what high DDAE tended to "go along with." If DDAE quality would serve, as we hoped, as an indicator of a school's responsible receptivity to change, then we would expect our measure of DDAE to relate in certain ways to the other facets of school life which our several questionnaires described. High DDAE schools should be different in a number of ways from schools with lower levels of DDAE.

Formal Organization of the School

From each of these schools we obtained information that allowed us to classify schools according to the predominant ways in which teaching was arranged. Over half of all the schools were organized in self-contained classrooms; a little less than a third of the schools had some form of cooperative arrangement in which groups of teachers worked together; the rest of the schools—about a fifth—operated with a mixture of self-contained and cooperative teaching.

These teaching patterns showed a strong relationship to the DDAE level of the schools. More than two-thirds of the high-level schools were organized in cooperative arrangements, and about four-fifths of the low DDAE schools were organized in self-contained classrooms (T5.6). Of course, this does not tell us which came first in these schools—whether cooperative teaching promoted higher-level DDAE in a school or whether high DDAE influenced change away from the traditional self-contained classroom. From what we observed in the League, however, we guess that pressures occur in both directions, that there is a continuing interaction between the quality of the DDAE process and the formal organization of the school once the staff makes a change in its organization or becomes strongly aware of its DDAE process. Thus, the creation of cooperative teaching arrangements increases the number of formal channels which are available for task-oriented communications and may even, to some extent, force the use of these channels. On the other hand, when a staff begins to assess its own DDAE process, it may well decide to set up cooperative teaching arrangements to overcome communication blocks among self-contained classrooms.

Informal Relations in the Schools

Whatever the formal organization of teaching in a school, some informal discussion usually takes place among teachers. We were able to get questionnaire information from two-thirds of the League schools and almost half of the non-League schools about the extent of these informal relations and whether they seemed to be based simply on friendship or consultation about teaching matters (Q5).

We found that there was a slight tendency for friendship contacts among teachers to be more widespread in higher DDAE schools. More interesting, however, was what we found concerning the discussions that teachers said they had about matters of instruction and discipline. These kinds of discussions seemed to be more extensive in schools which scored highly on the quality of DDAE in their *subgroups* (T5.7). (Remember that we had a separate measure of the DDAE process as it occurred in subgroups, such as teams or grade groups.) We found this reasonable, for our observation and the many reports we had from teachers told us that the DDAE process in subgroups was dominated by subject matter which was fundamental to teaching. We could expect then that an open, inquiring kind of DDAE in these subgroups would occur within the context of a broad and constant flow of informal advice-giving and mutual consultation about the tasks at hand. That is what these particular scores suggest, not that high DDAE can simply be equated with a friendly, sociable staff.

The complexities of the rapprochement between individual and organizational needs are suggested when we look at the relationship between formal structure of schools and the informal teacher contacts within them. Just as we would expect, we found more informal communication networks among teachers in schools which had cooperative teaching arrangements or a mixture of cooperative and self-contained classroom teaching (T5.8). We have already noted that both cooperative teaching and informal consultations tended to be found with higher-level DDAE. Putting these findings together, it isn't hard to imagine how staffs may move toward greater receptivity to change through various sequences of modifications in formal structure, informal contacts, and DDAE level. A change to cooperative teaching, for example, may necessitate more informal consultation, or an increase in teachers' exchange of information might lead to an experiment with cooperative teaching. The quality of DDAE might be affected either way. On the other hand, an original interest in the DDAE process could produce changes in both formal and informal structures. We think that we saw bits of all these patterns in the League.

The Role of the Teacher in the School Staff

We were particularly interested in looking at a set of scores which indicated how much influence or power teachers felt that they had in a number of areas of decision making in their schools (Q6). For at least two reasons it seemed plausible that the amount of power that teachers felt they had was to be reckoned with in describing responsible receptivity to change and so would be associated with the quality of the staff DDAE process. First, there has been a steady accumulation of evidence that a sense of control is a critical factor in determining the quality of performance of groups in a variety of organizational settings. This seemed relevant to the kind of performance that we would expect in a staff which confronted problems creatively, came to decisions about them, carried out some action, and assessed the new situation. Second, assuming that the teachers' perceptions reflected the influence that they actually exercised, greater influence should mean more resources at the teachers' command throughout the DDAE process. Too little power to manipulate the pieces which formed the daily pattern of school life might well limit the scope and flexibility of the decision-to-action sequences which teachers were able to carry out.

The scores on teacher power showed very clearly that teachers in high DDAE schools, as a whole, said they had more influence in decision making than did teachers in low DDAE schools (T5.9). This fit our overall expectation, but we also thought that there might be differences among schools in particular areas of decision making. If a high level of DDAE signaled a greater staff capacity for creative coping with school problems, then teachers on such a staff should be accustomed to wielding influence in decisions that had schoolwide impact. We looked at the scores on each item of the teacher-power questionnaire in order to find the percentage of teachers who said that they had influence in making decisions in different areas (T5.10). Now we saw that the least differences between high and low DDAE schools were generally in those areas that have traditionally been the province of classroom teachers—for example, daily classroom schedules, pupil behavior in classrooms, and parent conferences. The *largest* differences occurred in areas that pertained to the operation of the whole school, among them curriculum, selecting and assigning teachers, assigning pupils to classes, and unusual problems that affect the whole school. In such schoolwide decisions teachers in high DDAE schools claimed more influence than teachers in low DDAE schools. In sum, the teacher power that existed in low DDAE schools tended to be restricted to areas that affected only one or a few teachers at a time, whereas in high DDAE schools teacher influence was also found in areas which implied more coordinated assessment of and dealing with issues.

In addition to asking teachers to judge the amount of influence that they had, other questionnaires called for descriptions of several other teacher behaviors. When we looked at scores which had to do with the general morale and atmosphere in the school, we saw that the schools with higher DDAE showed generally higher scores than schools with low-level DDAE (T5.11). They were more likely to report, for example, that teachers liked working in the school and that the principal was helpful and less likely to say that teachers were critical of one another or that routine requirements hindered their teaching. Similar findings (T5.12) occurred in terms of school climate as measured by teacher responses to an adjective checklist (Q8). Teachers in high DDAE schools more often described their schools as developing, honest, or creative. Also, in high DDAE schools, teachers within each school were in more agreement as to how they described staff behaviors in that school than were teachers in low DDAE schools, which did seem reasonable since a high DDAE setting implies more open communication among staff members (T5.13).

Most interesting, however, was another finding. We were curious about how the descriptions of various teacher behaviors hung together in high and in low DDAE settings. Did certain kinds of behavior tend to go together in certain ways? In other words, did there appear to be consistent overall patterns of teacher behavior associated with DDAE level? The fragment of an answer that we were able to get intrigued us (T5.14). Looking at average scores for each school, we noted that within the group of low DDAE schools the scores describing various teacher behaviors tended to fit together in a fairly clear, commonsense arrangement, with traditionally good things associated with one another and not with traditionally bad things. A staff, for example, which was described as seeking opportunities for professional growth tended to be described also as having high morale and freedom from requirements that interfered with the business of teaching. Among high DDAE schools, on the other hand, a pattern was not as clear. Contemplating these results, we thought immediately of the destruction of firm patterns that is implicit in the notion of self-renewing schools and of the individual nature of school situations that is inevitably recognized by anyone who looks below the surface of problems of change. Now there was before us a hint that across a number of high DDAE settings the relationships among different aspects of teacher behavior varied—perhaps according to the problems and the situation at hand in each school?

We also took a look at the general school climate as indicated by the staff's response to a list of selected climate adjectives (Q8). How did they fit with descriptions of several facets of staff behavior? Again, there was no clear pattern in the group of high DDAE schools, but the scores among the low DDAE schools appeared to indicate that those staffs shared a quite conventional view of what constituted a pleasant work world—a view which seemed little affected by the fact that they were in different schools (T5.15). We would keep this in mind as we looked at further information.

The Principal's Role in the School Staff

We had asked a number of questions about how the principal behaved as a staff leader. Did he, for instance, set an example by working hard? Did he help teachers with personal problems? Did he correct teachers' mistakes? Did he hold meetings to a tight agenda? Did he encourage others to provide leadership? Did he communicate effectively? Both principals and teachers answered these questions. As we would expect, the overall quality of principal leadership was judged to be higher in high DDAE schools. He was more apt to be seen as especially helpful to teachers, as setting a good example by hard work, and as possessing considerable professional skill. Also, in high DDAE schools, which presumably had better staff communication, there was greater agreement between the principal and teacher descriptions of principal leadership behavior (T5.16).

None of our data could tell us whether the principal's behavior caused certain teacher behaviors, vice versa, or a bit of both. A few sets of scores, however, offered information as to how teachers and principals recognized and reacted to power wielded by the other party. One such set of scores came from a question which asked teachers to indicate why they did what the principal suggested or wanted them to do (Q9). We found that, in general, the principal's influence in high DDAE schools was attributed to his professional competence and to his likeableness as a person, but in low DDAE schools more teachers responded that the principal could pressure or penalize those who did not cooperate (T5.17). Low DDAE schools were also more apt than high-level schools to consider seriously the principal's power to reward teachers and the principal's legitimate right to be obeyed.

We caught a glimpse of the other side of the coin when we looked at how principals assessed the amount of influence that teachers had on decision making in their schools (T5.18). These scores showed that principals agreed with teachers that there was indeed greater teacher influence in high DDAE schools than there was in low DDAE schools (compare T5.9 with T5.18). Perhaps of greater significance were other scores of high DDAE principals which indicated that principals who perceived more teacher influence in their schools were apt to give more favorable evaluations of their own leadership, their staff, and the climate of the school (T5.19). In other words, these principals seemed to perceive teacher power as a generally good thing. This was not so with the principals of low DDAE schools; that group tended to view the amount of teacher influence as either unrelated or negatively related to the caliber of principal leadership, staff functioning, and overall school climate.

Of greatest interest, however, were certain outcomes which hinted again at variability among staffs in high DDAE schools in the way that they looked at their school worlds—a variability that was not evident in the group of low DDAE schools. First, looking at the average scores for each school, we saw that in the group of low DDAE schools, staffs apparently tended to make the same kinds of connections among the various aspects of principal behavior that we asked about. Their scores, that is, tended to go together in fairly definite ways (T5.20) generally associating good principal leadership with traditional values such as businesslike behavior and good staff meetings. The staff scores from high DDAE schools, however, didn't indicate much agreement from school to school on how different kinds of principal behavior were associated with one another. The same theme that had been sounded when we considered patterns of teacher behavior now recurred with the way a principal's behavior was perceived. And to us it made the same kind of sense. In schools where communication is fairly restricted, where things tend to remain the same (indicated by low DDAE), staffs of different schools share a traditional coherent view of the principal, but in schools with a more open and inquiring DDAE process, the various aspects of a principal's leadership behavior may fit together in different patterns, depending upon the situation of the school.

Next, we inspected the relationship between the teachers' scores on their own behaviors and their scores on principal behaviors. Was there any evidence of a pattern here—where one behaves this way, does the other behave that way? Once again the data evoked the same strong impression (T5.21). Among low DDAE schools if teachers rated themselves high, they tended to rate the principals high. By contrast the scores from the group of high DDAE schools showed no such neat meshing. To us the lack of overall pattern in the high DDAE schools spoke again of situational differences that are recognized by school staffs when they begin to open up to themselves the process by which they carry out their work.

Summary of School Characteristics

What kind of answer did we get to our question about how well a school's level of DDAE might serve as an indicator of a cluster of school conditions which we would expect to make up responsible receptivity to change? Let's list (from the foregoing pages) the school conditions that we found to be associated with high DDAE and those that we found to be associated with low DDAE.

In the group of high DDAE Schools	In the group of low DDAE Schools
There were more cooperative teaching arrangements.	There were more self-contained classrooms.
There were more friendship networks among teachers.	
There were more task-oriented communication networks among teachers.	
Teachers had more influence in decision making, especially in decision areas affecting the school.	Teacher influence was limited to decision areas which affected only a few people.

In the group of high DDAE Schools	In the group of low DDAE Schools
The quality of principal leadership was generally higher.	
The principal's influence was more likely to depend on his competence and his likeableness.	The principal's influence was more likely to depend on his power to reward and on his legitimate right to power.
The principal was more apt to see teacher influence in school decisions as desirable.	The principal was more apt to see teacher influence in school decisions as undesirable.
Overall school climate was more favorable.	
Teachers within a school showed more agreement on how they described their school.	
There was a greater agreement between a principal and his staff on how they described their school.	
There was no clear pattern from school-to-school on:	There tended to be a traditional pattern from school-to-school on:

The relationship among different teacher behaviors.
The relationship among different principal behaviors.
The relationship between teacher behaviors and principal behaviors.
The relationship between general school climate and various staff behaviors.

Even though, of course, the aspects of school life which we had considered were but a smattering of those one can imagine making up a staff's responsible receptivity to change, we felt that our measure of DDAE had not behaved badly as an indicator of that receptivity. The organizational arrangements that characterized our group of high DDAE schools and the evidence of the changes in them from the traditional roles of principal and teacher pictured school settings in which ideas could be generated from a number of sources and put into the mainstream of staff deliberations. Above all, there was the indication that those schools had not simply traded one mold for another but that, instead, each was making do with what it had, adjusting the principal's leadership style, teachers' skills and preferences, internal resources, external pressures—all these pieces and more in the search for a new individual pattern of carrying out its business.

DDAE AND THE MAGIC FEATHER STRATEGY

To return now to our story, we realized by the end of the third year that the time had come to combine our two major tasks into one effort—to incorporate the development of our new intervention strategy with our notion of DDAE as an indicator of responsible receptivity to change. Let's recap our whole concept of the magic feather type of intervention and see just how DDAE fits into it. First, we believed that the League schools *as a group* already contained enough resources within themselves and enough access to other resources to take care of a great part of the assistance and the intellectual stimulation which they would need in order to make changes. The magic feather principle directed us to build interschool communications which encouraged the recognition and use of these resources in sharing problems and solutions. Obviously though, we also had to think about what went on *within any single school* that could conceivably prod it to look for and to utilize the outside resources which were available in the League. That "something" within a school we called the staff's responsible receptivity to change, and we saw the DDAE process as the channel through which such receptivity could be fostered and, alternately, implemented in the conduct of school business. Therefore, just as we believed that the schools together had the ability to provide support and stimulation for one another—if they learned to recognize that ability—so, too, we believed that each school possessed, in the form of the basic mechanism of DDAE, a means for increasing the staff's responsible receptivity to change—if the staff came to recognize its own DDAE process for what it was and for what it could be.

The magic feather principle now suggested that we draw the schools' attention to the DDAE process and encourage them to observe how it was operating and to be critical of it; in other words, that we use the interaction among schools to build awareness of DDAE and inquiry about it. Thus, DDAE might function in our intervention strategy, as it did in our description of responsible receptivity to change, as a convenient handle by which we might grab hold of the larger objective. We decided to do it. A focus on DDAE didn't seem to involve anything totally different from what the schools were already doing. Principals and teachers would continue to share interests, problems, and resources (as one of our staff was wont to say, "you have to DDAE about something"). Now we would simply try to spark their interest in how problems were identified and solutions attempted.

Consequently, in the last two years of the project we worked toward one objective. The objective was to get the League schools to help one another increase each school staff's ability to "see" its own DDAE process and to consider how that process was helping or hindering it to meet the expectation that a League school would engage in self-scrutiny and be alert to new possibilities. The objective encompassed our two major tasks, for it allowed us to gather evidence as to whether or not the peer group approach was an effective and feasible intervention strategy, and it directed us toward DDAE as a concept which might ultimately serve to organize information about the processes of change in schools. Before we begin to describe the actual intervention activities through which we tried to accomplish this objective, a word is in order about the general stance we took in our work with the League principals and teachers during this final period. The magic feather principle directed us to strengthen the peer group—that is, to increase communication among schools about their problems and to help them find more effective ways to share their resources in relation to those problems. We accepted this direction, and we were able to *talk* about playing a facilitator role rather than a direct helper role. But it all made us definitely edgy—for reasons that seem clearer at the time of this writing than they did then.

For one thing, we were sensitive, particularly at the start of this period, to the fact that several of our staff who had established close contacts with the schools had left the project because they did not want to give up what they believed was essential consultant assistance in order to test the peer group approach. We made no effort to hide this situation from the League schools and frankly explained the staff departures as the result of disagreement about an organizational decision to devote the last two years of the project to an intervention which would try only to build the League as a peer group of schools helping each other solve problems and learning more about the DDAE process. Principals, for the most part, voiced professional understanding about how upsets occur when there is staff disagreement on organizational goals. (It was almost, "Welcome to the club!") Many teachers, furthermore, were willing or eager to get on with finding out what they could do together. Still, we were not to get away easily with the change that we were proposing. From the schools there came an almost continual dribble of chastisement and innuendo which never let us forget that a number of people out there grieved the departure of the lost SECSI staff members and resented the changes we were trying to make in our role. The fact that we had known it would happen was small aid or solace in coping with the realization that there was no way for us to know exactly how many strikes we already had against us.

Even without such feedback from the schools, however, we would have had qualms as we set about planning our intervention tactics. We were no different from the staff members who had left in that we cared very much about what happened to the schools, and we, too, had been trained to act as experts. The shape in which the new facilitator role first appeared to us looked meager indeed, for it was shorn of many familiar practices and spoke to us only of what we should *not* do. We would, for example, have to forego much leaping into the breach and guard against being too easily convinced that we were the only ones who had the skills that the situation of the moment demanded. We were constantly catching each other trying to rationalize a comfortable old behavior on the grounds that *this* time they really couldn't do it themselves, we owed it to them, and so on.

So there we were. The schools would have been content for us to play from the same old repertoire, allowing them to venture on their own only as far as the cord of dependence on us would reach. We could have turned away from that first bleak vision of an intervention stripped of the regular kicks of saving the day for this or that school. Instead, we stuck to our plan. We were going to find out if the magic feather strategy would work. We had no choice but to learn new behaviors.

Our high resolve didn't seem to get us very far for a while. Just leveling with the schools about our intent to change our ways didn't automatically erase old patterns. It was months before they truly came to expect us to suggest resources within the League whenever they asked us for expert advice. And we wrestled again and again with the question of just how we should behave with League people when we weren't actually arranging interschool contacts. We never did really think through an answer so much as we stopped seeing our new role as a "question" and simply became more comfortable about behaving as what we were—people who had a legitimate job to do in studying some of the aspects of change in schools and who were absorbed with finding different ways of going about the job.

Yet, at the start of the last two years it was with something less than a sense of confident control that we set out toward our objective of developing the League into a self-reliant group which encouraged all its member schools to be aware of how the DDAE process might be used to discover a wider range of alternatives in schooling. We concocted as a guide a master chart which laid out our main assumptions about how the peer group approach might be used to encourage responsible receptivity to change through attention to the DDAE process and how those assumptions could be translated into appropriate activities for the League schools. The chart directed our attention to activities that would

1 Encourage roles for teachers and principals that could maintain an open and inquiring DDAE process

2 Maximize the communication of ideas that would tend to continue each staff's assessment of its own DDAE process

3 Provide for sharing resources that could alleviate certain potentially troublesome consequences of an open and inquiring DDAE process

4 Promote the kind of visibility to a larger public that would make the schools proud of their League membership—proud, that is, of their concern about responsible receptivity to change

Of course, many activities were planned to serve simultaneously more than one of these four purposes. The logic of the strategy will probably be clearer to the reader, however, if we describe for each of the stated purposes the major League activities which we perceived to be directed toward that purpose and some of our findings relevant to that purpose.

In the next three chapters we will try to do just that.

NOTES

1 As it turned out, we were able to collect some interview data from the non-League schools in California.

2 Throughout this chapter (and Chapters 7 and 8, also), references will be made, when appropriate, to Appendix C, which contains the measurement instruments referred to in the text. For example, (Q3) refers to questionnaire three in Appendix C.

3 Relevant data are presented in tables in Appendix D. They are cross-referenced by the chapter in the text in which they are cited. For example, (T5.4) refers to the fourth table for Chapter 5 listed in Appendix D. This system of cross-referencing is more fully explained in the introductions to Appendixes C and D.

4 The out-of-state schools are described in Appendix B.

CHAPTER 6

CHANGING THE ROLES OF PRINCIPALS AND TEACHERS

The crucial assumption behind the notion that a self-conscious, self-help group of schools could encourage responsible receptivity to change was that peer interaction in such a group was capable of modifying traditional expectations about what principals should do and what teachers should do. As we worked on our concept of DDAE, we saw that process as the primary context in which staff roles were enacted and perhaps changed. The development of the idea that a League principal should be a monitor of the DDAE process lent early support to these assumptions, and all of our work with the schools was permeated with efforts to continue their thinking about principal and teacher roles.

In the final two years, frequent reassessment of the traditional teacher-principal relationship occurred as an outgrowth of a perennial problem which at that time assumed central importance to League school staffs. How could new staff members best be assimilated in League schools? In their first meetings during this period the principals discussed the problem frequently, and we took the opportunity to encourage them to think of ways to involve the entire staff in assimilation of new members.

A few principals began to experiment with having their teachers participate in selecting and assisting new teachers. As they talked about what happened, the concept took form that evaluation of new teachers was a legitimate decision-making area for League teachers together with League principals. All right, then, what about having all teachers help to evaluate one another? What about having teachers participate in firing as well as hiring? Now, difficulties were recognized. Teachers were at first reluctant to select staff members for dismissal, yet in several League schools, faced with disastrous budget cuts, the decision about who should go and who should stay was made by the entire staff or a representative committee, not just by the principal. Generally, however, while the principals felt that teacher-to-teacher evaluation was indeed desirable, they tended to favor easing into it, with new teachers only as the first object of evaluation. As Steve M. noted, it was a scary thing for many teachers, and while teachers did want to talk about it, a staff was apt to say for quite a while, "Let's just talk about it."

The principals may have misjudged the threat that peer evaluation posed for teachers. Certainly, informal evaluation of this kind was going on in most League schools and was an implicit element in the interschool activities. Whatever the case, the role of the teacher in League schools was undergoing change. The concern among principals and teachers about the assimilation of new teachers was both recognition of what had already happened and impetus (through constant spillover from this concern to other areas of decision making) for continuing the process.

As we look back we are able to make out a kind of sequence which, generally speaking, occurred in the League schools throughout the project as the roles of principal and of teachers underwent modification. The sequence which is described here has much in common with Lieberman and Shiman's observations of changes in school programs which are made in another report from the SECSI project.[1] The interested reader will find that interpretations in that report enlarge the picture presented here.

The Change Sequence: Stage 1

At the start of the project most of the League schools were not very different from other schools in terms of the roles which principals and teachers played in the DDAE process. Staff meetings, for example, were largely occasions on which the principal talked and teachers listened. The common definition of roles in this first stage grew from the assumption that the principal had the special knowledge needed to make all decisions outside of individual classroom matters.

As long as principal and teacher roles were based on this assumption, teachers and principals alike had a very fuzzy view of the DDAE process in its entirety. They saw pieces of dialogue, knew about certain decisions, and each person in some way took part in action and evaluation; but there was little comprehension by the staff as a group of the whole picture of the DDAE process in their school. Perhaps the most striking characteristic of the typical DDAE process, we discovered, was its invisibility as a process to those who carried it out. The laughter of sudden recognition, for example, came once during a principals' meeting when Steve M of Antigua School recounted the story of a recent hassle in his staff about how the pupils were supposed to use a certain piece of playground equipment. Teachers who had been at the school for many years claimed that a rule about the equipment was being broken.

"What rule?" Steve wanted to know.

"The one the principal, Mrs. H., made," was the reply.

"Mrs. H?—You mean the one who's dead!" And Steve suddenly saw the problem. The rule dated from some thirty years back and had only just now come up for evaluation or even, for many of the staff, recognition.[2]

Stage 2

As the League schools became interested in trying to devise new ways to cope with problems, the DDAE process did become more visible, but fresh difficulties arose as the role of principal and the role of teacher then drifted away from traditional expectations. Particularly troublesome at this stage was learning the tricks of risk-taking and of really open staff communication. The established roles of teacher and principal had very little to do with risk-taking (to put it conservatively), and some staffs now toyed with new ideas but kept trying to avoid adding an occasional element of risk to their plans. They usually did so in one of two ways. There were those who pretended that risk-taking was impossible, for reasons beyond their control. One research assistant described this position as follows:

> "Rather than suggest ideas for change, the staff obstructed changes by consistently pointing out existing hazards. Unconventional ideas were judged in light of conventional structures. Team teaching, for example, was considered impossible because of existing grade levels, conflicting schedules, and inflexible physical plant. Few suggested redefining schooling so innovative ideas could be tested." (Field report, Indian Flat)

Then there were those who pretended that they were already engaged in the risk taking needed for continuous consideration of changes. An example of this claim:

> "The staff showed eagerness, confidence, almost cockiness. They con-

sidered themselves to be progressive, alert, moving, willing to work hard at the process of change, and this they do. They work very hard but only within the norm and range that the group approves. They actively resist dealing with their own behavior. They look for the ultimate method. They must know it is right before they begin. Then they work hard and everything comes out okay, with no looking back." (Field report, Shadyside)

Another set of problems which emerged at this stage, as the DDAE process was brought increasingly into public view, was the woes of faulty communication within the staff. These problems perhaps did most to prevent the establishment of a staff's perception of itself as a task group. Only a few of the several varieties of these problems will be described here.

We had noted early in the game that principals were not, in general, doing a very good job of communicating information about the League to their staffs. Poor communication took on new dimensions when principals here and there decided to stick their necks out a little on innovation. If a principal had been unsuccessful in keeping up continuous dialogue with his staff about the new ideas he was listening to at League principals' meetings, his staff usually saw themselves being pushed when he himself decided it was time to move. "Often the principal goes to League meetings and brings back information that he wants implemented at once without any pre-planning," was the frequent perception of teachers who hadn't a clue about what went on in the principals' meetings. And of course, the shoe was sometimes on the other foot, as we built up League activities for teachers. After discussion with other League teachers a few teachers in a school might decide to risk implementing a new notion, then learn—often to their surprise—that the proposal ultimately would involve many staff members who had not yet even talked about it.

Another variety of staff communication difficulties was the familiar headache of learning how to handle personal values within a framework of the task to be accomplished. This agony so dogged the schools (as it does many groups in their initial attempts to concentrate on a task) that tempers often flew apart and staffs nearly gave up.

"In the principals' conference, Andy S. was explaining how a try at team teaching in his school had dissolved into disaster. He attributed the calamity to personality clashes among the teachers. The consensus of the group of principals was that Andy should take a tough stand—teachers either see their professional duty to rise above personal differences or out they go. Yet, they noted, as Steve M. put it, 'You can't just say, "Now let's be professional, girls." Professional, hell, I hate her guts!' "[3] (Film notes, second year)

Through the years, League discussions among principals and teachers brought out in the open the problem of "not getting personalities involved." An early solution tried in many school staffs was a kind of willingness to go along with "the others" for a while, even without true agreement. But such willingness alone did not, of course, solve the root problem, and it often produced a situation that was ruefully and only afterward seen as comic. Several times principals described staff blowups about changes that had seemed to be going smoothly. "They gave me hell for it because they said they had only gone along because they thought a few of us wanted it, and it turned out nobody wanted it!" Still, League schools, by the time they reached this stage in the development of more visible DDAE, had acquired the fundamental understanding that a change in one part of the school could easily affect other parts, and they had developed at least a desire for consensus as a way of working together.

Stage 3

Movement toward the next stage in redefining roles came primarily with the growth of the idea of the principal as a monitor of decision making, for it forced the recognition of needed skills wherever they might be found. It dimmed the line between "administrative" and "classroom" responsibilities as staffs tried to work out the everyday meaning of having decisions made by the "appropriate" people. Again though, the going was not smooth. A number of principals, when they first bought the idea of monitoring, tried to bow out of decision making almost entirely. Part of the SECSI staff interpreted this reaction as an extension of the principals' original hope that we would tell them what to do. Now certain principals saw monitoring as another way to retreat from "the front line of educational change" and shift the burden from themselves to their staffs. Another interpretation was that the principals were buying time in which to fashion a new and more appropriate role for themselves. In any event, there was a point reached in a few schools where the role of principal came dangerously near being emptied, rather than being recast with the principal as a staff member who bore important responsibilities and contributed important skills to the total group.

In some cases this castration of the role of principal was performed by teachers as they themselves felt release from the sterility of the "stay-in-the-classroom-and-keep-your-mouth-shut" role. Just as principal-as-monitor became an expectation in the League, so did teacher involvement in decision making become an important characteristic of the League schools. In the excitement, teachers sometimes charged past sober attempts to carve out mutually productive roles and turned their energies to defending willy-nilly their right to make decisions.

When schools reached this stage, with much of the basic content of the principal role and the teacher role truly up for grabs, two major kinds of things happened. One was that a school, lacking clearly defined tasks, would proceed by sudden starts and stops. A group of teachers might, for example, fire up the whole staff with a new idea, but somehow the necessary follow-up discussions were never scheduled; later, another wave of enthusiasm would break, then wash away.

The other notable sort of occurrence at this juncture was out-and-out conflict between principal and teachers. At Dewey Avenue conflict erupted in the third year when a new principal, Edith B., came to the school. The Dewey Avenue staff were generally very experienced and very strong minded about their experience. With Stan M., the principal at the start of the League, they had come to agreements which allowed a wide range of teacher participation in decision making.[4] The teachers, in fact, had submitted to the district office a list of qualifications which they thought should be paramount in the choice of a replacement for Stan. The district apparently paid attention, for Edith B. was thoroughly experienced, extremely knowledgeable about curriculum, and absolutely dedicated to a continual search for better ways of schooling. But everybody had ignored one thing. Edith B. also had beliefs about the division of decision-making responsibilities in a school; her beliefs were every bit as firm as those of the Dewey Avenue teachers, and they were not the same.

For two years, the situation at Dewey seesawed between out-and-out clashes and cooling-off periods. The unhappy events, however, do illustrate the progress that had been made toward increasing the visibility of the DDAE process, for there was no withdrawal into isolated camps. Teachers and principal openly searched for solutions to the problems, and just as openly showed their frustration when tentative compromises broke down. Everyone apparently recognized the basic disagreement.

"Many teachers felt an urgent need for sessions directed to role definitions for teachers and administration and wished to pursue this with
Edith B. During the previous years, the role of the teacher as decision
maker and facilitator had so expanded that we felt that a new administrator might not understand this at all or know how it had come
about." (Teacher report, Dewey Avenue, third year)

"So the big hassle was in decision making. Whose job will it be to do
what and what roles will we each take? It's a totally new definition of
the role of the teacher, the role of the principal. So this whole struggle
for decision-making power has developed in this school. What decisions
should a teacher be making? What decisions should an administrator be
making? And after the decisions are made, how are they carried out?
If I don't agree with the decision, should I then be bound to carry out
the decision?" (Interview with Edith B., fourth year)

Although clarifying the problem at Dewey Avenue did not lead to
a solution, it was not because of a lack of mutual respect between
principal and teachers. All through the turmoil, teachers freely expressed their awareness of the new principal's knowledge about
schooling and their appreciation for her efforts to increase their freedom from certain district constraints. Nor did Edith B. ever fail to
recognize the high professional quality of the school staff. Still, it just
wouldn't wash.

"I came here with certain expectations. When I was offered this school,
I said to myself, this is going to be the greatest place in the world to
work. But though Stan and I were good friends, I never knew what the
faculty was like. I thought it would be the greatest faculty that there is
and that I could really use some of the skills that I have without fooling
around with all the falderal.

But the kind of situation that I came to was totally different. They
were asking of me things that I couldn't deliver . . . I really couldn't.
What I could deliver, they didn't want.

There is one thing that I can't do. I came to the principalship for
certain reasons and those reasons have nothing to do with what this
faculty wants out of a principal. This I'm not willing to compromise. I
came to the principalship only because I felt that it was a way of doing
a better job for boys and girls. I could possibly affect the education of
many more children. I really don't see any sense in being a principal if
you become a manager of equipment and money and these kinds of
things—if you cannot spend your time in helping teachers with their
approach to boys and girls, so that they, in turn, can work with the kids
more effectively. Otherwise, you may just as well be in a classroom."
(Interview with Edith B., fourth year)

Edith B. perceived her staff's expectations as, "the principal becomes, in their eyes, a tote-and-carry man." But the teachers' view was something else:

"Now we are feeling pressure from the administration to tighten up, and we want to feel our way, make our mistakes, and correct and enlarge in a creative, innovative way.

We feel we are losing our decision-making togetherness which we had with the previous administrator. Morale is low, and dialogue is one way." (Teacher report, end of third year)

The problem was not solved but was removed when ill health forced Edith B. to take a temporary leave and Stan M. returned to his old position at Dewey during the last year of the project.

Stage 4

Although no one will ever know, it seems possible that the conflict at Dewey Avenue might have been resolved had Edith B. stayed on. This conjecture is based on evidence that Dewey Avenue had moved to the next stage in the process of reworking role definitions for teachers and principal. Edith B. once described the need that triggered this next stage.

"So far as Stan was concerned, it was great. He started at the beginning of the League. Then it was great to get somebody to release teachers from traditional requirements. That was a tremendous accomplishment. So we're looking at it from different points in time and I'm saying that if we're to learn from this experience, we need to take a serious look at what it is we're trying to change and why we're trying to change it." (Interview with Edith B., end of fourth year)

The need for that "serious look" was the next stage in the change sequence. When the exhilaration of their first big breakthroughs in changing customary behavior wore off, school staffs began to have their doubts. Why were the new ways good? How were they good? Were they, in fact, good? It was as many schools reached this stage that we noticed the habit of self-evaluation becoming an expected behavior among League schools. We marked it as a step toward a responsible reviewing of possible change.

What happened first seemed to be that all the earlier questions and problems finally emerged for a thorough looking over. When they had originally appeared in the preceding stages, these problems had mostly been worked around, spottily dealt with, or tucked under some convenient cover. Thus, DDAE in a school staff tended to move from relative invisibility (Stage 1) to greater visibility (Stage 2), and on to disequilibrium in principal and teacher role definitions (Stage 3), all the while coping only cursorily with the problems that arose along the way. But there came a point where the staff tended finally to turn a great part of its DDAE process to critical examination of the changes it had made—changes made directly in principal and teacher roles as well as changes made in programs. That point is here identified as Stage 4.

As these questions arose in schools staffs, particularly in the staffs who reached this stage in the early years of the project, the usual first reaction was to look around for an expert who would give an answer. The SECSI staff was often asked to pass judgment on the current state of "innovation." As time went on, however, schools became more accustomed to our refusal to play judge, and more importantly, schools began to trust their own assessments more than those of out-siders.

Second thoughts about changes that had once seemed good ideas drove some staffs to search further for comfortable patterns of prin-cipal-teacher and teacher-teacher relationships. Frequently up for eval-uation, for instance, were team-teaching arrangements which had been created to handle broad areas of daily decision making. In certain cases large teams caused more headaches than they were worth; the time spent in thrashing out plans by a five- or six-person team led Seastar to cut down team size. The staff at James School abandoned a team organization which placed too great an intercommunication requirement on their old, inadequate school plant and turned to less demanding forms of cooperative decision making. Other staffs were less successful. The large team at Country School could find no way to pick up the pieces that fell from its clash of different teaching styles and educational beliefs; most of the teachers in the team left the school.[5] In several schools the split between the few teachers who were committed to teaming and those who decided against it grew into permanent communication barriers. The staff at Frontier suffered this and other divisions which totally incapacitated it as a working group—a state of affairs quite different from staffs which deliberately accommodated and used the variety of teacher preferences that emerged from evaluation of changes.

Another situation came to light when staffs began to consider critically what they were doing. Some principals had, in effect, mandated changes in school organization which outran the understanding or agreement of their staffs. In certain cases, the principal had seemed to be acting out of frustration—he wanted his school to conform to the expectation that League schools would break away from convention, yet he was faced with a cautious or reluctant staff. Other principals might have been anxious to produce quick evidence of changes which would meet with district approval, even though the districts had technically agreed to let League schools follow their own course.

Whatever the motivation, changes dictated by the principal could not finally escape review of some kind. Outcomes varied. At Independence, the staff quietly and persistently cut down to size and made workable the steady flow of directives from an enthusiastic principal. At Shadyside it was a new principal who unobtrusively led the staff to evaluate (and eventually drop) a program which had been laid out for them by the previous principal. In some cases when principals at last came to understand that changing from traditional patterns was going to take time and would not always look pretty, they developed real skill in using the rhetoric of change to allay misgivings of higher administration and so buy time for themselves and their staffs to do what they had to do. But there were instances of stalemate as well. The incoherent, yet effective, resistance of the fragmented staff at Frontier, for example, brought to naught a number of attempts by several principals to forge staff consensus on a way of working together, and we have seen that the conflict between the new principal and staff at Dewey Avenue ended in a draw.

While not all the problems which surfaced yielded easily to staff introspection, it is notable that we never heard any staff suggest that it go back to the traditional roles for principal and teacher. For a few schools the habit of conscious evaluation led to a sort of chronic discontent; others were able to move on to create new and productive relationships among principal and teacher roles.

Stage 5

These successful arrangements formed the basis for the kind of DDAE process that allowed a school to be more open to the possibility of change and more thoughtful in selecting the changes to be put into practice. The newly defined roles, that is, seemed to provide for wider participation in the process, for higher probability that the process would be important and relevant to school problems, and for greater flexibility in the conduct of the process—the critical characteristics by which we were describing a DDAE process that signaled responsible receptivity to change.

This is not to say that the working arrangement which marked the cooperative effort that we call Stage 5 looked the same in all the schools where it was found. Principals revealed different leadership styles to meet successfully their different situations. For example, Andy S. at Country School acted as a strong task leader in a staff which held several potentially divisive educational beliefs, whereas the performance of Chris M. at Hacienda could afford to be very low key on task leadership since that staff expressed almost total allegiance to a single approach to schooling.[6] Teachers' relationships with one another also attested to several successful cooperative patterns. In certain schools the greater part of daily concerns was handled by subgroups; the pod construction of the Woodacres building, for example, encouraged delegation to subgroups, as did a deliberate staff decision to subdivide the large Dewey Avenue staff. On the other hand, a number of schools, such as the relatively small staffs of Seastar and Rainbow Hill, maintained the full staff group as the major vehicle for conducting business.

Although the patterns of work varied, at Stage 5 there were nonetheless signs of a staff which saw itself as an integrated work group, whatever its pattern. Among these signs, a cluster of three stands out in a perusal of the SECSI records.

1. The successful new patterns of principal and teacher role relationships proceeded in an atmosphere free of many fears about evaluation.

> Question: "Do you think that the teachers are maybe just making decisions to please the principal because he has the power to evaluate them?"
>
> Hacienda teacher: "No—no, he's just one of the team. I honestly don't think there'd be anything on an evaluation of his that we didn't already know about." (Meeting of principals and teachers, spring, third year)

> "At Antigua School this year, a committee of teachers has been supervising and will provide the official first-year evaluation of a new teacher whom they selected. The new teacher seems very relaxed in this group, speaks of what she is learning from them. The senior teachers are reluctant to write the usual formal evaluation because they see it as inappropriate. Perhaps this reflects lingering fears, or perhaps the typical form really doesn't describe this situation. Certainly they speak frankly

with one another about the strengths and weaknesses of each—the senior teachers as well as the new teacher." (Film note, fifth year)

Several members of the group talked about the value of using one of the DDAE measures to let the teachers evaluate the principal. Dave W. told (in an approving and relaxed manner) about an experience he had had after he had rated himself low on a questionnaire item having to do with the principal's equitable treatment of all teachers, and his staff had rated him high on the same item. They had talked over the discrepancy.

> "Dave said, 'You can't rate me that way—isn't it obvious to you?' And they said, 'What it really boils down to is: though you may not like somebody, our perception of you is that you try to deal with the facts and issues, and you try to handle them. In other words, if you don't like somebody, you don't like what they did, not that you don't like them.'
>
> Well—I don't really feel that way. I just don't like certain people. But that was not their perception, and we talked about it—quite a bit. And now, because of that discussion, the reverse happened! [Laughter] The second time we filled out the questionnaire, I said, well, if that's the way the teachers think, you know, that's the way *I* ought to think about it. I rated myself as respecting all the teachers and that I treat them all fair and equitably. And, they said, 'Like hell you do!' The second time around, they rated me down." [Laughter] (Principals' meetings, spring, fourth year)[7]

2. The new relationships within school staffs seemed to encourage the recognition and use of special knowledge wherever it was found. For one thing, the teachers, as Mike D. of Peace Valley early noted, "don't necessarily view the principal anymore as being the god up here who has the right answer." And the principals, thinking about their role as monitor of the DDAE process, were not upset by the loss of godlike attributes. (Dave W. of Seastar confessed that he had in the past frequently felt inadequate because he was so conscious of the limits of his own knowledge.) In the new staff patterns the principal's role took on another kind of importance.

> "I was pleased and surprised to see how much had taken place in the two days that had intervened since the visit to Hacienda School. Already teachers had decided to set up a multi-age, multi-grade primary arrangement. They had established a set of criteria based on teacher relationships and pupil maturity and readiness and were ready to begin placing pupils. It was very obvious that they were beyond the principal in their thinking and that he could offer little, if any, advice. What he

could provide—and had—was the freedom to move ahead, even though they might make mistakes." (Report of observation of primary teachers' meeting, Indian Flat, fourth year)

"The principal invited me to a faculty meeting held after school in the faculty lounge. Refreshments were served and teachers proposed questions for group discussion. They entered easily into the discussion, disagreed at times among themselves, gave examples of what they were doing; and all in all openly exchanged ideas and concerns. They became so excited inquiring into each other's style of teaching that the meeting ended by some of the group going down to one of the classrooms to see how the teacher had set up a social studies inquiry center." (Report of a visit to Shadyside, third year)

And a number of principals were quick to use teachers' new perceptions of one another to open the DDAE process further.

"What was apparent was the difference in the quality and quantity of dialogue going on among the various teams. Teams did not seem to be exchanging problems and ideas, but certain teams were obviously deeply involved in their search for ways to improve learning opportunities for children. Others continued to spend their time on what amounts to trivia: supplies to order, playground duties, etc. The principal, however, discussed with us some informal meetings which were planned at his home for the entire faculty. He seems quite aware of the uneven quality of dialogue and action among the teams and hopes for cross-fertilization through these home meetings." (Report of a visit to Woodacres, third year)

3. The ways in which the principal and other staff members came to relate to one another was based on a clear expectation of mutual support. In interviews at the end of the fourth year, each League principal was asked to whom he would turn if he had a problem. "To the teachers" was the response of principals in schools where new role relationships were apparent. (Several went even further saying that there was probably nothing that they and their teachers couldn't work out.)

Teachers in these schools expected and for the most part felt that they received support from the principal. One of the clearest expressions of this expectation (and an example of the dramatic prose which they often used) came from the Dewey Avenue staff when they were describing the kind of person they wanted to replace the departing Stan M. "We do not want somebody who verbalizes a philosophy but who really is unwilling to be the kind of principal Stan has become.

The role of principal is changing and our school proves this. We need a warm, sensitive, supportive human being. We need a guy who will support us, one who we can expose ourselves to, one who permits us to fail. He cannot be laissez-faire, either. He has to be committed to fight for the things we need. And he needs to be willing to go out on a limb to support and protect us. We have nervous stomachs, hives, meet on Sundays, have to do lots of explaining to our husbands, but we feel it is worth it."[8]

It would be gratifying to say that by the end of the project all the League schools had worked out effective new patterns of principal and teacher roles, but it didn't happen. We do think it fair to say that at some point every school did reach the stage of evaluating what had been tried, and most schools took on at least a few of the attributes that, together, seemed to characterize successful, cooperative role patterns. Still the advent of a new principal or new outside pressures (which we will discuss later) at times precipitated afresh problems which had once been solved, and a few schools seemed forever barred from reaching satisfying solutions.

As we look back over our intervention activities, we recognize that we did not bring principals and teachers together into frequent across-school discussions of the changes in role behaviors which were being attempted. For the most part, we remained trapped in our initial pattern of separate meetings for principals and for teachers, with only occasional activities in which all joined. Some principals were reluctant to take away time from the comfortable small group that they had become, and there was always the headache of how to release teachers for meetings. But we cannot excuse ourselves. We should have paid more heed to the problems that obstructed joint meetings of principals and teachers because, we believe, frequent opportunities for sharing might have enabled more schools to search more effectively for alternatives to traditional school staff roles.

DATA ABOUT NEW ROLES FOR PRINCIPALS AND TEACHERS

The steady flow of information which came to us from observation in the League schools and interactions with League people has produced most of our picture of what happened in the League; but we can draw, also, upon the data obtained from questionnaires. We will present certain questionnaire data as they seem pertinent to our account of what we tried to do during our intervention and what we believe occurred in the schools.

The presentation of questionnaire data will take the general form of comparisons between the League schools and the non-League schools who answered the questionnaires at the end of the study. Let's be clear at the start, however, why we think these comparisons are useful and what we do not expect them to tell us. First of all, they do not allow us to make statements about what we would probably find if we gave the same questionnaires to other schools. So, differences between our League scores and non-League scores do not by themselves prove that treating another group of schools as a League would produce the same variations—for a number of reasons, not the least of which is that we'll never know what parts, if any, of the sundry League experiences were critical determinants of those League scores. We recognize, in other words, that a search for statistical significance in our questionnaire data is an inappropriate (and, we think, inadequate even if it had been appropriate) basis for inference from this study.

Still, the questionnaires did afford a glimpse of League schools and some other schools at one point in time, and that did have value for us. The questionnaire data spawned new guesses and monitored old certainties. The scores for our questionnaires were a boundless source of hunches about what might have happened, what might be if. . . . Contemplating them stirred up thinking in a way different from our reactions to personal encounters with the school people. For the scores, the nameless patterns of numbers, allow prying; they can be pushed around, combined, arranged in juxtapositions that would prove indelicate if not downright impossible to achieve in face-to-face questioning. Often in the course of playing with numbers, having in mind a question we had posed for ourselves, we would notice a persistence or an oddity of scores—"Hey, maybe that means . . ."—and we'd be off again rummaging through our records and recollections.

Yet we are aware that in such numerical schenanigans we do assume that we know what the items on the questionnaires meant to the people who gave the answers (from which we got the scores), and we realize that this assumption is surely not true for all the people who gave answers. Just as surely, we inevitably misinterpreted some proportion of the answers obtained in interviews, observations, even in thoroughly informal conversations. There are several accepted research procedures which try to minimize this omnipresent uncertainty in human communication. In this study we opted for taking with a large grain of salt any one set of answers from any one data source. We looked for descriptions from different sources that seemed to hang together, that seemed to be trying to tell us something. In this sense, the questionnaire responses acted as quite another variety of information, which served at times to underline, or at times to make us wonder about what we thought we'd seen in League schools.

What did the questionnaire data suggest about the roles of principals and teachers in League schools? First, it didn't surprise us at all to find that League teachers were reported by both themselves and by League principals to have more influence in decision making than teachers in non-League schools (T6.1).[9] This difference between League teachers and others was apparent at all DDAE levels and for all types of formal school organization. That is, whatever subgroup we looked at—high, middle, or low DDAE schools; cooperative, self-contained, or mixed formal organizations—the League schools always showed higher teacher-power scores than the non-League schools in the same subgroup. Furthermore, there was not as much difference among League schools as among non-League schools. In other words, although high DDAE schools always had higher average teacher-power scores than low-level schools, and schools with cooperative organization always had higher average teacher-power scores than schools with self-contained classroom organization, the difference in teacher power between any two types among League schools was not as great as the differences between the same types in the non-League schools. Furthermore, a greater proportion of League teachers saw themselves as influential in making decisions that had impact on the total school (T6.2). League teachers, for example, claimed more influence than did non-League teachers in making decisions about the time and the content of staff meetings. Since the staff meeting is usually the direct vehicle for carrying out general school business, we find this difference in teacher-power scores altogether in keeping with the League emphasis on the staff acting as a group in conducting affairs that affected all.

A bit of questionnaire data added somewhat to other evidence that the role of the principal in a League school had taken on more of the character of a team member rather than a leader set apart. When teachers were asked to indicate why they complied with their principal's wishes, there was a greater tendency in the League to refer to the principal's competence and likableness, and a greater tendency in the non-League schools to give weight to the principal's ability to punish teachers (T6.3).

In these questionnaire scores we saw the shadow of the phenomenon, discussed in Chapter 5, that had appeared in comparisons between the group of high DDAE schools and the group of low DDAE schools. The scores of League schools, like those of high DDAE schools, were, on the whole, less apt to fall together in a pattern of associations among different facets of teacher behavior or in a pattern of relationships between principal behavior and teacher behavior. Traces of traditional patterns were more plentiful among the scores of non-League schools (T6.4 and T6.5). This difference between the League and non-League scores of course suggests that if the disruption of patterns in the League had occurred over the duration of the project, earlier League scores should look different from the latest scores. And so they did. In the first year there had been a marked tendency for League school scores on various staff behaviors to go together in definite ways; in succeeding years such patterning became weaker (T6.6).

These bits of evidence from the questionnaires would, by themselves, weigh little, but they appeared as altogether reasonable when placed alongside the mass of other information that described the turmoil of tinkering with principal and teacher roles that took place in League schools. We had observed the upsetting of old patterns, saw some schools continue to flounder without much form, and watched most League schools put the pieces together in arrangements as varied as what each school had to work with. These scores seemed to jibe with our observations.

The only general statement that we can make about what happened to the way in which teachers and principals worked together in all League schools is that in no League school did the DDAE process slip back into the cloak of invisibility carried by traditional principal and teacher roles. To that extent we believe that our strategy was successful. Though weakening the old molds of staff roles in League schools did not always bring order or satisfaction, it did at least reveal the DDAE process to the eyes of those who lived it.

NOTES

1 Ann Lieberman and David A. Shiman, "The Stages of Change in Elementary School Settings," in Carmen M. Culver and Gary J. Hoban

(eds.), *The Power to Change: Issues for the Innovative Educator,* McGraw-Hill, New York, 1973, pp. 49–71.

2   This incident appears in one of the films from the project, *A Matter of Trust,* Part II of *The League: Film Report on |I|D|E|A|'s Study of Change,* Information and Services Division, |I|D|E|A|, Melbourne, Florida, 1972.

3   This incident appears in Part I of the League film series.

4   Lieberman and Shiman, however, recount other aspects of the first changes in this school which reveal that even with its early successes, Dewey Avenue had not made everything come up roses. Lieberman and Shiman, op. cit.

5   This story is told in *Case History of a Teaching Team,* 16mm film, available for purchase or rental from Information and Services Division, |I|D|E|A|, Inc., P.O. Box 446, Melbourne, Florida 32901.

6   Information about principals' leadership styles in the League and in a comparison group can be found in Ann Lieberman, "The Power of the Principal: Research Findings," in Culver and Hoban (eds.), op. cit., pp. 35–47.

7   The incidents just described appear in the film series, *The League,* op. cit.

8   The sexism implied here and in other statements of both teachers and principals raises interesting questions which we had neither the time nor the resources to confront. The pressures created by and means of adjusting to the traditional hierarchy of female elementary school teachers and male principals offer a fertile field for study as does the special situation of the female principal. Our hunch is that such factors have an important influence on the workings of a school staff, and we invite the attention of researchers.

9   Data tables are found in Appendix D. See the introduction to Appendix D for an explanation of the numbering.

CHAPTER 7

FOCUSING ATTENTION ON DDAE

While our intervention activities during the last two years of the project were almost all related in some way to exploring new behaviors for principals and teachers, we were much more focused when it came to our second major intervention target—setting up interschool communication that would heighten each school's awareness of the quality of its DDAE process.

In retrospect it seems that the activities which we planned in order to keep League schools inquiring together about what constituted a receptive DDAE process and how they stood in relation to that kind of process were closely bound up with the role we came to play with them. In the search for behaviors for ourselves that would not encourage the schools' dependence on us, we more and more fell back upon simply acting honestly as researchers, with a few bees in our bonnet about DDAE and a great faith in the possibilities of helping one another. We talked together as much about our interests and questions as we did about theirs. Truth to tell, we first adopted this stance simply because we were groping about to dress with daily actions our theoretical model of a "facilitator" interventionist, but we very soon realized that the way we were behaving led readily to League activities which could turn the schools' attention to critical assessment of the DDAE process.

We found that our candid concern about our own learning in the company of principals and teachers was increasing their familiarity with the research orientation, and this kind of thinking was basic to the sustained, self-evaluation that we hoped the schools would develop. We were hit occasionally with flare-ups of the hostility that school people are said to harbor against researchers, yet they did not out of hand reject all research activities. Two years earlier, after the principals had come to grips with the idea of principal-as-monitor, they had asked us to "research" that notion somehow; they wanted systematic evidence about how their ideas would work out in practice. And dozens of teachers had all along offered dozens of suggestions about how we researchers might more profitably spend our time looking for answers which they felt they needed. Thus, while we suffered certain discomfort from scattered accusations of not studying "the right things," we looked with hope upon the interest in research that was clearly growing. Even if it started as an effort to make sense out of our work since they were stuck with us, we figured that a general interest in systematic inquiry as a way of discovering alternative practices would have to contribute to a better understanding of more open DDAE.

One kind of League activity which we encouraged was indirectly but, we felt, substantially related to building the schools' awareness of their DDAE process. We urged schools to inquire for themselves into those questions which they thought important. Two other |I|D|E|A| projects offered them some assistance for particular kinds of inquiries. One project provided free films and filmstrips to those League schools which would design and carry out small studies to explore the usefulness of the materials.[1] Ten League schools participated in the program, and the |I|D|E|A| staff member who acted as coordinator worked closely with the SECSI project to reinforce the general League intervention strategy in every way possible. The series of meetings involving these schools, for example, emphasized comparing notes on the problems encountered and lessons learned. Another |I|D|E|A| project involved a few League schools (who volunteered an interest) in the development of a measure of pupil attitudes[2] and a planned sequence of activities to improve staff problem solving.[3]

These projects, of course, provided outside guidance and even occasional instruction about formal research techniques. The SECSI staff, on the other hand, offered suggestions about how school inquiries might be carried out but left the actual procedures up to the schools. More often than not, during the last two years small action-research projects proceeded in the schools without our participation or even our knowledge until we heard about them in some League meeting. At least part of the staff of every League school attempted systematic inquiry about problems or interests. Usually the topics had to do with evaluating pupil progress or with school-community relations, and a whole staff might devote a major part of its time to the inquiry. Rainbow Hill and Woodacres, for example, developed and tested techniques for assessing the amount of agreement on educational goals that existed between parents and the school staff.

Of course, the number of starts exceeded the number of projects that reached discernible completion. We do not know the exact numbers, nor do we have any way of knowing how League schools compared with other schools in this respect, but our observations and the records we were able to obtain lead us to believe that League schools came to expect members of their group to gather and organize information about whatever concerned them.

To spark directly the schools' awareness of the quality of the DDAE process, our first step was to communicate how we saw DDAE, why we thought it important to them and to us. While topics for League meetings during the last two years were left almost entirely up to the schools, we, as the researchers in the group, did reserve the right to ask for periodic discussion of the concept of DDAE and its relationship to responsible receptivity to change. The discussions dealt with how DDAE might look in school life; we did not try to teach the League schools any specific techniques for doing "good" DDAE. They ended up working out their own definition of good DDAE (as we shall see shortly), but our initial intervention tactics were confined to having them talk about and, we hoped, think about the range of possibilities for the DDAE process.

For a while, DDAE was seen largely as our bag. The schools were polite and humored our idiosyncratic interest, but they were not exactly turned on by the concept of DDAE. We persisted in trying to make our case and in emphasizing the need for all-round give-and-take in this sort of inquiry. A couple of times we invited principals to join our research staff meetings to help us work on the concept of DDAE. The first reaction was instant frustration; then the basic goodwill of all parties led us to discover patterns of language and thought through which we could communicate.[4] Even more important, however, than the contributions made by these joint meetings toward an understanding of DDAE was an outcome we had not anticipated. The meetings were the principals' first observation of us doing our own thing in our customary way (for we made no attempt to change our staff meeting procedures for them), and the great revelation to them was that we were not always sure of what we were doing. Every one of them talked about it. They hadn't imagined that we ever had this kind of trouble, that in our work, too, there was more than one way to skin a cat, and the best way wasn't always indisputable. We had beefed up a bit our image as comprehensible people with a job to do.

Our most sustained tactic to build a partnership in inquiry about DDAE, however, was the creation of the League Reporter. In the third year of the project, we asked each school staff to select a League Reporter—a teacher or teachers who would write to us twice a month about the things that were going on in each school that, for better or for worse, made a difference; the contacts that were made with other League schools; and the kinds of staff meetings that were held in the school.[5] We referred to the League Reports as our research assistants, and in the final phase of the project we asked them to concentrate on giving us information about the DDAE process in the schools. At the start of the last year all League Reporters attended a training session with one of our research staff members, where they learned to use the several forms which we had by that time developed for observing the DDAE process. (In the development of these and other measures of DDAE we also involved teachers. We would get our first ideas for questions from our own observations, put these in a tentative form, then discuss them with a few teachers in each school and use their suggestions to modify the form.) Throughout the year the Reporters used the observation forms, often discussing them with other teachers and relaying information to us about how we might improve our descriptions of DDAE.

THE SCHOOLS MEASURE DDAE

There did finally emerge from the League schools their own definition of high-quality DDAE. It began (as had their statement about a changed role for principals) with about half of the principals holding a series of discussions with a SECSI staff member. Originally, the group had taken on the task of developing criteria, for ultimate adoption by the entire League, which would describe "a good League school." The task force was formed in late autumn of the fourth year when the question, "what do we value about the League," was much in the minds of League schools. The end of the project was not that far away and touched off pervading anxiety: "How do we continue to try to be self-renewing schools after the project is over?" We had introduced to the schools our notion of DDAE as the vehicle for responsible receptivity to change, but we knew that they would have to make the concept their own if it were to be truly a key to understanding and a guide to change. It seemed fitting then for the League to start work on a description of what they hoped to be, for themselves, for us, and for those they might in the future need to convince. Hence, the formation of the task force of principals.

We suggested at the start that the group try to think of the criteria they were going to develop as a measuring instrument—a means by which each school could rate itself against what it wanted to be and check its progress from year to year. The suggestion met with approval, and over the next two and a half months the group met periodically to sift out the items that it wanted. In between meetings most of the principals got teacher reactions to the items which were being considered and brought this information to the group. Alex R. at South School tested the early forms of the instrument at length by having his staff use them to describe their regular meetings. By midyear a tentative form was presented to the entire group of principals, who took it back for testing in all the League schools. Revisions were made with help from us, and the instrument was used at the end of that year and the next year in League schools and in the other schools which cooperated in the project.

The instrument, called CRITERIA (Q2),[6] does not constitute a complete list of criteria for the League idea of a good school. To the surprise of no one, the group found that they could not manage a complete picture all at once, so they agreed to start with six aspects of staff life in school. Thus, the CRITERIA questionnaire describes desirable *dialogue, decision making* and *action,*[7] which were by now household words around the League. The other three facets of staff life described in CRITERIA reflect the League's awareness of the redefinition of roles that they had been undergoing; criteria are given for the behavior of *the principal, the teachers,* and for the most common, formal setting of their interaction, *meetings.*[8]

The CRITERIA questionnaire, though it can be easily faulted by sophisticated test makers, provided necessary and relevant information about the DDAE process in the school. But more than that, the schools took pride in it, and it was of immense value to them as well as to us. Above everything else, developing the questionnaire had much increased daily awareness in the League of the responsible receptivity to change that we were now all trying to describe.

We used CRITERIA as one measurement of the quality of DDAE and of other conditions making up responsible receptivity to change. We were not especially dismayed at the prospect of possibly one more imperfect instrument (being less than certain of what constituted perfection anyway), and we wanted to see how the behaviors that the schools had singled out in their criteria seemed to fit with our four basic qualities of DDAE. We were, of course, risking distorted responses from League schools on the instrument since the principals and many teachers knew it as a League product, but we faced the same problem with any measurement of DDAE. As we have pointed out before, we were, after all, intervening to call attention to the very process that we were trying to describe. We simply had to live with the possibility that League staffs would develop such a "DDAE orientation" that it might color their responses to all requests for descriptions of the process.

We can, of course, never be sure about just exactly how our intervention affected the data we got from League schools, but we do have enough information to make what seem to be two good guesses. First, we have little reason to believe that the League schools tried, for the most part, to give the "correct" answers when they described their DDAE processes. The quality of the process, as measured via all our methods, varied from school to school and over a period of years (this fluctuation is part of the content of Chapter 9). Furthermore, when League schools were compared with other schools, the comparisons showed no special bias in the League toward the "correct" answers about DDAE. Second, we believe that the awareness that existed in League schools about the DDAE process did lead those staffs to think more carefully about their answers, and that this greater self-consciousness may have resulted in slightly different interpretations of questions that appeared on the Basic DDAE Questionnaire, on CRITERIA, on observation forms, and in questions asked in interviews. The evidence suggests that the League schools did not treat questions about DDAE in as all-of-a-piece fashion as the non-League schools did (T7.1).[9] Furthermore, we hoped that our intervention strategy, in its design to promote open interaction in the schools, would implicitly promote both open interaction in the schools and an independence between teacher characteristics (such as age and teaching experience) and teacher perception of the DDAE process. Indeed, our data, when viewed at the school level, suggest little or no relationship between teacher characteristics and DDAE for the League schools; on the other hand, substantial associations are evidenced for the non-League schools (T7.2).

FEEDBACK FOR THE SCHOOLS

One of our intervention tactics was deliberately designed to help schools think seriously about the answers they gave to questions; that is, we gave feedback to the schools about the information that was obtained from their responses on questionnaires. Even during the first phase of the project we had occasionally given information of this sort, but this tactic had not prevented the growth of antipathy toward questionnaires in general. By far the most burdensome part of the project, as perceived by League schools, was the packet of questionnaires which they filled out near the end of each school year. These were the questionnaires (see Appendix C) through which we obtained information on DDAE and other school conditions which we thought might be related to it. Each time we gave the questionnaires we explained our purpose and asked that teachers add whatever comments they wanted to their answers. Nonetheless, filling out the questionnaires remained a chore which League schools would have been happy to do without.

For one thing, they had been beset since the League was formed with certain doctoral studies related to our purposes and a miscellany of other studies not really connected with the SECSI project. Such fine distinctions were not made by the schools, however; they tended to identify all questionnaires as "League" duties. Still, the dislike of the questionnaires seemed to have less to do with the actual amount of time spent on them (about an hour for our annual packet) than it did with the difficulty that teachers and principals had in understanding how the information might prove useful to them. That is a common failure in communication during research in schools; we knew about it, expected it, tried to overcome it, and still didn't score a smashing success. We did spot several underlying difficulties but lacked the personnel (or perhaps, the imagination) to handle them as well as we would have liked. It took time, for instance, to process the data and prepare feedback; any report, therefore, was in danger of looking stale, especially if a summer had intervened and there had been much staff turnover in a school. It also required a certain kind of skill and intimate knowledge of each school situation to make the findings come alive to the school staff to whom they were presented. What might be a fascinating finding to us did not necessarily send them. These different interests are often quite legitimate, but that doesn't solve the feedback problem. Above all, the disparate pieces of information, uncovered over many months, cried for organization, for accumulation into an ever-current and ever-enlarging description of each school—a summary that would enlighten each staff. With limited resources we were unable to keep all the data in the form of an up-to-the-minute, comprehensive, easily distributed view of the League world.[10]

By reason of these difficulties and others, the sporadic titillations of interest occasioned by our feedback sessions never entirely dispelled the black looks that greeted any bearer of questionnaires to a League school. However, with the considerable involvement of the schools in the CRITERIA questionnaire, we were, during the last two years, somewhat better able to provide coherent and meaningful feedback. After the schools' first go-round with the instrument, we presented and discussed the League average scores in a session with the principals and then gave each principal the scores for his own school to be used in further discussion with his staff. In many of the schools these follow-up discussions proceeded in great detail; each item was considered—why did they score that way, how might they change (or did they want to change) the behavior in question? After each subsequent administration of CRITERIA, we provided that kind of written report to every school: the scores for that school and the average League scores. During the last year a SECSI staff member discussed with each school staff a summary of all its DDAE scores.

SOCIALIZING NEW TEACHERS

We received confirmation in what we heard and saw that in most League schools questioning was indeed becoming the order of the day. Not often formal, not always organized, it was spreading to all areas of school life and did sometimes focus on the very process (DDAE) of which it was a part. Of course, the questioning was closely tied up with the concurrent upsets in role expectations as well as any increase that might have occurred in kindly feelings toward a research stance. (We noted earlier that while we can separate several categories of intervention happenings on paper and after the fact, the whole ball game really took place at once.)

Several features of this low-key but persistent ferment may convey our impressions of it. One thing that struck us was the growing concern of League staffs to socialize new members into schools which they saw as different from the old mold. Perhaps the most common setting used by League schools to acquaint new staff members with the way things were done was a work-social combination. This was not the obligatory, special-occasion staff party but a regular use of outside-of-school meetings expressly planned to discuss school affairs in the relaxation of a private home. These gatherings obviously served to increase total staff solidarity as well as to initiate newcomers. (At least one school, Independence, institutionalized the informal get-together as a Friday afternoon happening.) Related to this tactic of divesting professional socialization of some of its sober character were efforts by some staffs to diversify their in-school meetings. Mike D., while principal at Peace Valley, called certain meetings specifically for decision making but set separate and regular periods for voluntary, informal (and well-attended) problem-sharing sessions.

A quite different approach to training new teachers took advantage of traditional work settings. Shadyside negotiated with its district administration for special in-service programs for new teachers that would be related directly to the concerns of the Shadyside staff. Indian Flat also made use of in-service programs and suggested new ones, not only as a means of helping their new staff members but also as a means of communicating what the Indian Flat staff had learned to other schools in the district.

In many schools the burden of socializing new teachers fell primarily upon subgroups in the staff. Hacienda was organized into four teaching units based on pupil age groups, and new teachers learned how to relate to the school as members of these units. At Antigua, a team selected and trained its own new member. More common were small teams and informal cooperative teaching by which the newcomer was shepherded to understanding what was expected in that school.

Though care was taken not to leave the newcomer to fend for himself, the schools which had moved toward more daily questioning of what went on did not try to shield new staff members from unpleasant events that might arise. These, too, were part of what was to be learned. A striking example of such a baptism by fire occurred at the beginning of the dispute between teachers and principal at Dewey Avenue. Even though they disagreed about what role behaviors should prevail, teachers and principal did agree that new staff members should learn to see the situation for what it was and become a part of it.

"The first Teacher Committee meeting adjourned after it was decided that more new teachers would be invited to each meeting in order to increase their participation in school affairs and to bring their reactions and ideas.

The first Steering Committee meeting, held the next morning with the principal, did not go well. Most teachers left this meeting and rushed to their classrooms stiff-necked with tension.

The Teacher Committee met again to specifically face the problem; would we continue to meet as usual, or would we meet with the principal as a steering committee? New faculty members had been invited to this meeting. It is a tribute to the skills developed through team teaching that, in an hour's time, impassioned pleas, reasoned rebuttals, and a complete exchange of representative opinions produced a decision. In the interest of developing a working arrangement so that we could get on with our program, the teachers voted to meet as a steering committee with the principal." (Teacher report, Dewey Avenue, third year)

"I started with a group of new teachers just to talk about how we proceed in a school like this—what are things we're trying to do? Some of the older teachers wanted to sit in on the meeting and they did. It's easy to talk to new teachers about the kinds of things that the staff can agree upon, but what is hard is to say to new people, 'Look, this is a divided faculty and you could be hearing strange things. In this kind of a program we're treading on paths that we don't know about, so there is a lot of tension, and from time to time we're not very nice to each other, but then it blows over.' I say this to them. I think they need to know." (Interview with principal, Dewey Avenue, fourth year)

There were other occasions too when bitterness marked the questioning that went on in League schools, but more noticeable was a growing ease in working with people who did not all think alike. The SECSI reports are full of comments that try to capture this indefinable ambience.

"Open and frank discussion by all present. A warm, friendly atmosphere. They say they agree on outcomes, and it doesn't bother them much that they disagree on the methods." (Observation, Seastar)

"They were able to express their feelings quite freely, insisted on dealing with issues at the 'gut' level, and were unafraid to examine very critically what they were trying to do. Perhaps even more impressive was their unbridled enthusiasm. At the end of the session they were saying they couldn't wait to get back to their classrooms the next day." (Observation, Hacienda)

"Joe did say that he had changed the way he feels about his work with teachers. He does not feel as threatened. He's more at ease with them. He said that when he used to make arbitrary decisions and someone didn't like them, he felt very much threatened. Now, it doesn't bother him that teachers sometimes disagree with him. Joe feels that this new attitude works on the teachers' side, too. He said that now he and the teachers never walk away from one another with a sour mouth." (Interview with Joe A., James School)

"The principal had called an early morning faculty meeting, and almost everyone was there by 8:00 in spite of inclement weather. There seemed to be a relaxed feeling among the group, with some joking among the members and between the members and the principal. It seemed that they were feeling good about being members of an innovative school.

They were talkative during the meeting and were anxious to meet in small groups. The principal had arranged a schedule, but they freely objected to it and rearranged it informally before the end of the total staff meeting. The small groups were also talkative and engaged in quite a bit of cross-conversation answering each other, raising questions with each other, etc. Later when one of the more innovative teachers talked to me, she reported what an exciting lunch hour they had had talking over new possibilities in the primary grades. She said that after discussing individualization during the morning, they had many more questions and concerns which they shared with the middle-grade group (more innovative) during the lunch hour. Apparently the middle-grade team functioned as consultants for the primary teachers who were not as far along. Again in the afternoon, one of the teams mentioned that they knew the middle-grade team disapproved of what they were doing and were trying to give them different suggestions; and they also admitted they were changing their program after some of these discussions with the middle team. They appeared to me to be quite free to evaluate their own programs and to make changes as they discussed plans with one another. The principal seemed to be close to the action and quite supportive of their decision-making responsibilities." (Observation, Rainbow Hill)

DATA ON DDAE QUALITY

Again we can turn to the questionnaire data for more information, this time about the communication that went on in League schools. Some questionnaire data bore directly upon features of staff communication; some offered information about conditions in which the communication took place.

In Chapter 5 we discussed briefly how the formal organization of a school could be related to the openness of its communication networks. League schools were about equally divided among the three types of formal organization—self-contained, cooperative, and mixed. Non-League schools were dominated by the self-contained classroom; over 60 percent had this type of organization, less than a third could be classified as having cooperative patterns, and very few were mixed (T7.3). Furthermore, the division among the three types of formal organization early in the League schools (1967) was predominantly in the self-contained mode (T7.4), resembling the pattern in non-League schools.

We see in these differences and similarities an indication of the general search in the League to find formal organization patterns that were compatible with a staff's evaluation of what it needed and what it could do. That the League had largely moved away from the teacher isolation that is so easily fostered by the self-contained classroom is obvious; more interesting to us is the relatively higher proportion in the League of the mixed type of organization. In the course of other analyses, we noticed that these League schools had average teacher-power scores considerably higher than non-League schools of the same type and, in some areas of decision making, even higher than the League schools classified as the cooperative teaching type (T7.5). This supports our hunch that the mixed type of organization in the League at the end of the project was a different animal from what it had been earlier and perhaps different from its namesake in non-League schools. League schools, we feel sure from all our information, learned to view the mixed type of organization as one possible way to accommodate legitimate individual differences among teachers or pupils or both. For these kinds of reasons, staffs sometimes chose to set up the mixed pattern after careful deliberation; the mix did not simply happen to them as an uncomfortable transition to be endured on the way from something bad to something good.

Other questionnaires offered further glimpses into the work world of the school. We have seen in Chapter 5 that teacher ratings of climate adjectives (Q8) were higher in high DDAE schools. Here we found that the rating of overall school climate showed generally more favorable feelings in the League group as compared to the non-League school (T7.6).

On another questionnaire (Q10) teachers and principals listed what each perceived to be the major problems facing the school. These responses told us a little more about the contexts in which the

DDAE process might be carried out. We were able to sort the problems into twelve categories of content; then we grouped these categories into three types, according to the implied sources of the problems (T7.7).

The first type of problem talked about characteristics of students which were seen as troublesome and often beyond the staff's control. When we inspected the proportions of staff members who had mentioned problems of this sort, we saw that the proportion was smaller in League schools, primarily because considerably fewer League teachers spoke of discipline problems.

The second type of problem also came through primarily as complaints about conditions largely unchangeable by staff efforts—unfavorable community characteristics, lacks of necessary facilities and various kinds of restrictions imposed on the school by outside bodies. Here the picture was somewhat more complicated. Relatively few staff members in any of the schools listed community problems, while a high percentage listed lack of facilities, but in both cases the proportions were smaller for League schools. This was not so, however, when it came to problems which cited constraints on the work of the staff such as school board battles or new legislation; a substantially higher percentage of League teachers mentioned these restrictions as problems.

Finally, there was a type of problem which was located in some part of the daily work of the staff (staff morale, principal-teacher relationships, organization of teaching, communication with parents). All categories of this type of problem were cited by a slightly higher percentage of League teachers than by non-League teachers.

All this information fits with our observations that League school staffs, in viewing their own DDAE processes, had become more sensitive to actions that they themselves might take in coping with problems. Thus, League teachers seemed more apt to look critically at internal school operations, while at the same time certain external demands on the school were more widely perceived in the League as inhibiting legitimate staff efforts to create appropriate daily conditions for schooling. Furthermore, the goodly number of League as well as non-League staff members who chafed at inadequate facilities counters the argument that League schools, as a group, might have had significant additional physical or monetary resources which somehow made it easier for their staffs to develop a less passive view of school problems.

The somewhat larger proportion of League teachers who identified problems concerning staff relationships we take as a direct reflection of League attention to the roles of principal and teachers. We believe further that the expression of these problems in the League was essentially task-oriented. The problems, that is, were "real" enough in the sense that we, too, could spot them; and League staffs generally perceived them as a legitimate focus for group thinking and effort. We base that assertion, of course, largely upon our total experience in the League, but we can mention in passing that the questionnaire data didn't show any particular connection between the frequency with which staff problems were mentioned among League staffs and the way in which those staffs rated their overall school climate. The scores, in other words, did not indicate that such problems might have been perceived as just another facet of an undesirable school situation.

Finally, we were able to get from the questionnaire data a bit of information about the extent to which the members of a school staff agreed in describing various features of their school. The extent to which teachers within a school agreed on their school descriptions generally was greater in the League schools (T7.8) In Chapter 5 we noted that agreement within a school staff tended to be greater in high DDAE schools than in low schools, and we remarked that the finding was consistent with the notion of generally more open communication in situations which were presumably marked by high-level DDAE. The assumption, in other words, was that the characteristics of what we call high-quality dialogue, decision making, action, and evaluation provided more opportunities for staff members to observe, discuss, and, perhaps tacitly, come to common assessments of their own behaviors, whether those behaviors were seen as desirable or undesirable.

We found, however, that when compared to non-League schools, the League schools, as a group, showed the same sort of tendency for a staff within a school to agree among themselves on their descriptions of their school. The League schools varied in their DDAE levels just as the non-League schools did; we couldn't simply say that a higher level of DDAE within the League schools accounted for the larger proportion of League schools which showed relatively great staff agreement. Yet we do not think that we have to abandon our basic premise that common understandings about staff behaviors are promoted by communication concerning those behaviors. We note two conditions in the group of League schools that might have increased this kind of communication across the board. First, the thrust of our intervention, remember, was to increase the visibility of the DDAE process, and we have a lot of nonquantitative evidence that League staffs did become more self-conscious about the way they worked together. It seems possible that this awareness might have generated kinds of communication within the school that were not picked up by our limited measure of only four characteristics of DDAE in essentially formal settings. Second, we know that opportunities for communication about professional behaviors—what they looked like, what they meant—were provided by League activities to League staffs at all DDAE levels, and we conjecture that these opportunities may have in a way compensated for some of the communication deficiencies in League schools with lower levels of DDAE by building up certain "League" interpretations which served as common reference points when each staff described its own school behaviors. For example, the widespread League discussions about the desirability of shared decision making within a school probably created a mental yardstick which was commonly used in assessing a number of staff behaviors.

In later chapters we will have more to say about the existence and functions of such "League" definitions or values. At the moment we will touch only one other aspect which seems relevant to the topic of a staff's agreement on the way it perceives its work world. We had lots of discussion in the SECSI staff about just what the optimal level of agreement within a staff would be for that staff to be responsibly receptive to change. While we believed that staff agreement would have to be great enough to get group effort on the job, we suspected that it shouldn't be so great as to squelch questions about how the job might be done differently. A staff in which members have come (for whatever reasons) to see everything pretty much the same way might have trouble if faced with a new problem that would not yield to any attacks already within its repertoire. On the other hand, a staff which has agreed to disagree—within limits—might possess more effective habits of searching for ingenious solutions.

This line of reasoning led us to think about what was required in the latter kind of staff. At least one necessary ingredient would be that the staff members value differences. Our experience in the League had made us believe that a League climate was developing in which individual differences among pupils and staff were accepted and, upon occasion, found exciting. We were curious to see if we could find any reflection of this in the questionnaire scores. We did not have a direct measurement of how much school staffs valued different opinions, but we could see how the teacher agreement scores were related to the good feeling that a staff expressed about its life in the school.

When we looked at these scores, we found that in the League there seemed to be several parts to their relationship (T7.9). Better school climate ratings didn't seem particularly connected one way or the other with the amount of agreement that the staff showed in describing a number of teachers' work behaviors. Poorer climate scores, however, tended to accompany greater disagreement among the staff's descriptions of certain task-oriented behaviors of the principal, such as the way he conducted meetings. Among non-League schools these several relationships were not in evidence; there it was pretty much a case of poorer school climate scores being found along with more staff disagreement in the way any behavior was described—either teachers' or principals'. We are willing to surmise that League schools might have moved a step toward greater selectivity—perceiving some areas in which it was more desirable to have wide agreement whatever the local situation and other areas where lack of agreement was not necessarily bad. The non-League schools looked more like an either/or proposition: to agree is good, to disagree is bad.

All in all, the League activities which were designed to increase awareness of the quality of DDAE seem to have had fair success. An item in the last set of questionnaires asked the respondent to choose from several sentences the one that best described the way the League was supposed to be. About 60 percent of the principals and about 30 percent of the teachers who answered chose the statement, "League schools are supposed to try to improve the process of dialogue, decision making, action, and evaluation."

Another 30 percent of the teachers chose "League schools are supposed to exchange ideas and help one another solve problems," a response which indicated some success also in another of our categories of League activities. We had planned, remember, a set of activities which sounded our (by now) old refrain—there needed to be ways for the schools to support one another as they laid themselves open to possibilities of change. The next chapter recounts how we addressed this need.

NOTES

1   The Encyclopaedia Britannica Educational Corporation supplied materials for this project.

2 The instruments, *School and Learning Attitudes Scales*, are designed primarily for sixth graders. They are available in the Experimental Series of the Educational Testing Service, Princeton, New Jersey.

3 Samuel G. Christie, Adrianne Bank, Carmen M. Culver, Gretchen McCann, and Roger Rasmussen, *The Problem Solving School*, Institute for Development of Educational Activities, Dayton, Ohio, 1972.

4 The principals were not at all reticent in confessing confusion. Once when we solemnly solicited an opinion about the problems of self-renewing schools from a principal given to colorful phrasing, he shrugged, "Beats my ass—I don't know what you're talking about."

5 We paid fifty dollars a month for six months each year (October, November, January, February, April, May) to each League Reporter, or the fifty dollars was divided among however many reporters there were in a school. This was the only money we ever paid to the League schools.

6 Instruments are found in Appendix C. Numbering is explained in the introduction to that appendix.

7 The reader will recall that we did not treat evaluation as a separate element until the last year. The CRITERIA instrument, therefore, does not give a separate score for evaluation.

8 The CRITERIA instrument is discussed in detail in Bette Overman, "Criteria for a Good School," in Carmen M. Culver and Gary J. Hoban (eds.), *The Power to Change: Issues for the Innovative Educator*, McGraw-Hill, New York, 1973, pp. 209–220.

9 Data tables are found in Appendix D.

10 For an unusually perceptive discussion of the problems and needs involved in providing truly appropriate feedback to schools, see Ruby Takanishi-Knowles, "Collaboration between Educational Researchers and School Personnel: Some Reflections and Proposals for Reducing the Research-to-Practice Gap," paper presented at the American Educational Research Association Annual Meeting, February 26, 1973, New Orleans, Louisiana.

CHAPTER 8

BUILDING AND ENHANCING LEAGUE BONDS

A general push in the League schools toward reassessment of what they were doing and how they were doing it could make for a fair amount of discomfort. That sort of self-scrutiny could spell for a staff uncertainties about how to do x, y, or z and nervousness about looking the fool, consequences which seemed to us not unmanageable with existing League resources. All of our experience since the beginning of the League had led us to identify two major kinds of resources that the schools could share with one another: first, very practical information about daily school affairs and second, that assemblage of compassionate communications usually called moral support.

MOBILIZING LEAGUE RESOURCES

We have a hunch, thinking back over it, that teachers in general emphasized the first kind of resources in their exchanges, while principals set more store by the second. The League principals, who met at least once a month from the beginning of the project, cherished their group and were bound more closely each year to their idea of themselves. Three times each year they spent several days together, shared business, rooms, and recreation. Their persistence in coming together (absences from principals' meetings were not common) might bear thinking about. On the face of it, there was nothing in it for them except interaction with one another and with a few of us who regularly attended —no coercion from us or their districts and no Brownie points either. The prestige of association with our organization might be considered reward enough to keep them coming, but this does not explain altogether what we saw. Our prestige over the years was rubbed down by friendship, and familiarity with us tempered the miracles that we might be expected to perform. A few principals, true, probably never recovered completely from the bedazzlement of keeping company with the big time, but they were very, very few, and even they were not immune to the larger clout wielded by the group itself. Its power lay in the excitement of freedom to grope together for possibilities at the outer edge of the imagination, coupled with the warm certainty that if you toppled from reaching high, you would land among buddies and you could join without hurt in the jokes that analyzed your predicament and set you up to have another go at it. We, the researchers, were good enough guys; we provided the opportunity and we could be counted on to toss in a bit of grist for the mill now and then, but time and again in the last two years, the principals unabashedly husbanded their time for just talking together.

In the last phase of the project, however, the principals did work on distinct tasks related to assessing DDAE and exchanged information about what they had learned at every meeting. A SECSI staff member, for example, got them started on investigating the informal communication networks in each school and on gathering simple but systematic data about general problems they had identified. The stories told during principals' meetings about these ventures and about various action-research projects in different schools disseminated in the group a lot of practical information about techniques that might be used and warnings about lurking dangers. As a final mutual assistance project in the last year, each principal assessed his own strengths and weaknesses as a school leader; then principals met in small discussion groups where they tried to share success and diagnose needs.

The principals also communicated outside of regular League meetings, although the pattern was uneven. Over the last two years, several League principals in the more isolated areas (Peace Valley, James, Fairfield) had very little contact with other schools apart from League meetings, but centrally located principals, especially those facing problem situations (Independence and Shadyside), frequently sought advice from others in the group. In some cases principals made use of resources not actually in a League school but by way of a League school. Thus, Adam S. of Mar Villa was able to set up informal, nonthreatening observation and critiquing of his school with an able consultant from the Woodacres district office, and when Frontier tackled staff reorganization, Carl C. got pertinent suggestions for the Frontier staff from several consultants known to other League schools.

We mustn't give the impression though that the League principals' group proceeded through its affairs, during the last years, in an altogether orderly fashion. Quite the contrary; in a way they never did get everything sorted out, as far as we could see. (The qualification may be important.) We didn't help much—deliberately. Although our earlier move to turn over to principals the planning and execution of League activities had aborted, we now held to working out a new role for ourselves. They must handle their own business. We would help write up the records they wanted, but we would not carry the whole group. We would not call or chair meetings; we would claim meeting time only for our research needs. Otherwise, we would offer suggestions when asked, which they could take or leave. As time went on they asked less and less and certainly didn't take all our suggestions. But they had big problems. One—in the sheer mechanics of group operation—seemed to stem from an overriding reluctance to formalize relationships among members, even to the extent of empowering their appointed leaders to hold the group to some regulated progression through a planned agenda. Another problem was a continuing struggle to keep three balls in the air by allotting meeting time to take care of (1) a variety of individual interests, (2) tasks that they thought important for the whole group to undertake, and (3) loose brainstorming sessions.

Meetings often resulted in a certain amount of frustration for them and bitten tongues among us, yet there was an ebullience that was never quite squelched. They usually acknowledged their foul-ups and caught themselves trying to dump a muddle back into our laps. Steve M. (Antigua) labeled their trials yet another phase in the weaning process that had been going on since the League began and principals and teachers had expected us to tell them precisely what to do. Gene G. (Rainbow Hill) once offered the group small solace in his wistful comment that, "We used to be really confused—remember? Well, I guess we're still confused—but on a much higher level!"

It did seem to us, too, that their strivings now were a far cry from their earlier timid peeks outside the status quo. And they did conduct their own affairs, albeit without much in the way of style. During the fourth year, they appointed temporary groups to arrange and direct their several three-day conferences and to guide the work on the CRITERIA questionnaire. By the start of the fifth year they had selected six of their number to serve as a yearlong planning committee with a permanent chairman. In that last year they were able to steer their way through two major group tasks (to be described later), employing such techniques as input from outside speakers, discussions and writing in small groups, and decision making by the total group.

The Teachers

The teachers had much less difficulty in taking the reins for League activities. The Teachers' Activities Group, consisting of one representative from each school, was formed in the last two years and met three to four times a year to plan interschool contacts. (Principals joined in planning large activities which included both teachers and principals, but the bulk of the decisions about meeting content were handled by teachers.) The activities and some of the problems encountered in teacher-to-teacher communication have been described at length in another publication.[1] Here we will note only that the planned activities included several all-League one-day conferences, area workshops for subgroups of schools, special interest groups that met on Saturday morning in our library, school visits for specific observations, and in the spring of the fifth year a "League Fortnight," in which each school displayed its program and its problems for visitors from other League schools.

The teachers' planning sessions tended to give full, though gossipy, attention to the tasks at hand rather than straying into indecision about group mechanics. The Teachers' Activities Group, of course, had no considerable history either to embroider or to get in its way. We can guess what longer or more frequent association might have done to it, but as it was, we observed teachers spending precious time together (for time to plan was generally scarce, particularly for teachers from outlying schools) as efficient representatives of a larger group of people who wanted to air and share professional concerns.

The content of the League activities which were planned by teachers did not often call the DDAE process by the name we had given it, although teachers in most of the schools were explicitly involved in the development of the CRITERIA questionnaire to measure several aspects of DDAE. Instead, when it cropped up in their discussions, DDAE appeared in its around-the-house dress as teachers exchanged tips and cautions on how to manage team teaching, swing reluctant staff to an experimental program, convert to a nongraded school, etc.

The importance of the DDAE process, whatever its guise, was especially emphasized in the initiation of new staff. League teachers, as well as principals, were mightily concerned that incoming teachers learn that League schools were not places where things stayed the same, and they wanted new teachers quickly to become comfortable in joining the continuing self-assessment. To this end the Teachers' Activities Group planned special orientation meetings for all new League teachers near the start of the fourth and fifth years. These meetings were occasions for several old-time teachers to explain to the newcomers "how we do it in the League" by recounting their own learning experiences. The presentations were lighthearted, often amusing, and the chitchat over the food which followed eased new teachers into the information exchange; but the visible evidence of a group of schools which talked about themselves as a different breed effectively alerted the newcomers to certain expectations for League school staffs.

With the best will and effort, however, neither teachers nor principals could execute, alone, a system of interschool contacts which could respond quickly to school needs and interests. To match the resources that existed with needs as they arose required current knowledge of each. It was this requirement for a central bank of information about the schools which became the basis for the role we played as facilitator of interschool contacts. In order to make League resources available to schools as they wanted help or encouragement, we first had each school supply a specific description of what it felt it had to offer by way of skills, programs, or experiences. To keep these descriptions up to date, however, we could only rely upon the barrage of information we received almost daily through all the kinds of contacts with the League. It was not practical for us to try to keep written records of everything that we learned was going on out there. Instead, we utilized our very real pool of knowledge about the schools to take care of the requests for help which came to us through informal sharing among SECSI staff members.

Our clearinghouse function was beefed up by our curriculum library and the League newsletter, which we continued to distribute. The SECSI librarian assisted schools in their search for materials and kept them informed of newly available titles. As a result, some 3,000 library items were checked out each year by League school people, and the habit of referring to the literature and comparing notes on it spread in the League. The League newsletter, which is described in detail elsewhere,[2] in the last two years featured much teacher-written material and strove primarily to supply the schools with information that would enable them to initiate contacts with one another without always going through us. By its very existence, of course, the newsletter served as periodic reaffirmation of the existence of the League as a group aware of itself.

To give the reader an idea of how intervention tactics were used to enable League schools to help one another, we offer in the table on pages 134 and 135 an outline of a typical sequence which occurred over a period of several weeks.

PROMOTING THE VISIBILITY OF LEAGUE MEMBERSHIP

The final set of activities which guided our intervention during the last two years of the project grew from a belief that to be successful our magic feather strategy had to have two basic thrusts. One, the building of each school staff's identification with the League group, we have already discussed. It is apparent, however, that a school staff might feel a part of the new group, know what the group expected, have the wherewithal to meet the expectations, yet fail to do so because those expectations might run counter to other expectations which the staff considered more important. It was the possibility of such conflict between expectations that a League school should inquire into its own DDAE process and counter pressures to hide the DDAE process that made us alert to every opportunity to increase the prestige of League membership. That membership had to mean enough to the schools to make them feel it was important to behave as a "League school."

We had, from the beginning, kept the schools apprised of information about the League which the SECSI staff disseminated through speeches, articles, and a variety of professional contacts. We had also used League people as resources in several workshop-type activities which were directed by SECSI staff members for personnel from non-League schools. In the last two years we stepped up the use of League people as resources; whenever appropriate, we tried to fill outside requests for consultant help, particularly requests that touched upon staff relationships, by recommending League people or visits to League schools. Given the opportunity, League teachers and principals were not slow to talk about what League schools were trying to do. In the process, of course, they clarified their own purposes and strengthened their own commitments.

League schools were particularly interested in spreading the word within their own districts. Each League school was, after all, a member of another group of schools—a district—and there was a great deal of variation in district support of the League expectation that each school staff would assess its own problems and test solutions. For a League school to act as a resource in its own district, then, had the twin value of lending prestige to the League and legitimacy to the practice of new behavior in the district. Consequently, we lent a hand from time to time as a League school would arrange a meeting with other school personnel in its district to "explain the League," and we encouraged other such events which occurred without our presence. Additional exposure to the districts came during the last two years as each League principal brought a "buddy principal" and non-League teacher guests were invited to certain League meetings.

As soon as the CRITERIA questionnaire was completed, most League principals began to show it around as a League product, and a number of the districts began to make use of it. Three other written records of parts of the League experience were produced during the last two years in order to help the League gain wider visibility. First, a group of ten teachers decided to put together in a monograph all that they had enjoyed and endured in the process of change. Their title came in an early burst of insight—*Tell Us What to Do! But Don't Tell Me What to Do!*[3] A SECSI staff member arranged meetings for them and provided coordination for the writing-editing process. By the time this product was finished, we began hearing noises from more teachers about writing up what they had been trying to accomplish in the individualization of instruction. We began work with this group, which did not finish its book until some months after the official end of the project.[4]

From the principals came the third expression of what the League schools felt that they had learned. During the final year, all the principals' meetings were focused on arriving at a description of a hypothetical school district which would embody their beliefs about what was required for true "school accountability." The SECSI staff member who worked with them has included much of their thinking in another report from the study.[5] The model that the principals had in mind emphasized flexibility to meet a variety of needs of pupils, parents, and school staffs, and recommended evaluation appropriate thereto. As did the teachers' writings, the principals' model reflected their years of getting comfortable with asking questions about the conduct of schooling.

Perhaps the greatest spur to the feeling that, according to one principal, "we're on a championship ball team" came with the signs

Events	Intervention Strategy	Data Sources
Teachers from Seastar call |I|D|E|A| for help. *Problem:* Need to develop criteria for promotion and placement from kindergarten to first grade.		Telephone logs.
SECSI doesn't send a consultant, but talks about situation at Seastar and how we can help them.	Preparation for interschool contacts by informal sharing among SECSI staff.	Accumulated information about schools which is possessed by SECSI staff.
SECSI staff arranges meeting for concerned Seastar teachers and teachers in other schools who are either facing similar problems or have handled them in the past.	Provide opportunity for teachers to act as resources for one another.	Telephone logs. Accumulated SECSI information.
Meeting held at SECSI offices. Teachers start discussion of the immediate problem of criteria for promotion and placement of children. Teachers' discussion moves into broader questions of continuous progress and nongrading. Teachers realize that curricular and instructional questions also involve the questions of how decisions are made in the school. Teachers share strategies for promoting changes in school decision making in order to achieve goals.	SECSI member attends meeting and suggests work on pupil assessments as a kind of action research in the schools.	Tape recording. Meeting observation forms. Field notes written about meeting.
SECSI staff discusses outcomes of meeting.	Build SECSI bank of information.	Informal sharing.

Events	Intervention Strategy	Data Sources
	Alert staff to watch for evidence of follow-up in schools.	
Seastar teachers act in their school. Teachers continue dialogue among themselves. Gradual emergence of general, though not school-wide interest in question of nongrading. Growing staff realization that whole school should confront question of organization/nongrading. Teachers and principal have meetings. Teachers agree to decide as a staff about direction of school program.		League reports. Telephone logs. Interviews. Field notes from |I|D|E|A| observations.
Seastar teachers come to curriculum library for research about continuous progress, nongrading, multi-age grouping.	Support flexible decision making.	Correspondence. Telephone logs. Library records.
Seastar teachers visit other schools and talk to teachers to get relevant information. Interest is sparked in other schools.	Assist, when asked, in arranging visits.	League reports. Telephone logs.
Seastar staff meets. Staff discusses philosophies and research information. Do not reach total agreement. Staff consensus is that school will experiment with overlapping multi-age clusters.		League reports. Telephone logs. Interviews.

that the League concept itself was spreading. In the fourth year, the schools learned that a League type of organization had been adopted in a nationwide |I|D|E|A| program.[6] About the same time League districts and other districts in the area began to speak of starting new Leagues. Finally, there appeared exciting indications that teachers might be introduced to a League structure upon entry into their profession, for the schools were invited to confer with John Goodlad and others in the UCLA Graduate School of Education about a new teacher training program in which new teachers in training would join, essentially, the staffs of changing schools.[7]

CHANGES IN THE LEAGUE PEOPLE

At the end of the project, in the final packet of questionnaires, League teachers and principals were asked to state what they felt had been the advantages and disadvantages of being in the League. In 13 of the 18 schools, the advantage most mentioned by teachers was sharing ideas with, or simply having contact with, people in other schools. Over 52 percent of all advantages listed by all teachers were of this nature, while the remainder of the responses spoke of within-school advantages such as improved instructional programs (34 percent) and improved staff relationships (14 percent). As for the 13 principals who answered the question, 8 said sharing ideas among schools was an advantage, 9 mentioned improvement of staff relationships, and 4 mentioned improvements in instructional matters.

The disadvantages that were perceived were scattered—there was a variety of concerns but none that seemed to be felt by a large number of people. A smattering of responses from teachers decried the time spent on questionnaires, and a small number indicated undying disappointment that we had not provided explicit how-to-do-it instruction. A few teachers and principals (mostly those in distant schools) wished there had been greater teacher involvement, and another few were uncomfortable about disagreements which their new activities had spawned in district offices or in the community or within the school. More than a quarter of the teachers and four principals simply stated that they saw no disadvantages to the League.

And at the end of the project how did the schools see our relationship with them? We got some information from answers to another question which asked the League people what, if anything, they thought we had expected of League schools. About a third of the teachers and over half of the principals said that we had expected them to work with us on finding out about the change process in schools. The phrasing varied, but the message seemed clear: "Our cooperation in trying to determine how change takes place"; "Report successes and failures to the SECSI staff"; "Honest reporting"; "Exchange of ideas—our feeling"; "Help with research." Another third of the League people felt that we held some kind of expectation that they would try out new ideas. About a fourth of these said that we wanted League staffs to develop more open attitudes and internal staff processes which would allow them to communicate freely with one another.

Of course, it is gratifying that a considerable number of League people spoke of a kind of partnership with us; that makes us feel some success in the role we tried to put together, especially since we had altered our role midway. Perhaps we should be disappointed that just as many teachers and principals indicated a more lopsided relationship (that *we* expect *them* to change), but disappointment is tempered by our acknowledgment that we could not, with any firm grasp on reality, have hoped by our uneven strategy to sweep the League clean of all traces of the traditional image of the interventionist as the guy who tells me what to do. Furthermore, the fact that a number of League people felt that we expected the schools to change does not preclude the possibility that they also expected this of one another.

When we talk about new expectations or behavior and people learning to act in accordance with those expectations, we are talking about socialization. Out of the League project there has come to us a notion of socialization occurring at two levels. At one level a school which was a member of the League had to try to meet the expectations for "a League school"; most importantly, its staff, as a unit, was supposed to conduct business in a way that allowed exploration of new ideas. On another level was the socialization of individuals within each school. A League school had to, in a sense, process particular people so that they could form a staff which met League expectations for the school.

We have offered evidence from a variety of personal encounters which speaks to socialization at both levels in the League; and we have discussed questionnaire data relating to the first level, that is, data indicating that the staffs of League schools, when they were considered as *school units,* were different in a number of ways from staffs who had not been in the League. So far, however, we have not looked at what the questionnaires might tell us about *individuals*. Now we will investigate some of that information in order to consider the socialization of individuals within the schools.

SOCIALIZATION OF TEACHERS

There are so many possibilities of new behaviors and new beliefs that League teachers might have learned that our questionnaire data seem terribly inadequate. Nevertheless, one questionnaire (Q11)[8] particularly interested us because it asked about educational beliefs which we thought would be basic to a staff's willingness to try out new ideas in schooling—beliefs about desirable goals for instruction, how discipline should be maintained, and to what extent pupils should make decisions in the classroom. The questionnaire was scored to indicate traditional or nontraditional beliefs in these areas. For example, a desire for maintenance of quiet classrooms and little pupil participation in decision making were considered traditional beliefs. Setting different learning goals for each individual student was seen as a nontraditional belief. Although teacher discussions in the League did not have a single focus, we felt that these discussions had been permeated by a growing realization that traditional beliefs about a teacher's relations with students simply narrowed too much their vision of possible solutions to problems. We thought, in other words, that there had grown up in the League a considerable pressure for nontraditional educational beliefs.

And when we inspected the school scores on our measure of educational beliefs, it was clear that League schools were far more likely than non-League schools to be found in the ranks of the non-traditional staffs (T8.1).[9] In terms of our notion of socialization at two levels, it appeared that League membership might have indeed carried with it expectations that League schools would not be hamstrung by traditional beliefs about educational practices. We could, of course, wonder if it might not have been the other way around—if schools had started in the League already committed to nontraditional beliefs. There are no comparable questionnaire scores to prove the case one way or another, but neither can we, with all the other kinds of information that we have, accept that proposition as an explanation for more than one or two League staffs.

Therefore, we can presume that being in a League school puts some pressure upon a staff as a whole to move toward nontraditional beliefs. Now what about the other level of socialization that we have proposed; how might these beliefs have been inculcated in individual staff members within a school? Earlier discussions have pointed out that the League schools were by no means alike in their methods for conducting business, including the business of socializing staff members. For many purposes it is important to keep those differences in mind, but in order to look at the educational beliefs of individual teachers, we are going to take account of only one kind of difference among the League schools—the level of DDAE. We will consider the educational beliefs of teachers who worked in high DDAE settings and of those who worked in low DDAE settings.

Before we do that, however, we should glance first at a few other characteristics of these teachers. Some people might argue, for example, that younger or less experienced teachers would be more apt to accept nontraditional beliefs. Were the League teachers very different in these respects from teachers in other schools? Our data indicated that, on the whole, there were practically no differences between League teachers and our sample of non-League teachers as far as age, years of experience, or tenure in a school were concerned (T8.2). In the case of low DDAE schools, League and non-League seemed pretty much alike in possessing more mature and less mobile teachers. If we looked at just the high DDAE settings, however, a couple of interesting differences did appear (T8.3). First, teachers in the high DDAE League setting were spread rather evenly over the age range from younger to older, but in the high setting outside of the League there tended to be a higher proportion of young teachers. Second, about 60 percent of the non-League teachers in high DDAE schools had been in their schools more than a year; but in the high League schools, about 85 percent of the teachers had been in their schools for longer than one year. One gets a feeling of younger teachers on the move in the non-League schools with high DDAE, while there is a hint of more holding power in the League schools at the same level.

Individual Teachers and High and Low DDAE

We will keep these points in mind as we turn now to the question of how high and low DDAE settings might have influenced the educational beliefs of individual staff members. It would have been nice to see whether or not the beliefs of individuals changed over the time that they worked in particular types of schools, but unfortunately, we do not have the data to do that. We can only look at the beliefs which were expressed on one questionnaire by teachers who had been in their schools for varying lengths of time. We began by dividing these scores into three groups according to how long teachers had been in their respective schools: (1) the scores of those teachers who had been in their schools a year or less; (2) those who had been in their schools from two to five years; (3) those who had been in their schools for six years or longer.

The educational beliefs of these groups showed several interesting things, which, however, are exceedingly difficult to describe with words alone. (We strongly urge the reader to refer to Table 8.4 in Appendix D as an aid in understanding the following discussion.) First, the League teachers in all three groups expressed less traditional beliefs than did the non-League teachers in the same group. We see this as another reflection of the prevailing pressure for League schools to move toward less traditional beliefs. Now, what about the beliefs of teachers at different DDAE levels? In the League, teachers in low DDAE settings expressed more traditional beliefs on the whole than did teachers in high DDAE settings, and the beliefs expressed in low settings were pretty much the same no matter how long the teachers had been in their schools. There wasn't any difference either in high League schools between the beliefs of teachers who had spent only one year and those of teachers who had spent as much as five years in their schools. But then came a distinct difference; the League teachers with the longest tenure in high DDAE schools (six or more years) expressed by far the most nontraditional beliefs of any group.

This meant that the most striking thing about the League schools, as far as DDAE level was concerned, was the considerable gap between the beliefs of the longest-tenured teachers in low DDAE schools and the beliefs of the longest-tenured teachers in high DDAE settings. Was the same gap apparent in the non-League schools? Quite the contrary. Non-League teachers who had spent six or more years in their schools showed very little difference in the beliefs that they expressed whether they were in high or low DDAE settings.

In keeping with our notion of considering socialization in terms of what may happen both to school staffs as units and to individuals on those staffs, we speculate as follows. Nontraditional orientations toward teaching practices, such as those described in our educational beliefs questionnaire, probably are formed largely through professional discussion and support for experimentation. With limited opportunities for this kind of stimulation, teachers may tend over time to adjust their beliefs to the better-known and more traditional orientations of the profession. While the openness and flexibility implied by higher levels of DDAE should provide a degree of professional discussion within a school, one school alone, even with high-level DDAE, may not possess resources for enough intellectual, task-relevant interaction to encourage the adoption of less traditional beliefs about teaching practices. The development of such beliefs may require provocation from exchanges with a wider range of professional experience and, perhaps more importantly, a sense of support for group efforts to explore diverse approaches to schooling. The non-League schools, we believe, were relatively cut off from regular outside contacts which might have provided reinforcement for new perspectives about education. Under those circumstances it would not be surprising to find that more years of experience in such schools, whatever the quality of their DDAE processes, would tend to encourage the same orientation toward teaching—some set of acceptable traditional beliefs which seemed to work in moving through standard teaching assignments.

The critical difference in the environment for a League school was the interaction and identification with the League group. Considering the scrutiny of programs and the bandying about of new possibilities which took place constantly in League activities, it would have been odd if nontraditional educational beliefs had not to some extent appeared in these schools. We think, as we said earlier, that new expectations developed in the League which supported such beliefs, just as the prevailing norms in the non-League schools supported more the more traditional attitudes of the educational establishment. Our data, which show all groups of League teachers expressing less traditional beliefs than non-League teachers, say to us that the impact of these League expectations was felt even in low DDAE schools and even by teachers who had had only one year of experience in a League school setting. The restricted interaction of a low DDAE process, however, seems not to have added much to the outside influence of the League network, for in low DDAE settings there was no differentiation between the beliefs of teachers who had spent a little time or a lot of time in those settings.

In the high DDAE schools in the League, however, it looked as though internal openness and flexibility might have maximized the impact of new League norms. Certainly, on many occasions we observed staffs in the high-level schools discussing, trying out, evaluating ideas picked up during League encounters, and the questionnaire scores indicated that League teachers in the high DDAE settings expressed, on the whole, the least traditional beliefs. The beliefs of the teachers who had worked longest in those settings, furthermore, were outstandingly nontraditional.

Why should that be? We cannot, of course, prove with the questionnaire data that the latter group of teachers had not held the same educational beliefs before the League began. Our familiarity with the League teachers, however, leads us to believe that only a minority of these veterans had in fact found the experimental nature of the League altogether congenial right from the start. Resistance was the more common initial reaction. Much later a longtime teacher at a high DDAE school recalled the way it was.

> "The other day a group of non-League people was invited to participate in our meeting. These people by most standards are well-informed, but I found that their reactions to the panel mirrored my own reactions, way back in the early days of our League—frustration, confusion, and anger, intermingled with sudden understandings." (Teacher report, fifth year)

When the sudden understandings did strike League teachers, those who worked in high DDAE settings were prompted to act upon their insights primarily, we think, because a new set of rewards became available to them. In addition to satisfactions from classroom accomplishments (usually the sole source of professional reward for the teacher), high DDAE settings now offered the excitement of collegial exploration and experimentation, the support and encouragement of a principal, and often the involvement of the community. In all this commotion, the school veterans had the advantages of great ease in handling the tools of their trade and familiarity with the conditions of their particular schools. With these advantages they by and large maintained positions of informal leadership within their staffs and within the League. Only now they became the spokesmen for a fresh look at old ways:

> "Mrs. X (a veteran teacher) and I discussed various ways in which she could explain what she does. She was very excited about talking with teachers, but her central concern was that she cannot show a finished product—that every day she learns new things about the children and that she never feels completely happy about her performance. I assured her that this was part of the change process and this is the very reason why teachers can be such valuable consultants for each other." (Field report, third year)

As they struggled in their own classrooms and tried to convey to other teachers the changes they were making, the challenge to old beliefs became explicit to these veterans in high DDAE settings. In low-level settings, on the other hand, new rewards in the form of professional sharing and support were quite limited within the school (for example, the principal might not evidence a strong desire for experimentation or there was little teacher-to-teacher communication), and any change efforts by senior teachers remained fragmented and less likely to trigger profound reassessment of established patterns.

Teacher Power and High and Low DDAE

If the growth of nontraditional educational beliefs was to be expected in the League atmosphere, so too was an increase in teacher influence in school decision making. We believe, in other words, that League membership put pressure on schools to widen participation in decision making, and earlier we discussed the questionnaire data which told us that League staffs, as total groups, did claim greater teacher influence than non-League staffs. Now we want to consider what the teacher-power scores can tell us about what might have happened to individual League teachers who worked in high and low DDAE settings.

When sorted into the same three groups of teachers who had spent varying amounts of time in their respective schools, the teacher-power scores fell into a picture similar to that of the educational beliefs scores. (T8.5. Again we urge the reader to consult the data table.) Outside of the League the lines on the graph which showed the scores of teachers in high DDAE settings and those of teachers in low-level settings came closer together as years of school tenure increased. All groups of teachers in high-level settings saw more teacher influence than did those in low-level settings, but with increasing years the teachers in high-level schools claimed less influence and the teachers in low-level schools claimed a little more—as if there came to be a rapprochement between the confidence which stemmed from seniority and the recognition of constraints on the role of teacher. Within the League, teachers working in high DDAE settings also uniformly perceived more teacher influence, but the graph lines for both high and low DDAE settings started by going up. That is, teachers who had spent two to five years in their schools, be they high or low DDAE, perceived more teacher influence than did those who had been there only a year. Then, for teachers who had been longest in their schools, the graph line for high DDAE settings continued upward, with the senior teachers claiming the most staff influence, while the line representing low DDAE settings dropped with the scores of these veteran teachers. The resulting picture, of course, is a dramatic gap between the teacher-power scores of the most senior teachers who worked in high DDAE settings within the League and the scores of their counterparts in low-level settings.

We think that this difference between the two groups of senior teachers in the League is related in part to our earlier description of an increased sense of control which senior teachers gained in high DDAE settings, where there was internal organizational support for new behaviors as well as external League expectations. In addition, however, we suspect that the League expectations for broader teacher participation in decision making brought to senior teachers working in low DDAE settings a large measure of confusion and unresolvable frustration. (The senior teachers, it is important to note, were those who had been in their schools before the project began, and the advent of the League created a more profound change in condition for them than it did for teachers who had known their schools only as "League" schools.) In high DDAE settings the expectation of wider participation in decision making was apt to reveal to senior teachers new possibilities for leadership. In low-level settings the senior teachers knew that something was afoot, or so their experiences in League activities led them to believe, but the changed expectations were hard to get hold of in the daily mechanics of school life. We observed signs of increasing uncertainty among these teachers as they tried to rescue their rightful confidence of seniority in a world that had got somewhat out of hand. This uncertainty, we believe, colored their view of the amount of teacher influence that was present in their schools; they could no longer trust the old rules, and the new rules weren't very clear.

CHANGES IN LEAGUE PRINCIPALS

In discussing what we think happened to League principals, we will draw primarily upon information gathered in personal encounters with them. We have more of this kind of information about the League principals for they were fewer than the teachers and we observed and conversed with them more frequently.

Work with the School Staff

We have touched upon certain differences in principal-teacher relationships within the League as compared with schools outside it. In interviews during the final two years, we asked principals to comment on how the League experience had affected, if it had, their way of working with teachers. All of them mentioned a move toward a more informal but task-oriented total staff group. As Steve M. of Antigua put it, "I used to go in and demand they do this and that. Now I encourage them. Also, now I encourage things I would have condemned formerly." Even the very few principals who expressed some reservations about greater teacher involvement in decision making seemed to feel compelled, as League principals, to try to change. (Occasionally, we caught a glimpse of how such a principal talked himself into it. "Having teachers make the plans? I'm not all one way, but it may make it easier when the unions come because then the authoritarian principal may run into problems.")

Were the League principals different to begin with? Our descriptions of how the League began indicated that they were not simply a group of willing volunteers. True, the average age and length of experience of League principals were slightly less than the averages for non-League principals, but this degree of immaturity was not found primarily in the League principals of high DDAE schools. Instead, there was no difference in average age or experience between League principals in high-level schools and those in low-level schools. Nor was there a difference between League principals who led schools organized around cooperative teaching and those whose schools were organized in self-contained classrooms. Outside the League, on the other hand, younger and less experienced principals did tend to be found in high DDAE schools and to be associated with cooperative teaching arrangements. It seems then that while in some circumstances principals may show greater flexibility earlier in their careers, an explanation along these lines cannot adequately account for the behavior of the League principals.

Personal Development

The League principals, of course, differed among themselves in the ease with which they accommodated the expectations to be innovative. Some of these differences we have spoken of in earlier chapters and in the descriptions of League schools (Appendix A). Nearly every principal, however, reported great personal growth in what was usually called "my awareness of what's going on in education." Obviously, much of this new knowledge began with the speakers invited to a number of League meetings (especially in the early years), with materials in the League library, and with information from the SECSI staff. It is critical to understand, however, that words from these expert sources were not simply received and assimilated by eighteen separate principals (or, for that matter, by the individual teachers who were also exposed to them). Rather, the input was many times hashed over during League interactions which continued long after the original source had conveyed the message. The milieu of the League itself was also explicitly recognized by principals as a source of new knowledge. They spoke of the perspective that they had gained in learning about what went on in other districts, of new insights from the constant trading off of woes and delights during conversations with one another. In the eyes of one principal, the League supplied knowledge "about things the principal has more control over."

We were curious about how the League association compared with the principals' experiences in district groups of principals to which they also belonged. In one series of interviews, each principal was asked to compare his feelings about his district group with his feelings about the League group. All but four principals reported that they felt closer to the League principals. Of the four who did not, two were in schools far from the center of the League cluster; they mentioned specifically the difficulties that distance posed for their League participation. The other two principals simply felt well established in their district groups, with long-term friendships and professional relationships there.

The latter two were the only principals who did not cite greater intellectual stimulation in their League experiences as the major difference between the League and the district groups. The uninspiring character of district meetings was emphasized; as one principal put it, "There we talk about the color to paint the flagpole and the height of toilets." The principals elaborated on the more exciting League environment, with comments that revealed another meaning which the group had for them. In interviews we heard that in League interaction principals were "more honest, less defensive," that they had "more compassion," that there was "less feeling of dependency, less competition . . . you talk of more things than in the districts. I don't discuss school problems with friends in the district. Even in the League we hold back a little, but we are more open. We've covered a lot of different areas."

Many of the principals also generally credited the League with a growth in professional confidence. Some told of this kind of change in themselves; some claimed to have seen dramatic shifts in others. Increased confidence was often attributed to the informative, open, accepting atmosphere of League discussions. Another reason was, in the words of Chris M. of Hacienda, "League principals were able to stand up and talk to strangers because they said, 'I am a member of this group, and we're something special.'" The League principals did finally view themselves as avant-garde. Many noted with elation and a small wonderment that they felt able to make contributions in education just as well as superintendents. It was a long way from the early uncertainty with which the principals had first approached the task of defining school projects.

They had tasted the heady freedom of spurning rewards which were doled out for getting reports in on time, but at the same time they had acquired new habits that punctured their self-content. They had accustomed themselves to constant self-evaluation as well as to that sound of a different drum. With mixed feelings we observed signs that increased League experience brought to most of the principals a measure of skepticism about their own performance, resulting in more work with satisfaction less easily come by. Still, of course, it was that forever-appearing next step that fueled the excitement, and the excitement held them. Fourteen principals were in the League at least four years; eleven were in their schools for the entire project.

We are absolutely certain that for most of the principals who were involved in it the League was a critical professional experience. The bulk of our certainty, however, comes not from displays of figures but ultimately from the long time that we lived together trying to work out new ways of doing our respective jobs. The principals granted that the SECSI staff learned a few things, too.

WHAT DO YOU MEAN BY THE "LEAGUE"?

"I used to think of the League as eighteen guys meeting with the resource people. Now I feel that it is much deeper than that. At first we depended on consultants too much; now we are on our own. The League is more of a feeling about people and the kinds of problems people have in working on school staffs. It isn't an organization like a club. It could dissolve tomorrow, but I'd still feel that I was part of something important." (Principal interview, fourth year)

The League project came officially to an end in June 1971. A big party was arranged by a committee of League teachers and a couple of us. The party went the way of such affairs with considerable warm feeling, a few final reminders that some teachers still resented the loss of those who had left the SECSI staff, a lot of hard work on decorations, and an inadequate public-address system which turned the planned entertainment into a debacle.

But after the ritual fanfare to signal its demise, the League went on. Throughout the last year of the project the schools had been mightily preoccupied with "what will happen to us next year—can't we keep the League?" During that year plans got under way. The principals drafted a letter which stated that the League schools wanted to continue their association with one another and requested each district to contribute a small amount toward the part-time services of one person who would act as a clearinghouse for interschool information, arrange meetings, and produce a League newsletter. The letter was approved by the teachers, and district consent was granted to fourteen of the eighteen League schools. Nine additional schools were invited to join the new League.

NOTES

1 Carmen M. Culver, David A. Shiman, and Ann Lieberman, "Working Together: The Peer Group Strategy," in Carmen M. Culver and Gary J. Hoban (eds.), *The Power to Change: Issues for the Innovative Educator*, McGraw-Hill, New York, 1973, pp. 73–98.

2 Ibid.

3 Ann Lieberman (ed.), *Tell Us What to Do! But Don't Tell Me What to Do!*, an |I|D|E|A| Monograph, Institute for Development of Educational Activities, Inc., Dayton, Ohio, 1971.

4 David A. Shiman, Carmen M. Culver, and Ann Lieberman (eds.), *Teachers On Individualization: The Way We Do It*, McGraw-Hill, New York, 1974.

5 Richard C. Williams, "A Plan for an Accountable Elementary School District," in Culver and Hoban (eds.), op. cit., pp. 221–244.

6 Information about |I|D|E|A|'s Change Program for Individually Guided

Education (IGE) may be obtained by writing to |I|D|E|A|, IGE Program, 5335 Far Hills Avenue, Dayton, Ohio 45429.

7   John I. Goodlad, "The Reconstruction of Teacher Education," *Teachers College Record*, 72, September 1970, pp. 61–72.

8   Questionnaires are found in Appendix C.

9   Data tables are found in Appendix D.

THREE

THE LOOK OF CHANGE

CHAPTER 9

HOW SCHOOLS CHANGED: CASE STUDIES

When the League project was over, we finally had time to think about what had happened, although at first our phones still rang a lot as old League members wanted to tell us or ask us about events in the new League. After all, a close five-year relationship can't be ended in one day. Still, we did have another job to do by then and so did they, so after a while our communication grew infrequent.

Our new job, of course, was to inspect the data, review our thoughts, and begin to put together our story. As we did, we tried ways of grouping the League schools to arrive at some framework within which we might summarize the major elements that we had seen at work when they tried to change. By clustering schools according to their DDAE level at the end of the third year (that is, at the time of our earliest actual measurement of DDAE) and their level at the end of the project we arrived at four groups:

Group 1: Those schools whose DDAE level was high at both the first and last measurements; the "High-High Group"

Group 2: Those schools whose DDAE level was lower at the first measurement than it was at the last; the "Low-High Group"

Group 3: Those schools whose DDAE level was higher at the first measurement than at the last; the "High-Low Group"

Group 4: Those schools whose DDAE level was low at both the first and last measurements; the "Low-Low Group"[1]

In the rest of this chapter we will describe in some detail one school in each group; then we will look for similarities and differences between conditions in that school and conditions in the other schools in the same group.[2] We will try to identify several major themes which appeared to be played with variations through all the groups, so that we can explore them in the last chapter.

THE HIGH-HIGH GROUP

This felicitous group numbered three schools: Hacienda, Seastar, and Woodacres. Seastar and Woodacres housed grades K through six, and Hacienda extended from K through eighth grade. The school descriptions in Appendix A indicate that although these schools had several demographic characteristics in common, they were not, on the face of it, all alike. We will need to look more closely to uncover critical conditions that they may have shared.[3]

The Case of Seastar

Seastar School was located about ten miles from the SECSI offices on a quiet residential street in one of the many "satellite" cities that are interwoven among the boundary lines of the city of Los Angeles. When the League began, teaching at the school was "mixed" in organization. Some teachers were involved in various forms of formal cooperation, including full-fledged team teaching, while others taught alone in traditional self-contained classrooms. The Seastar staff was somewhat older and more experienced than were League staffs as a whole, and as Dave W., the principal, used to say, "They hang around. We may not get but a couple of new teachers in several years." Teachers and principal, moreover, were quite nontraditional in the educational beliefs which they expressed on our 1971 questionnaire and in what we were able to see of their daily work.

The Seastar staff indicated on a 1971 questionnaire that they followed the suggestions of Dave W. primarily out of respect for his competence. This reason was ranked highest by the staff in 1969 and 1970 as well and was followed in all three years by respect for the principal's personal qualities. The questionnaire data were backed up by interviews with teachers which were sprinkled with approving comments on Dave's considerable knowledge about education, his sensitivity in human relations, and the freedom he allowed to his staff.

Dave W. was shown by sociometric analysis to be clearly the central and most chosen person in the school for informal discussion of curriculum and instruction and for discussions of classroom discipline. Overall, the informal organization at Seastar was quite well developed when our sociometric data were gathered there in 1971. At that time nearly three-fifths of all the teaching staff were engaged in stable mutual interactions with other staff members in the school on each of the three dimensions of informal association (Appendix C, Q5). The cohesiveness of the Seastar staff had appeared even earlier in data which Dave himself had collected at the start of the fourth year, when he and the other League principals tried to gather systematic information about the social structure of their staffs. Dave had reported his findings to the principals' group, tracing out with delight the intricate web of relationships that bound the Seastar teachers together.

Let the reader not conclude, however, that throughout the project, Seastar was simply a school blessed with good relations between a principal and staff which possessed shared values and beliefs providing a strong basis for cooperation. There is substantial evidence which suggests that Seastar's participation in the League influenced change within the school. The evidence came from both questionnaire data and our amassed records of observations, communications, and impressions about Seastar's experience in the League. For example, certain questionnaire scores having to do with staff behavior changed consistently over the 1967–1971 period in the direction of general openness, heightened staff morale, and decreased close supervision by the principal. Furthermore, the scores describing teacher influence in school decision making rose steadily over that period.

We can flesh out these bare numerical bones with material from other sources. We referred earlier to the fact that Seastar was not initially a willing participant in the League. Upon seeing a newspaper story which announced their impending League involvement before they had been informed by their district office, the staff had voted not to join the League. When told by the district superintendent that they would be in it anyway, neither teachers nor principal made any attempt to conceal their hostility toward the SECSI staff.

The antagonism seemed to stem primarily from two perceptions. First, the staff was professionally quite experienced; most had served on curriculum committees, several were seeking advanced degrees, and the principal was in a doctoral program. To be "assigned" to a project which was labeled as our effort to learn about innovation in education to them smacked of an expression of doubt in their current ability to function at a high professional level. Their pride was hurt. Second, the Seastar staff was clearly distrustful of their new superintendent, who had come from outside the district and was pushing very strongly for more emphasis on research. Dave W. and his teachers quite openly surmised that Seastar was in the League more to accrue prestige for the district than for any advantage that the project might offer the school.

The first year seemed an unending hassle, and the second year was not a whole lot better. But the processes through which the staff was conducting its business were increasingly exposed to view. Before, Seastar teachers had been accustomed to working alone; now teachers were arguing out in meeting after meeting what on earth they might do as a League school. As Dave W. brought reports back from League principals' meetings, and Seastar teachers were finally engaged in communication with other League teachers, they did come to identify a sort of League school responsibility (though at first it brought little pleasure).

In the second year Dave became deeply involved in the effort to define a decision-monitoring role for League principals, and he became exceedingly nondirective with teachers in order to encourage his staff to take over more areas of decision making. The teachers reached an uneasy agreement to experiment with team teaching as a better way of coping with individual differences among pupils. The short-term results of these early efforts were thumping failures in a number of the teaming ventures and a fair amount of apprehension about what some took to be their "leaderless" condition.

Still, the staff found itself less and less dismayed when something didn't quite work out and more and more possessed of ideas about what might work better. Before long Dave and the teachers decided to confront their district problems. They invited their superintendent to meet with them to discuss district support for Seastar's attempts to take advantage of their League association in order to improve the school. As a result, Seastar received assurance of a minimum day for teacher planning, additional secretarial help, and the knocking out of a few walls between classrooms.

The walls came down and staff confidence in their own ability to make changes rose. Seastar participation in League activities increased as the staff sought ideas from any available source. In addition, change in the district superintendency soon relieved pressure on that front.

Although there was disagreement about what the school should be doing and how, the staff developed great skill in using its differences productively and maintained a great commitment to keeping the whole process out in the open. Little by little the staff found effective ways of acting as a group.

For example, several teachers felt that the standard report card form used for children's grades in the district was inappropriate. They brought the matter to a staff meeting as a problem and found enough support to form a committee of interested teachers who volunteered to develop an alternative report card. That committee sent inquiries to other schools in the League (and to some non-League schools as well) to determine what had been tried or discarded in parallel circumstances. The ultimate product of this effort was an anecdotal report form which sought to describe the child's progress, his relevant attitudes, etc.; in addition, the plan called for parent-teacher conferences as part of the assessment and reporting procedure. The plan was approved in a staff meeting (Dave W. having been content to take a more or less neutral stance and leave the matter in the teachers' hands), and the procedure was tried out in the school. After the first use of the new system, the reactions of parents were obtained via a brief questionnaire, and appropriate changes were made.

Faced later with another occasion for change—the development of a learning or "resource" center—the staff agreed to take on a slightly increased pupil load in order to make the necessary hiring of new staff possible. They persuaded the principal of the merits of their plan and participated in the selection of two part-time resource center staff members.

Halfway through the last year of the project Dave W. left Seastar to take a superintendency in another district. The very real sadness and well-wishing from the staff during Dave's last weeks at the school left us with no doubt about their regard for the colleague they were losing. At the same time the staff made Paul S., their new principal, welcome and settled into helping him learn the way of life at Seastar. Paul openly expressed his respect for what he had heard about the staff and his expectation that he would begin by learning from them.

Seastar and the Other High-High Schools

To what extent is the case of Seastar typical of the group of schools which we have called High-High? Not in the maturity and stability of its staff, for both Hacienda and Woodacres had staffs that were considerably more youthful, and both schools had high turnover. Nor did these two other High-High schools have the markedly nontraditional educational beliefs scores of the Seastar staff, for although the Hacienda staff, too, expressed such beliefs, Woodacres' score was not especially nontraditional for a League school. It is hard, however, to judge the meaningfulness of the "more traditional" score of the Woodacres staff when we remember that, compared with non-League schools, the entire group of League schools was decidedly nontraditional.

Yet a bit of nonquestionnaire data does indicate that, at least at the beginning, teachers at Woodacres were not altogether comfortable with new possibilities in schooling. As the League began, Woodacres opened its new ultramodern plant with movable partitions but no permanent walls to form rooms. Teachers immediately spread out and constructed private spaces for themselves. This did not correspond to the initial resistance we saw at Seastar. The first principal—and soon to be superintendent—at Woodacres could not have been more enthusiastic about belonging to the League, but the staff remained skittish for a year or so until Leonard B. became principal and the group gained confidence in coping with its problems (see Chapter 4). And the utterly opposite pole from resistant Seastar at the start of the League was Hacienda, where principal and teachers greeted the new League impetus to be innovative as the only way to go and the way that they were going anyhow.

Just as the three High-High schools seem to have traveled different paths through the League history that preceded our first measurement of DDAE, so too did they vary in their styles of DDAE during the period when, according to our measurement criteria, we were able to designate them as high DDAE schools. Thus, for example, while the Seastar staff was apt to be considering possible changes in several areas at once, the Woodacres staff tended to focus on one area at a time; Hacienda fell somewhere between the two others and made more use than they did of the principal as a source of topics for discussion.

Nonetheless, these three schools, insofar as we were able to determine from the observations and questionnaires that we were using then, seemed to have possessed at the time of the first measurement of DDAE a number of the same characteristics that we found were associated with high DDAE in the final (1971) data. The formal organization of each staff possessed some provision for cooperative teaching; teams predominated at Hacienda, and both Seastar and Woodacres worked with a mixture of teams and self-contained classrooms. The staff's recognition of the principal's professional competence ranked high in each school as the basis for the principal's authority over teachers. Teachers felt that they had considerable influence in decision making; there was high agreement between the description of the school given by teachers and that given by the principal; and the overall climate of each school was generally portrayed as open, friendly, and stimulating.

Here were three schools, then, where staffs reached and maintained, at least over our two-year measurement period, a high level of DDAE and its concomitant conditions. What might their League membership have had to do with it? First, let us note that these schools were active as League members. All three principals were elected to the principals' steering committee, and all discussed League activities with their teachers. Our records of such indicators as interschool visits, attendance at League meetings, and use of the League library, show that teachers from these schools also participated substantially in League matters. But did they participate primarily as the ones out in front, the consultants rather than the learners? Even the numerical records suggest not. For example, teachers from these three schools were visitors to other schools about as frequently as they were hosts to visitors.

When we consider all the information we have, we get a distinct impression that membership in the League was a source of support as well as stimulation for these High-High schools. We have already told, for example, how the Seastar staff was in the early years badgered into new action by its identification with the League. Also the staff successfully made use of its League membership to back up requests to its district office. For the rest of the project Seastar had few problems in its relations with the district.

The story played in reverse at Hacienda and again suggests the power of League identification. Hacienda began the project as the showplace of the League. The district administration, as well as the school staff, bubbled with excitement about their exploration of new patterns in schooling. Hacienda's freewheeling staff communication and unabashed enthusiasm about school tasks did look a bit different. Among League schools and the SECSI staff some viewed Hacienda as a fairy child; in others it aroused distrust. For whatever reason, the question was often asked, "How could Hacienda get anything out of the League?" Still, representatives from the jaunty Hacienda staff were rarely absent from League events, and the school (as we observed earlier) was probably oversold as a visiting site.

Then, not quite halfway through the project, there came a change in the district administration and with it an about-face in the district expectations for Hacienda. No longer was Hacienda encouraged to seek better answers to its own problems; greater conformity among district schools was now desired. Commitments to outside projects tended to be valued only to the extent of any clearly material benefits that they might bring. In spite of repeated attempts by Chris M., Hacienda's principal, to explain the intangible worth of membership in the League, blocks to the school's League participation mounted. It became difficult, and more often impossible, to free Hacienda teachers to go to League meetings; Chris M. had to justify every attendance he put in at a League principal's meeting.

Though the Hacienda staff was beginning to feel the crunch by the time we took the first measurement of DDAE, things got even worse. Yet, in a very real sense, Hacienda remained a League school to the end of the project. There are several reasons. For one thing, Hacienda's presence in the League remained highly visible to other League members; they continued to visit the school and to expect certain things from it (in the final year teachers from six other League schools visited Hacienda). Perhaps that first, and otherwise undesirable, "star" status bestowed upon Hacienda had created a kind of fat off which the school could live for a while. Therefore, it was not allowed to forget that it was a League school, even though it didn't get around much anymore. We would hear from time to time how by hook or crook the Hacienda staff was still trying, as best it could, to inquire into and to experiment with its own operations in spite of district restraints, and during our last year teachers from Hacienda managed to visit and consult with teachers in four other League schools. The final questionnaire data, however, as well as our encounters with the staff revealed small erosions in the climate of Hacienda. Nonetheless the school did maintain its high DDAE standing to the end of the project.

Unlike the other two High-High schools, Woodacres enjoyed the support of its district administration throughout the League project. The strength of this solid backing for the school was demonstrated when, about midway through the project, an outspoken, militant minority in the community tried to halt the staff's efforts to test alternatives in school organization and instructional programs. Drawing on its broad base of support in the district office and in the League, the Woodacres staff developed a strategy for improving communication and was able to ride out the storm. Indeed, through the powerful technique of bringing parents into the school to observe and assist with the daily program, by the end of the project the staff had won the approval of some of its former detractors in the community.

From the beginning of the League strategy, we had recognized the possibility of conflict between the expectations held for a school by its district and the expectations held by the League. We have observed several configurations of these expectations in the High-High group, and we will keep the potential problems in mind as we move on to consider the other groups.

THE LOW-HIGH GROUP

The seven schools whose final DDAE level was higher than when it was first measured may perhaps be labeled more as "success stories" than the High-High group, where schools simply held their own as far as DDAE level is concerned. Three of the schools moved from middle rank to high over the two-year period; four of the schools moved from low to middle rank.

The Case of Independence

The title of this story might well be "How to Succeed under Great Handicaps," for Independence represented what must be a classic example of physical and organizational conditions calculated to interfere with the development of a healthy DDAE process. The circumstances with which the staff at Independence had to contend included the following:

1 At the close of the first League year, the school was forced to move from its original location (the building having been condemned), and the principal moved to a new position in another city.

2 In the following year, with a new principal, the staff and pupils were split and sent to three different school plants. Though Independence continued to exist formally as a unit, it was a school with noncommunication and dispersion built into its very organization.

3 The classes were on double session for the duration of the second year.

4 The school was reunited at the end of the third year in a set of portable buildings and remained in these temporary quarters until the conclusion of the League project.

5 At the beginning of the final year, the school was changed from

K–6 to K–3. In addition, several new special programs were instituted which brought a substantial increase in the size of the staff.

6 The pupil population at Independence was a markedly transient one
throughout, and during the last year of the project a high proportion
of the 1,000 pupils were bussed in from other neighborhoods.

It goes without saying that these features of life at Independence
might all have made for serious problems with DDAE and League participation. Indeed, at the time of our first measurement of DDAE, the
school ranked low. Yet, beginning with the second year of the project,
the Independence staff was quite well represented in League activities.
Arnold Z., who became principal in the second year, was openly dedicated to the concept of sharing problems and resources via the League
structure. He himself played an active role in the League principals'
group, and he encouraged staff participation in the League by working
out ways for teachers to attend meetings and visit other schools.

Independence teachers had a strong professional orientation and
quickly came to view the League as a source of valuable opportunities for improving professional skills. Besides attending League meetings and playing both host and visitor to other schools, Independence
teachers made great use of the League library and contributed written
material in the form of League reports, League newsletter stories, and
selections for publications by League teachers.[4]

In the fourth year of the project we had several indications that
the DDAE process in the Independence staff might be improving. Data
from a SECSI substudy reported that a number of organizational characteristics of Independence school appeared to be fairly favorable for
the integration of individual and group goals.[5] And a highly qualified
observer who visited the school in the spring of that year commented,
"In general, the involvement of teachers and of children seems to me
to be very high. These teachers seem to know what they are about.
They work very hard and seem happy in their work. My guess is that
it will not be difficult for this group to adapt to any kind of organizational changes which they might institute."

This prediction, it turned out, was correct. Within a very short
time the Independence staff was informed of a district decision to convert the school from K–6 to K–3, as part of a plan to meet the requirements of a court order to desegregate. When they received the
news, the Independence staff immediately began intensive planning
to meet inevitable difficulties. For example, they held a series of meetings to decide whether (and which) teachers wished to leave, con-

sidering among other things that a change in customary teaching duties was involved for those who, at the time, had upper-level classes. Most of the teachers elected to stay; only four out of forty left. Both the teachers and the principal encouraged decisions to stay by working out plans and programs to ease the transition—most particularly, by developing a nongraded approach and an organizational plan of both self-contained and team-taught classrooms to aid in coping with the new situation. (By contrast, in a similar situation a non-League school in the district lost half of its teachers. Here, little school-based discussion took place to prepare for the change, even though district-sponsored workshops in intergroup relations were offered.)

We do not wish to overemphasize, however, the quality of staff characteristics or the principal's leadership at Independence. Both had their weaknesses; at our final measurement the school's DDAE process was in the middle range of quality as far as the League group was concerned. The striking fact was that Independence managed, under the circumstances, to improve at all. A variety of evidence attests to the staff's continuing attention to new possibilities and the accompanying rise of professional satisfaction. Questionnaire data, as well as observations, indicated that the staff made much use of informal consultation about their work. The content of the DDAE process at Independence gave heavy emphasis to the exploration and implementation of innovations in curriculum and instruction. Furthermore, when asked about what they perceived to be effects of their League membership, more than three-fourths of the Independence staff attributed these innovations to their participation in the League.

The school problems which were cited by the teachers provide other insights into the events at Independence. Most of the staff mentioned the lack of various facilities, which was surely a realistic assessment of their situation, but they did not indicate that much of the DDAE process centered on those kinds of problems, which was also realistic, since there was relatively little that could be done until the new school plant was completed. Very interesting, too, is a comparison of the problems which were mentioned when the school was anticipating the changeover to grades K–3 and the problems mentioned after the staff had had a year's experience in the new situation. Looking toward the K–3 structure and the bussing in of pupils, some 30 to 40 percent of the teachers foresaw problems having to do with racial differences, community understanding, and staff orientation. A year later, however, problems in these areas were mentioned by only 10 percent or less of the staff, perhaps an indication of the effectiveness of the staff's preparation for inevitable change. Probably related but with an interestingly different twist is the fact that problems with student discipline were neither widely anticipated nor cited after the change had occurred.

Other questionnaire data support observations of an increase in staff esprit de corps at Independence during the final two years. The score on general school climate rose, as did the measure of teacher morale. The amount of influence that teachers felt they had in decision making, however, did not change much and was slightly below the average League school score. Nonetheless, Arnold Z.'s style of leadership seems to have worked in the situation. The teachers' favorable assessment of their principal's leadership went up from the middle range of League scores in 1969 to among the highest in 1971. During that period, also, there was a strengthening of the tendency for Independence teachers to see the principal's professional competence as the primary reason for his influence over them. And about a fifth of the teachers stated that changes in this general area of staff relationships were direct outcomes of the school's involvement in the League.

There emerges a portrait of a school that survived rather well more than its share of vicissitudes. Independence made clear use of its League membership to investigate a wider world. It also put together a DDAE process which enabled it to cope with a succession of external demands in ways that preserved staff integrity and brought a reasonable measure of satisfaction.

Independence and the Other Low-High Schools

The other schools in this group were Dewey Avenue, Bell Street, Country, Antigua, Rainbow Hill, and Mar Villa. As far as demographic characteristics go, these schools did not look much alike. They ranged, for example, from the strongly urban settings of Dewey Avenue, Independence, and Antigua, through the suburban Country, to the distinctly rural flavor of Rainbow Hill. Size range was just as pronounced, and the pupil populations varied from mostly white middle class to several potpourris of racial and ethnic backgrounds. School plants included, besides the portables at Independence, the oldest permanent building in the League and one of the newest.

Nor do the questionnaire data reveal a clearly homogeneous group of school staffs. Most of the staffs had a predominance of members with substantial professional experience, but the Rainbow Hill group was rather new to the game, and at Country there was an even split between veterans and newcomers. The educational beliefs scores of these staffs spread from among the least traditional to among the most traditional in the League. (Again we note, however, that "most traditional" within the League was not very traditional, compared with non-League school scores.) The staffs were more similar in showing general improvement during the last two years on several measures of school climate, teacher morale, and principal's leadership, conditions which we would expect to accompany a move toward a more receptive DDAE process. Even here, though, the Mar Villa scores were sufficiently ambiguous to warrant some further explanation a little later on. Also in line with our expectations for higher levels of DDAE was the predominance of cooperative teaching in these schools. Only one, Bell Street, was classified as a self-contained classroom arrangement; five fell into the cooperative teaching type, and Independence, as we have said, had a mixed organization.

Perhaps even more germane to the change we recorded in the quality of the DDAE process in these schools was certain information about the problems perceived by the staffs and the sorts of things that tended to come up for consideration in the DDAE process. The Independence staff, remember, appeared to behave quite realistically, recognizing undesirable conditions that could scarcely be ignored, but spending most of its time on matters of curriculum and instruction. This same picture holds up very well for the other staffs in this group; the data indicate that they put heavy emphasis on discussions of curriculum and instruction, although a variety of problems from external sources came up for mention, and concern about their own staff relationships was made explicit by principals and many teachers. In our sociometric data, these staffs also showed a substantial amount of informal consultation on task-related matters. Another observation about Independence data can also be said to be true of the whole group: members of these staffs were not likely to cite problems of discipline or poor student attitudes.

The Low-High school staffs (with one exception) shared, too, the view that the basis for their principals' influence over them throughout the period between the two DDAE measurements lay primarily in his professional competence. The leadership styles of these principals, however, were very different, as we had frequent occasion to observe. We saw these observations reflected in data which indicated how nearly a principal's scores agreed with the average score of his teachers on questionnaires which described various aspects of school life. Some principals in this group, for example, described their own behavior quite differently from their teachers. We discovered from these scores, however, an interesting similarity among all these principals. Each of them considerably overestimated, at least in comparison with the view of his teachers, the staff esprit and the amount of influence that teachers had in decision making in his school.

We came out of all these excursions into the questionnaire data with a strong feeling of a group of schools which had, in a quite businesslike fashion, stuck closely to the manageable professional job at hand, whatever blocks might have been thrown in the way. Our observations confirmed this impression. With one possible exception, which we will talk about in a minute, things didn't seem to come easily to these staffs. But they stayed with it, worrying away at what they saw to be their responsibilities. The principal, however he handled the burden of leadership, had in all cases reinforced staff attention to specific tasks. It seemed quite reasonable to us, then, that he might have lightened the daily load a bit for himself (and, perhaps through his resulting optimism, for the whole staff) by perceiving a somewhat rosier world where his teachers were happily sharing with him the decisions that must be made.

At this point we must note that in all but one school there was only one principal at the school during the period we are discussing. (In fact, four of the others were in their schools throughout the project and two from the second year on.) The one exception was Dewey Avenue, and we think it is a somewhat special case in the Low-High group. It belongs in the group by virtue of the difference between its two DDAE rankings, but its history is quite different from the other schools. Its low DDAE rank came at the climax of the argument between the teachers and Edith B., the new principal (see Chapter 6), and its final high rank came in the year that Stan M. returned as principal. All our preliminary observations from which the DDAE measurement was derived indicated a high level of DDAE at Dewey Avenue during the early years of the project, and the evidence is simply overwhelming that the critical incident in the school was the change in principal. We would guess the DDAE path of Dewey Avenue over the duration of the League to have been High-Low-High. That cannot be surmised for the other schools in this group. They appeared to have followed a steady, if sometimes slow, upward path.

During the climb, the principals of these schools made use of the League, as did Stan M. when he was at Dewey Avenue. (It is interesting that Edith B. was one of the few League principals who felt closer to her district associates than to the League group.) Arnold Z.'s behavior at Independence was fairly typical of this group. All but one of these principals had taken advantage of League opportunities for themselves and for their teachers from very early in the project. Some managed more teacher participation than did others, and in part this was related to distance problems, for the Low-High group covered the whole range of ease of access to other League schools. Still, each of these schools sent and received at least a few League visitors, made moderate to high use of the League library, and was represented at most League activities. Of particular importance is the fact that these Low-High principals not only participated heavily within the regular structure of League activities, but more than any other group, they initiated additional contacts with League members.

The one principal in this group who was slow to make much use of League connections was Peter M. at Bell Street. There was reason for his hesitance, and it brings us back to our questions about the role of district support for a League school. All the other schools in this group had support from their districts in the form of no interference or verbal encouragement or special awareness. The district office for Bell Street, however, did not appear to be friendly to League expectations, and when Peter M. came to the school in the second year, he assessed the situation as one in which he dare not try to make any waves. The problems that this created with many of his staff who did want to venture out as a League school into new territory was part of the background for the first low DDAE rank of Bell Street.

Although Peter M. was absent from League meetings more often than most of the group, he did attend enough to learn very soon what the League was about. It was interesting to observe his quite outspoken efforts to reconcile what he saw as two conflicting sets of expectations. He was not, personally, that much opposed to trying out new ideas, and he enjoyed the League interaction, but he was fearful of the consequences for his career in the district. He sought advice from the SECSI staff and from League principals. Gradually, he moved to what seemed to be a policy of allowing more teacher freedom, of letting a few things happen even if he didn't make them happen.

Finally, in the last year, the district office indicated an interest in having Bell Street as a center for innovation, and Peter M. stepped up his efforts to involve his staff in League affairs.

Would the DDAE rank of Bell Street have improved as much if the district had not signaled at least mild approval for experimentation? We will never know, but we did see that it was not so much the approval itself that mattered here as it was the resulting relaxation of tension between principal and teachers. In another case we observed district encouragement of innovation create that same kind of tension, with somewhat mixed consequences. This occurred at Mar Villa, and there is much more to the story than we will be able to tell here. Briefly, the Mar Villa staff during the early years were rather apathetic about their League membership. Although Adam S., the principal, was a steady League participant, his generally laissez faire style of leadership had not been able to stir much enthusiasm in the staff. Nor was Mar Villa close enough to other League schools for teacher contacts to be made easily. The Mar Villa staff at the time of the first DDAE measurement was still pretty much set in ways that did not facilitate entertaining new notions.

Then the district office announced that the old Mar Villa building would be completely remodeled so that the school could demonstrate individualized instruction and team teaching. In preparation for the change, the Mar Villa staff was required to produce a statement of the school philosophy and educational objectives. Adam S. went along with the task. Although he had no illusions about great and rapid transformations, he did see the district decision as a possible way out of the rut—a beginning. The teachers, for the most part, were not happy. Many resented being forced into the new program, since they were requested to sign agreements in order to have their contracts renewed. Nearly all the teachers viewed the definition of goals as a low-priority item. Fearful of what they didn't know about the coming changes, and very soon finding themselves keeping school in the physical chaos of building demolition and construction, the staff saw as more important the need to learn new ways of organizing their daily efforts to do their jobs.

Nonetheless, Adam S. held them to the task which had been set for them, though he did recognize the staff's concerns and tried to draw upon League resources to provide at least some attention to them. The upshot was that in the final year of the project the Mar Villa DDAE process had clearly opened up considerably, the statement of goals was distributed to district personnel and to parents, and the principal and teachers were at last beginning to tackle the basic problems that they had to solve in order to exist in their new environment. All this, we think, lies behind that ambiguous display of scores which we mentioned earlier: a substantial rise in DDAE rank without the definite accompaniment of a more desirable school atmosphere. The times were somewhat out of joint at Mar Villa; a step had been taken, but we could not be sure of the direction of the next one.

The Low-High group offers additional information on the school-district-League relationships. On the whole, it supports the obvious conclusion that when district and League expectations were, or came to be, in line with one another, a school staff might more easily increase the openness of its DDAE process. Yet the case of Mar Villa adds a cautionary comment, for although the district demand for innovation certainly seems to have resulted quickly in better staff communication, we are left with a question as to whether or not supportive conditions of general staff climate in the school could catch up with the rapid, largely involuntary change.

THE HIGH-LOW GROUP

The six schools in this group are in many ways of greatest interest to us; they give us, we hope, a few clues about what may be the most difficult conditions for a change strategy to handle. Although we did not have earlier measures of DDAE comparable to those on which these groupings were based, informal assessments by SECSI staff members during the first two years did indicate that all but one school in this group had, by midproject, progressed from their initial conditions to greater receptivity to change. (The remaining school had shown, we thought, little movement in any direction.) These were, of course, our impressions, not ratings given by the school staffs. Nonetheless, we believe them to be worth mentioning since our later impressions of these schools agree with the teachers' ratings—we, too, would say that this group did lose ground in the last two years.

The Case of Shadyside

Two major changes, independent of the League strategy, highlight Shadyside's history. First, there were two changes of principal from the inception of the League to the project's close. One change occurred at the end of the first year when an experienced professional woman,

Lucy K., came to the school. At the end of the third year she moved to the district office and was replaced by a young man, Brad C., in his first job as principal. Second, the racial integration plan instituted in the district in the last year required that Shadyside convert from a K–6 plan to a K–3 organization. Word of the change came to the school too late for much planning by the staff. Many of the teachers were transferred to the "sister" school (designated to handle the fourth through the sixth grades), and new teachers (many from the sister school) made up 40 percent of the Shadyside staff. Thus, in the last two years of the League, Shadyside was the scene of relatively rapid and profound change: new teachers, new pupils, and a very new principal.

No doubt it would have been difficult for any principal to follow in the footsteps of Lucy K. An extraordinarily dynamic and personable leader, she had encouraged a climate of experimentation and teacher participation which centered on various programs for individualizing instruction. Shadyside developed a reputation for these activities within the League, and both teachers and principal participated enthusiastically in League affairs. Shadyside, in fact, was much favored by some of the SECSI staff—part of that questionable early practice of ours of tacitly anointing a few schools.

What the teachers thought about themselves in these high-point years of their League membership was glowingly communicated in the monthly League Reports provided by Shadyside teachers. One reporter commented that "there is an air of excitement and enthusiasm at Shadyside; the faculty is extremely open to new ideas and there is constant communication between teachers throughout the day." Another reporter wrote, "In my opinion and observation, Shadyside School is at a definite advantage in terms of educational innovation and initiative, due in large measure to the ability of the staff to talk, share, laugh, commit themselves, argue, and listen; in other words to communicate." And a third reporter summed it up with the remark, "Our staff at Shadyside has a certain magic about it that makes an experimental program exciting. Perhaps because we share team successes and failures, it becomes easier to open up and share individual success and failure."

While the "magic" probably sprang in part from a brilliant position in the League orbit, it certainly rested upon the wide-open, daily give-and-take among the staff. Then, in the last two years, the bubbling enthusiasm at Shadyside went flat; DDAE took on a humdrum air.

Brad C. was willing to try different ideas in education, but he was at the same time feeling his way into a new role. His earnest efforts to learn simply did not satisfy a staff which from the start of the League had been described as self-confident and which had thrived for two years on charismatic and professionally impeccable leadership. In interviews teachers expressed concern about a certain loss of cohesiveness and direction; they thought that the principal "should be far more persuasive"; they would have liked "to develop a more integrated staff"; they were "not quite sure what his role is" and believed that as a result he sometimes kept them "from knowing what they are supposed to do."

The staff decided that its experimentation with team teaching was not accomplishing what they had wanted, and they reverted to self-contained classrooms. A switch in the teaching organization must be added to the list of changes which occurred at Shadyside during the period of the decline of its DDAE level. Whatever the interaction of changes was, it seemed to show up not only in our observations but also in other school scores. The summary score on teacher morale dropped dramatically over this period, as did the general school climate score.[6] Teachers, on the other hand, saw little change in their influence in school decision making. The Shadyside scores on teacher power remained very close to the League mean throughout this period.

The staff's assessment of its leadership produced a far lower summary score on the quality of principal leadership in the last year than it had in the third year. Also changed was the weight given by teachers to several possible grounds for compliance with the principal's wishes. With Lucy K., the principal's "competence" was almost uniformly the teachers' first choice as the reason for their compliance. With Brad C., however, fewer teachers cited competence as their prime reason and more importance was assigned to the principal's legitimate right to command and to his power to reward.

The different leadership styles of these two principals can be glimpsed by comparing the extent to which each agreed with the teachers in answers given to several sets of questions about staff behavior. For example, Brad C. saw the teachers as more committed and less burdened by nonessential tasks than they saw themselves, and his view of his own personal consideration for teachers far surpassed theirs. Lucy K.'s judgments had been quite in line with most teachers on those matters. On the other hand, she had estimated the amount of teacher influence in decision making to be much higher than most teachers did, while Brad C.'s estimate was close to the teacher average.

A variety of evidence points to difficulties in staff relationships during this period at Shadyside. Yet Brad C. did not cite any such difficulties when he listed major problems which the school faced in those last two years; his overriding concern was for the staff to develop clarity and consensus about goals. More than half of the list of problems obtained from teachers midway through this period had noted staff problems, but at the end of the project, no more than a quarter of the teachers mentioned problems of this kind. We might suppose that the decline indicated that problems in staff relationships had been largely solved, but the rest of the data do not support such an interpretation. Rather, we are left with the feeling that staff attention had moved to other areas.

One of those areas seems to have been pupil discipline, for in the final questionnaire the principal and over half of the Shadyside staff saw pupil behavior and/or attitudes as a problem. The staff also indicated fairly traditional educational beliefs about discipline, but the principal's beliefs on this score were quite nontraditional. What part of the concern about discipline was related to the influx of new pupils, what part to the sizeable proportion of new teachers, we do not know, but whatever the cause, our information on the DDAE process at Shadyside revealed that the staff had spent at least a modest amount of time working together on discipline problems—and on problems in a number of other areas. The data show that the content of the DDAE process at Shadyside was among the most diversified in the League.

The school also continued as an active League member. During the last year, for example, Shadyside teachers exchanged visits with half a dozen other League schools. There was, however, a different flavor about the Shadyside participation during the period of its decline in DDAE level. More than most, the Shadyside teachers had expressed extreme displeasure with our decision to limit our intervention role to facilitating interschool contacts. They were distressed with the loss of SECSI staff members whom they had valued as expert consultants, and the loss had hit them just at the time when Lucy K. left the school. Although the Shadyside staff continued to attach great importance to the opportunities that the League gave them to make contact with other teachers, some of what had appeared to them earlier as League magic had now clearly vanished.

There are two obvious comparisons to make between Shadyside and other League schools. Independence had faced precisely the same problem of school reorganization to comply with a district desegregation effort, but in coping with the change the Independence staff had improved its DDAE level. Some differences stand out clearly. Independence had about a year for staff planning; the time allowed Shadyside was much shorter. At least as important probably were two aspects of the principalship. The Independence staff was not in the process of becoming accustomed to someone new. Furthermore, the assured, directive style of Arnold Z. did not seem to violate seriously the expectations of the highly professional Independence teachers, while the less mature, though quite self-confident, Shadyside staff was frustrated by what it saw as a lack of leader direction. Finally, though both schools used League resources (they were the top "visitors" in the last year), it seemed that Independence expected to be working forever on its own problems, while Shadyside sought a more definitive answer to their problems that never came.

In the early years Shadyside was also like Hacienda in its stardom in the League. But when the SECSI intervention strategy was changed, Hacienda seemed to take our new role in stride. At Hacienda no great internal changes coincided with the restriction of SECSI intervention: the same principal remained, and a high rate of teacher turnover had always been a part of Hacienda life. When external pressure hit Hacienda, it hit a staff confident about its own fashion of doing things and proud of its League membership. The final external demand on Shadyside, however, was a blow to a staff already punchy with internal doubts and bereaved by the loss of strong outside mentors.

Shadyside and the Other High-Low Schools

Once again this group does not contain schools that immediately look alike on the basis of demographic data or distance from other League schools. For example, South and James, like Shadyside, were in urban situations; Indian Flat was in a fast-growing suburb; Middleton was semirural; and Fairfield was in a definitely rural setting. Shadyside and South were close to other League members; Fairfield and James were far distant.

Certain questionnaire scores do show similarities throughout the group. In general, there was a decline in school climate, teacher morale, and teachers' evaluation of principal leadership, though Indian Flat and, to a lesser extent, James were clear exceptions. Except for the mixed organization at South, the other schools in the group stressed self-contained classrooms. Also, though the principals in the group did not exhibit a uniform pattern in the extent to which their scores agreed with their staff's scores, they were alike in that they tended to be out of line with a goodly number of their teachers in assessing their own consideration toward staff members. (Again, Indian Flat was somewhat different in its principal's closer agreement with teachers.)

The characteristics of Shadyside's perception of school problems and the content of its DDAE process hold true generally for this group. These principals, unlike the Low-High group, did not stress staff relationships as a problem, and the mention of such problems by teachers in these schools dropped off during the last two years to a lower level than was the case in the Low-High schools. These staffs (principal and teachers) were, furthermore, more likely than the Low-High staffs to mention pupil behavior and attitudes as a major problem during this period, though there were no striking overall differences between the pupil populations of the two groups. Finally, the DDAE process in these High-Low schools was marked by diversity of topics under consideration. The Low-High schools had conveyed an impression of concentration upon the professional work of teaching and awareness of the staff as a group. The High-Low schools' staffs appeared distracted by a variety of concerns.

We saw at Shadyside how overwhelming the buildup of problems on many fronts could become. Let us look at the rest of this group in light of the three major sources of problems that we spotted at Shadyside: internal sources, district sources, and League sources.

Internal Problems

None of the other schools experienced the sudden wave of new teachers that occurred at Shadyside, but South did get a new principal, Harry L., when its longtime leader, Alex R., retired at the end of the fourth year. Much younger and less experienced than his predecessor (or, for that matter, much of his staff), Harry L. nonetheless took firm hold of the reins at South. More importantly, what data we have suggest that although his leadership style was considerably more directive than that of Alex R., he was largely in accord with teachers' perceptions of staff behavior. In turn, the ratings given to Harry L. by the teachers were remarkably similar to those given to the man he had replaced. The change in principals at South did not, then, appear to be an important source of its problems. The trouble came from outside when, during the last year, changes in the school board resulted in enormous pressure on South's staff to provide constant justification of its program to a distrustful audience.

There was another school in this group, however, where most of the problems were obviously internal. Fairfield, isolated from the rest of the League in a small agricultural community, had a staff which was on the average older and possessed of more years of teaching experience than other staffs in the League. Turnover rate at the school, in addition, remained relatively low throughout the project. Aside from these biographical variables, teachers at Fairfield were the most traditional in the League in their educational beliefs. It was indeed a staff set in its ways. Ben U. was elated with the League because it put him in touch with the world outside for the first time in his long career. His ideas about leadership changed, and he tried to involve his staff in reaching decisions together. Very slowly, some small progress seems to have been made in opening up staff communication. Now and then a few teachers would try team teaching or follow up ideas that had been brought in from League activities that some of them had attended.

Even this snail's pace of change, however, bogged down. In the last two years staff communication laid open many disagreements but could rarely reach solutions. By far the major topic of concern was pupil discipline. A large majority of staff members cited discipline as a major problem, and far more discussions in total staff gatherings seem to have been spent on this than on any other subject. (The "discipline problem" at Fairfield smacked strongly of a self-fulfilling prophecy considering the tendency of many staff members to expect little else from the school's largely Mexican-American pupils.)

A stubborn cause of the failure to change the DDAE process was the widespread staff resentment of Ben U.'s efforts to construct a new kind of role for himself. It appeared that teachers at Fairfield carried over their traditional beliefs about classroom discipline into their thinking about the principal's leadership. They tended to emphasize the principal's authority over them just as they stressed their own authority in their beliefs about pupil behavior. Sociometric data indicated that there was indeed heavy reliance on Ben U. to provide direction for daily decisions about curriculum, instruction, and discipline. The data also revealed that there was little or no informal structure of regular communication among the staff.[7] Less than half of the teachers were involved in mutual friendship relationships, even fewer in task-based relationships. With scant possibility of teacher leadership that the principal could call upon for assistance, the situation drifted into unending, uncoordinated complaints.[8]

The school was extremely well supplied with outside consultants as a result of several federal and state projects in which it participated. The district was very supportive of outside involvements, including the League. For the most part, however, the teachers expressed annoyance at being given so many and varied suggestions by a parade of "theoreticians." They had voiced similar criticisms of the consultants the SECSI project supplied in its early years. On the other hand, most of the staff read the League newsletter, and a few made contributions to it. Yet in spite of Ben U.'s efforts to encourage them, League contacts dwindled for the Fairfield teachers. The physical isolation of the school simply made face-to-face encounters too cumbersome to arrange. Few of the Fairfield staff could manage the long trips, and almost no teachers from the other schools could come to see them. The lack of League visitors to their school caused disappointment and, probably at last, resentment among Fairfield teachers.

External Problems

In addition to South, two other schools in the group, James and Indian Flat, felt that they suffered a decline of district support during this period. In the last year the staffs at these three schools seem to have devoted a substantial part of their discussion time to problems that were coming to them from outside the school.

The situation at Indian Flat is interesting because it appears to be a kind of opposite to what occurred at Mar Villa. Mar Villa had received a mandate to experiment; Indian Flat was stunned when they were directed to give up parts of their innovative attempts by a theretofore supportive district. At Mar Villa while the DDAE level rose in the course of staff deliberations on their new orders, the cluster of conditions in which the staff process took place—school climate, teacher morale, and evaluation of the principal—dropped off. But at Indian Flat, those conditions improved although the DDAE level fell.[9] In the earlier story of Mar Villa we wondered whether a set of more supportive conditions would develop in the wake of the more or less forced march upward of its DDAE. Now we ask if the strength of the organizational environment at Indian Flat might arrest, or even reverse, the downward course of its DDAE.

A somewhat different kind of external pressure caused disturbance at James and Middleton when militant teacher-union activities erupted in those districts. We know that a temporary rift resulted between principal and teachers at James which, though apparently overcome, may have had residual effects.[10] Though we have sketchy information that lines which were drawn on this issue also split the staff at Middleton, we can say very little about what took place at that school, for the Middleton principal and teachers participated almost not at all in League activities.

Relationships with the League

League membership might also have been related to the High-Low schools' fall-off in DDAE. Along with Shadyside, the James staff was probably the most distressed by the change in the SECSI intervention, and we were frequently made aware that League activities had lost some of their charm for many James teachers. In addition, this school was quite far away from almost all other League schools. The result of disaffection and distance severely limited League participation by the James staff; the principal had the poorest attendance record (except for Middleton) at League meetings. He reported, however, that his absences were due to dislike of travel rather than to other displeasures.

We have already spoken of the extreme distance problems that essentially cut Fairfield out of League involvement. The situation was exacerbated as the Fairfield teachers began to attribute indiscriminately all of their annoyances to the fact that they were a "League school." Thus, the principal's absences from the school, of which they disapproved, were seen as League requirements, though most of the demands on his time came, in fact, from responsibilities to specially funded district programs. And the barrage of consultant help which they received from such programs became undesirable "League" disruptions of their classrooms.

Two schools in this group, however, made use of their League connections during the last two years. South's principal and teachers sought help in a variety of ways as they tried to cope with an increasingly hostile district atmosphere. Even more pronounced was the reliance on League support that was expressed at Indian Flat. Chet O. was one of the most assiduous of League principals in his use of League resources. He saw to it that his staff was well represented at League meetings, invited other principals to come to critique his school, and arranged numerous tactics for disseminating knowledge about the League to other schools in his district. Many of the staff at Indian Flat were quite articulate about the feeling of moral support that they derived from the League, and during the last year they conveyed considerable anxiety about what would become of them after the project ended.

As we would by this time expect, the High-Low group does not line itself up neatly in any obvious counter manner to the Low-High group, as far as school-district-League relationships are concerned. These High-Low schools do, however, lead us to make explicit a question that has been percolating underneath this discussion. To what extent might a school's recent history of DDAE level and the organizational conditions surrounding that process coupled with its current picture help us to guess what direction the school might take next? We will speculate on this question in the next chapter.

THE LOW-LOW GROUP

Two schools were assessed at a low level of DDAE at both the beginning and end of the last two years of the project. We shall try to look at these two together along several lines that have emerged from our consideration of the other groups.

Frontier was a small school; Peace Valley, a large school; and though both plants were only about a year old at the start of the League, Frontier was housed in several very plain finger units, while the more elaborate Peace Valley buildings had been designed for flexible programming. Neither staff was very stable, the result of rather high turnover at Frontier and rapid growth at Peace Valley. Yet the schools were obviously alike in a number of ways. They were the only two intermediate schools in the League. (All other schools contained elementary grades, though Hacienda and Fairfield extended through grade 8.) They were in semirural areas and were relatively remote from other League schools. Their pupil populations were comparable, as were most characteristics of their staffs.

It was another set of similarities, however, that we think was more important to the DDAE behavior of these schools. Above all, both schools had to contend with serious conflict between League and district expectations. The conflict for Frontier was more or less constant throughout the project, with the district reluctant to sanction much in the way of autonomous change by the school staff. Peace Valley experienced a wild yo-yoing of enthusiastic support and adamant disapproval, occasioned by bitter political battles for control of the school board. Both districts were small, and each school was the only intermediate school in its district—a situation which served to make each school highly visible to its upper administration and bring the attitudes of that administration quickly home to the school staff. At the end of the project, when the last DDAE measurements were taken, Peace Valley had completed a year of relative calm even with a district administration largely unsympathetic to the League association. The Frontier staff during a somewhat longer period had been not altogether willing participants in a district-initiated program to improve school-community relations.

A second similarity between the two schools was the fact that each had three different principals during the project. The turnover of principals was symptomatic of the turmoil in the district-school relationships. In each of the schools, for example, a principal was ousted because his actions, which included encouraging ties with the League, displeased the district. Nor did any principal in these schools, no matter what his general orientation, enjoy full support of the school staff. Staff members were divided about what the school should do, and there was considerable change in staff personnel from year to year.

Altogether, it was as if the various pieces that made up these schools would never hold one configuration long enough for anyone to do more than just hang on. The answers that these staffs gave when we asked them to list the major problems they faced indicate that although concern about discipline, outgrown school plants, and district interference was common, they also attached great importance to the difficulties that they experienced in staff relationships. More than in most League schools, for example, Frontier teachers were apt to mention unfriendly disagreement and lack of purpose in the staff ("What are we doing here?"), and Peace Valley teachers were apt to speak of their communication barriers, compounded by increasing size and staff factionalism which rose out of the bitterness of district politics. In both schools the teachers' assessment of their own influence in decision making dropped during the last two years. One got the feeling that the staffs had a sense of what was preventing them from even a concerted much less successful attack on problems.

Perhaps the League became, for these two schools, yet another source of frustration. As we said earlier, Frontier and Peace Valley did not have easy access to other League schools. Most importantly, they were about as far as they could be from one another. Both they and we recognized the desirability of contacts between the two staffs, but distance and the lack of freedom afforded them by their districts made teacher attendance at League meetings difficult and the visiting of other schools nearly impossible during the last two years.

Nor, by then, was there any sizable effort on the part of either staff to participate in the League. For Peace Valley the fourth year was the time of a critical battle in the district which climaxed in the firing of Mike D., the principal, and several teachers. In the fifth year the staff was picking up the pieces with a new principal; neither he nor the teachers were inclined to push for favors in order to participate more in League affairs. Many of the teachers, in fact, knew little about the League since the Peace Valley staff had continued to grow while the school maintained only tenuous contact with other League members. The much smaller Frontier staff was more generally aware of its League membership, and Carl C., who was principal during the last two years, wanted very much to increase the school's involvement in the League. In addition to district reluctance, however, he had to contend with a disgruntled staff. Whatever hopes Frontier had held for help from the League had been too many times dashed. The staff felt abandoned and would not court further disappointment.

The League project didn't work for these two schools, but the underlying idea of the peer group strategy was scarcely even tried with them. We are left with impressive examples of the potential power of higher administration to quash outside contacts for a school, but we really didn't learn much about how the staffs of these intermediate schools might have responded to opportunities to engage in mutual consultation with other staffs. We do know that the great majority of responses given at these schools to our questions about the advantages and disadvantages of having been in the League spoke of sharing ideas with other teachers as the chief advantage and, conversely, complained of lack of enough teacher involvement. But to what extent certain features of intermediate school staffs[11] might require drastic modifications in the League strategy remains for us an almost untouched question.

When the project ended and the new League began, the staffs of Fairfield and Frontier elected not to remain in the group. Peace Valley's district did not wish to participate, and Country's district office designated another school to participate.

NOTES

1   The League schools were ranked according to teacher mean scores on DDAE, based on the Basic DDAE Questionnaire in 1969 and 1971. For each year the six highest-ranking schools are classified as high DDAE schools, the middle six as middle DDAE schools, and the six lowest-ranking schools as low DDAE schools. In the discussion of change between 1969 and 1971, those schools which were classified as high at both time periods are categorized as High-High schools, and those schools which were classified as low in both time periods are categorized as Low-Low. Schools which moved from a 1969 level of low to a 1971 classification as middle or high or from middle to high are categorized as Low-High. Schools which moved from high in 1969 to middle or low in 1971 or from middle to low are categorized as High-Low.

2   In previous chapters, we have explicitly referred to various quantitative data which were obtained on a number of questionnaires. This chapter again makes use of much of these data, as well as a number of qualitative interpretations of anecdotal material and other SECSI staff experiences. Since the quantitative data have been tabled and referred to previously, this chapter handles all data in essentially qualitative terms presented in narrative form.

3   Other reflections on the cases used in this chapter may be found in Ann Lieberman and David A. Shiman, "The Stages of Change in Elementary School Settings," in Carmen M. Culver and Gary J. Hoban (eds.), *The Power to Change: Issues for the Innovative Educator*, McGraw-Hill, New York, 1973; and Richard C. Williams, Charles C. Wall, W. Michael Martin, and Arthur Berchin, *Effecting Organizational Renewal in Schools: A Social Systems Perspective*, McGraw-Hill, New York, 1974. It should be noted that conclusions in the latter are based on data collected at the end of the fourth year and so may vary in some respects from our interpretations.

4   Ann Lieberman (ed.), *Tell Us What to Do! But Don't Tell Me What to Do!* an |I|D|E|A| Monograph, Institute for Development of Educational Activities, Inc., Dayton, Ohio, 1971; and David A. Shiman, Carmen M. Culver, and Ann Lieberman (eds.), *Teachers on Individualization: The Way We Do It*, McGraw-Hill, New York, 1974.

5   Williams, Wall, Martin, and Berchin, op. cit.

6   We found it interesting that two of the adjective scales which made up the climate score accounted for most of the lower score in the last year. The school's "competence" was rated 5.62 in the third year, then dropped well below the League average in the last year to 4.55. The same kind of major realignment occurred in the depiction of the school as a "developing" one; the score on this adjective went from 5.78 to 4.86, again below the League mean. But there was little decline in the teachers' assessment of their "flexibility," "creativity," and "honesty." It is almost as if the teachers were saying that the school's output or product had noticeably changed (in its development and competence), but the staff's underlying predisposition remained more or less as it was in better days (i.e., flexible, creative, and honest).

7   Although our sociometric data are incomplete for the High-Low group, they do indicate less use of informal consultation networks in these schools than in the Low-High group.

8   It is interesting, however, that in spite of the staff's general orientation toward a strong leader, the teacher power score at Fairfield steadily increased during the project.

9   We think it is worth noting that Chet O., the principal at Indian Flat, also seemed to have overestimated the esprit and decision-making influence of his teachers—the sort of optimistic view that we observed in the Low-High principals.

10 Williams, Wall, Martin, and Berchin, op. cit.

11 It happens that neither Frontier nor Peace Valley would have provided a clear case of departmentalized secondary schools. Both tried some team teaching and Peace Valley experimented with modular scheduling.

CHAPTER 10

INTERVENTION IN SCHOOL CHANGE

Although it's probably a good idea for the last chapter to be a summary, it would be impossible to pull together in this space all the threads that we see woven through what has been written up till now. So, we will limit our final comments on the whole five years to three main topics. First, we want to reflect on what we learned in answer to a major question posed at the outset of the study: What does the process of change look like in the daily life of schools? A second question with which we began the study addressed the requirements for an intervention strategy that would be both effective and feasible for encouraging widespread change. Here we try to answer that question by summarizing the effects that our strategy did produce—effects both on the schools and on interventionists—and by presenting a proposal of how such a strategy might work optionally. This is not to say that our "answers" to these two major questions are complete, or even that they satisfy us. Rather, much of what we learned gave rise to still more questions, and these we will discuss as well.

The final set of reflections turns on ways in which our own experience in this project opened our eyes about what we were doing and what we might do.

THE PROCESS OF CHANGE IN DAILY SCHOOL LIFE

At the beginning of the project we weren't really discriminating between the process of change and anything else that might be going on in the schools; we were just trying to get to know those eighteen collections of people with whom we were going to be working. Since, however, we did start with the principals, and since it was congenial with the beliefs of the SECSI staff to care about how those principals worked with teachers, it seemed natural to concentrate our attention on staff relationships. From there it was no distance at all to DDAE as the basic concept around which we organized our thoughts about the process of change.

We think that it is important to take note of how we arrived at DDAE. Other people might have come to something altogether different or proceeded in a different fashion. As we said in Chapter 4, we did not start out with the rationale of the DDAE process that we present in this book. While our current array of ideas, observations, and hunches, therefore, may not conform very well to the standard dress code of many research concepts, we do argue that what we have pictured as DDAE has a ring of authenticity to anyone who has spent much time in school staff life.

For there is an area of that life which is legitimately conducted outside of classrooms. Of course, the professional activities of a staff, apart from teaching, are closely related to instructional matters, but the two cannot be just lumped together. Nor will it do to dismiss them off the cuff as simply the difference between "administration" and "instruction," and so, it is often implied, essentially a distraction for any but formally designated administrators. We cannot safely assume either that several individually competent teachers will automatically produce a staff that copes effectively and creatively with changing demands on the school. At least that was not the way that we of the SECSI staff had read our own previous school experiences or interpreted what we saw in the League. And what struck us above everything else in all the talk that had gone on about self-renewing schools was that the task of really bringing off such a school had to be a group enterprise for the school staff. Hence our focus on the interaction within the school staff as basic to the process of change in the school.

Along this general line, most readers have probably recognized the similarity between our DDAE and the general "problem-solving" model which has generated a lot of insights and several important intervention tactics in work with school staffs. Still, we see a noteworthy difference between the two. The problem-solving approach when used as the primary tool for bringing about change in schools has, understandably, tended to stress adequacy of performance in light of criteria for "good" problem-solving techniques, at the expense of attention to the fact that school staffs who do not proceed properly through all these steps are nonetheless solving problems daily. While we certainly concur in the importance of what we've called high-level DDAE, the basis of our intervention strategy lay in the development of peer groups of schools, and our fundamental notion of DDAE is of a process that goes on all the time in every school, closely reasoned or willy-nilly.

We look at DDAE as useful for two kinds of thinking about the process of change in schools. First, we can view it as the daily tilting ground on which the school staff reaffirms or juggles a bit the way that it handles its affairs, the way it considers or rejects proposals for change. From this vantage point we could watch how a host of conditions comes into play that make up the people, the setting, the action. Or, we can focus on the appearance of the DDAE process with its attendant conditions at a given time in order to get a reading on the configuration of the pieces at the moment. It is in this latter sense that we have talked of some "measurement" of the DDAE process as indicative of the level of staff receptivity to change.

The extent to which we were able to get data on this picture was limited indeed. We've said that before, but it should be said again. Perhaps it will be helpful to sketch our mental image of how DDAE and the descriptions we obtained reflect a staff's responsible receptivity to change and a school's capacity for self-renewal.

The figure on page 186 can be viewed both as a product of the League project and as the image that we were trying to check out as we went along to see how well it held up in the schools. It makes clear how much more checking needs to be done, yet the information that we did collect seems generally consistent with several of our fundamental assumptions. That is, the four characteristics of the DDAE process (scope, importance, relevance, and flexibility) on which we based our ratings of DDAE quality not only sound as if they themselves might reasonably be connected to a staff's receptivity to change, but also they were connected with other conditions in ways that built up larger and still more logical pictures of school staffs at varying levels of receptivity.

First, the very essence of DDAE is communication within the staff, and our data showed higher levels of DDAE associated with formal and informal staff arrangements which facilitated interaction and greater agreement among staff members (principal and teachers) about what was going on in the school—good or bad. Second, the idea of DDAE as the staff's major vehicle for dealing with its concerns suggests that the quality of DDAE might vary with different distributions of influence among members of the group. Here we found high-level DDAE associated with wider participation in decision making, mutual

Conditions Affecting Capacity for Self-Renewal

External factors (e.g., relations with outside resources and powers)

Internal factors (including factors not considered in this project)

Staff's responsible receptivity to change (including factors not considered in this project)

Elements interacting with DDAE not considered in this project	DDAE process
Elements considered in this project as conditions modified by and within which DDAE process occurs	
Limited description of these elements obtained from our data	Limited description of this process obtained from our data

respect for professional competence between principal and teachers, and an overall sense of willing attention to the tasks at hand. Finally, since it is inconceivable (to us at least) that there is only one best way for many different schools to reach their goals, we would expect staffs with high-level DDAE to be quite unlike one another in their assessments of what mattered most and what worked best for them. Our evidence indicated that high DDAE staffs did not set the same priorities as often as did low-level staffs, and we observed a great many instances of very different styles of task accomplishment at higher levels of DDAE.

Characteristics of the DDAE Process

We can't begin to enumerate all the questions that we accosted in looking at DDAE, but there are a few we want to mention because we think that they point directly to other characteristics of the kind of DDAE which indicates staff receptivity to change and because we turned up some interesting leads on them. One obvious set of questions has to do with the specific content of DDAE. The assessments of the quality of the process which teachers gave us concerned examples of DDAE about "changes," "problems," and "plans," but we were not able to complete more than a cursory analysis of the content of these examples. What we did uncover turned us immediately to this question: How do staffs at various DDAE levels differ as to the amount of time they spend on what they identify as their major problems? We suspect that they do differ, and we have a hunch that the differences relate to how they define problems in the first place. From the Low-High group in the League (see Chapter 9), for example, we got the feeling that while they duly listed as problems a number of situations about which they could do little, they spent most of their time on the implications which these problems had for adjusting daily school activities to new demands. In some of the schools on a downward course in terms of DDAE level, the reverse appeared to be true; fewer problems were perceived as instructional or having to do with staff relationships and more time was devoted to DDAE about unmanageable pressures per se. We're not at all clear about it at this point, but we do recognize the possibility that one aspect of DDAE which signals greater receptivity to change is that it facilitates worrying problems into some shape that can be handled by the staff. (This, it seems to us, is closely related to the often reported phenomenon that acceptance of change is more likely when the group sees the change as easily incorporated into what it is already doing.) None of this is to deny that outside pressures must sometimes be dealt with head on if they are to be dealt with at all or that sometimes school staffs persevere on particular topics (for example, discipline) to avoid considering anything else.

Another group of leftover questions has to do with the amount of agreement that is expressed in the course of the DDAE process itself. We have reported a little questionnaire information which indicated that agreement on descriptions of staff behavior was, on the whole, greater at higher levels of DDAE. This seems sensible enough as far as it goes, but it doesn't tell us about what goes on in the DDAE process itself. As we've said before, an important feature of our mental picture of the DDAE process which is receptive to change is the interplay of differing perceptions and opinions which are brought to bear on school problems. A lot of our nonquantitative data spoke to spirited debates in the course of high-level DDAE, but we also observed staffs at lower levels incapacitated by differing beliefs, and we can easily imagine staffs who harbor few differences among their members scoring quite high, for example, on one of our DDAE characteristics, breadth of participation in DDAE, but not very high on the flexibility dimension.[1]

Much remains to be sorted out, but it's clear to us that more attention should be paid to the similarity of views expressed by staff members. Some of our data hinted that similarity of views might be more important in some areas than in others. While we think that it may well be important for receptive staffs not to look unkindly upon differences of opinion and to have a DDAE process which regularly airs and copes with such differences, we suspect that there are limits to effective combinations of differences, on the one hand, and open DDAE on the other. We envision a sort of bounded optimal zone. Beyond it on one side we see staffs whose mélange of viewpoints is hidden in restricted DDAE processes which routinely isolate those different perceptions from one another. Out of bounds in the other direction lie staffs whose wide participation in DDAE serves only to reiterate agreement.

Perhaps the most prominent cluster of questions which we touched but lightly concern the amount of DDAE that takes place in a school. We did not try to "count" quantity of DDAE in our determination of levels. We did notice differences in the amount of DDAE that was reported occurring in subgroups of the staff, and this seemed to vary roughly with the staff's general fashion of handling its affairs— in a total staff group or in subgroups. But how does the sheer amount of DDAE that occurs relate to receptivity to change? We think that the relationship does have to do with type of organization (e.g., teaching teams) and staff size. For example, the large staffs at Fairfield and Peace Valley, both low DDAE, complained of having few opportunities to get together as a total group. But we doubt that these relationships are altogether obvious.

We suspect instead that the amount of DDAE required to produce staff receptivity to change also has something to do with the staff's style of carrying out DDAE in different settings. Our descriptions of DDAE were pretty much confined to the formal setting of meetings. Observations, reports from teachers and principals, and the sociometric data on informal communication networks, however, indicated the need for attention to the DDAE that is conducted during coffee breaks, in the corridors, and on the playground. This informal DDAE would ultimately have to be considered in determining quantity, and it raises questions about the effectiveness of various combinations of formal and informal settings. Would we, for example, find that in stable high DDAE schools there is always a straightforward, rational integration of DDAE in all settings, as most of the problem-solving types of intervention seem to assume? Or, might some staffs (and we believe we saw instances in the League) appear to the passing observer to be forever on the point of falling apart and forever pulling themselves together for one more week?

The recognition of informal DDAE suggests also the possibly relevant comparison between amount of informal DDAE and the amount of the nontask conversations that go on in the same settings. We'd guess that the proportion of informal DDAE would be greatest in schools moving toward a higher level—judging from our impression of the nearly unrelenting attention to doable tasks in the League Low-High group. And what about the proportion in stable low DDAE schools; is it quite small, as some of our sociometric data suggest?

The notion of DDAE in different settings also leads us to take note of DDAE through written communication within a staff. League principals had several discussions, for example, about increasing their use of bulletins in order to conserve staff meeting time for matters that required group deliberation. Our data, however, are only suggestive as far as principals' bulletins or any other aspects of leadership as a characteristic of DDAE are concerned.

DDAE and Leadership

We have reported a number of observations about the principal's leadership style and the extent and kind of teacher leadership at several DDAE levels. These observations could send us off in a good many directions, but one of the possible paths interests us most. In the following discussion, the reader should keep in mind that we are using the term "leadership" very broadly to refer to both principal and teacher behavior which initiates, directs, or dominates stages of the DDAE process.

We would like to follow the notion of perceived legitimacy of decision making as a characteristic of the DDAE process. This, of course, gets us into what is often called having decisions made by the "appropriate" people; only we are pretty sure that "appropriate" can't just be determined on rational grounds by an outsider and applied to all school staffs with the expectation that a staff will then be more satisfied or do its work more effectively.

Let us illustrate with what we learned about teacher participation in decision making. Teacher power scores were clearly related to high DDAE. Furthermore, all our data indicated that teacher influence in school affairs increased in all League schools over the period of the project, and we believe that this increase did in many ways contribute to more openness to change on the part of League staffs. Our knowledge of the League schools, however, (as is evident in Chapter 9) does not lead to the conclusion that increased opportunities for teacher decision making is the whole story of the relationship between teacher influence and high-level DDAE. A new principal at Dewey Avenue tried to close off from teachers certain areas of decision making which they perceived as legitimately open to them, while at Shadyside a new principal failed, in the eyes of the staff, to do his own decision-making job. In both cases DDAE level dropped. The Woodacres teachers moved into more decision areas and maintained high DDAE, but the Fairfield staff remained at a low level and rejected the principal's attempts to share more responsibility for the operation of the school.

Still other variations were found in other League schools. Altogether they suggest two ways in which the perceived legitimacy of decisions may be related to a staff's receptivity to change. First, receptivity may require some minimum agreement in the staff (principal and teachers) that the decisions being made do come from sources which are legitimate; and second, it may be that the perception of more sources as legitimate accompanies greater receptivity.

The DDAE Process and New Staff Members

Finally, we would like to consider briefly the DDAE process as the arena in which new staff members learn how staff business is conducted. In Chapter 8 we offered several hypotheses about how DDAE level might be related to inculcating certain educational beliefs and ideas about teacher influence, particularly with older teachers. Here we want to offer a few observations about how new staff members are socialized to the school's way of carrying out the DDAE process itself. Presumably they do learn this. If they don't, that fact could contribute to a change in the school's mode of DDAE.

During the project, most of the League schools exhibited relatively stable proportions of new teachers, though the proportions in various schools ranged from one or two new members a year to about a third of the staff group. Seastar and Fairfield were at the extreme low end of number of new teachers; one was high DDAE and the other low, and at neither school did the DDAE level change much, though the level at Seastar probably did rise early in the project. That's about what one would expect, simply on the grounds that it wouldn't be much of a job for the great majority of a staff to "teach" a few newcomers at a time how business was done at the school or, conversely, that a few newcomers wouldn't have much chance to change the style of the staff.

Higher proportions of newcomers might conceivably hold more potential for change, but in the League we found relatively high percentages of new teachers somewhere in each of the groups that we discussed in Chapter 9—in schools that maintained the same DDAE level and in those that showed a change. And in all cases the input of new teachers was only one of a number of factors that might have affected DDAE level. We will offer here, therefore, only a few observations about how a staff with a relatively high-level DDAE process might differ from one with low DDAE in the way that it routinely treats a large incoming group of new members.

A possibility that should be considered, of course, is that the new members are selected to begin with on the basis of how well they will fit in with the staff. That should lighten the load of what must be taught later. There is evidence that attempts to select in this way did occur in a good many League schools. We cannot be sure at which DDAE level those attempts were most prevalent and most successful, but we are sure that selection was not the sole tactic which high DDAE schools counted on to integrate incoming personnel.

There are characteristics of the DDAE process itself which seem to be obviously related to a staff's routine socialization of newcomers: what we have called the scope of the process (that is, the proportion of staff members who participate in it), the quantity of DDAE that occurs, and the number of legitimate leadership sources that are recognized by the staff. A school that ranked high in these respects should be offering many opportunities to newcomers to observe and to practice the behaviors expected in the conduct of staff business. In such schools the DDAE process itself helps teach newcomers how to become proper members of the group that uses the process.

What does the flow of newcomers learn where DDAE is a relatively restricted or fragmented process? One could say that they learn another way of carrying out staff business, but one could also note that there is not much of a staff group to become a member of. A newcomer to a low DDAE setting might learn to choose up sides in a divided staff or join a small clique, or the newcomer might learn that it's pretty much a matter of everyone for himself. Other possible variations will occur to the reader; our point is simply that the newcomer does not learn to behave as a member of a total staff problem-facing (even if not problem-solving) group. And this is the case, it appears to us, not so much because socialization techniques used in low DDAE settings are some less effective version of those used in higher DDAE schools, but more because there is little group concern about socializing new members to any set of school expectations at all.

The idea of a lack of groupness as one characteristic of low DDAE has run throughout much of this book. The extent of "groupness" that is perhaps partly defined by certain qualities of the DDAE process would seem to be a critical ingredient of the situation in which a staff confronts newcomers. What we have called a relatively open process tends to integrate new persons and so preserve the group and the group style of openness.[2] A restricted DDAE process, on the other hand, may preserve the weak group ties, of which it is a part, simply by not affording much opportunity for anyone to get anything else off the ground.

While we do think it important to recognize the lack of group effort to socialize new staff that may occur in low DDAE settings, we do not deny that a staff may attempt to socialize new members and fail. Of the numerous conceivable variations on this theme, we will note only one situation in which failure might happen, that is, when there is a sudden drastic increase in the number of new staff. We observed two examples of sudden increases, at Independence and at Shadyside.

We can think of a sudden increase as potentially overloading the mechanism by which a staff customarily socializes new members. The Independence staff made specific plans to increase its socialization efforts, while the Shadyside staff did little. (In fact, reverting to self-contained classrooms, as they did, may have decreased the number of settings in which newcomers could have participated in DDAE.)

Although we can't say just how it worked, we have a strong feeling that the Independence staff made special provisions to maintain its integrity as a group, while Shadyside showed signs of being swamped by more than it could handle and, finally, signs of disintegration in its grouplike qualities.[3]

Socializing a new principal to the school's DDAE process is, of course, a somewhat special case because of the principal's position as the formal leader of that process. A key notion here, we think, is the group to whom the principal is "listening," as it were, as he builds his role in the DDAE process. One possibility is that the new principal will come with the expectation of learning to fit in with the style of the staff—the sort of smooth succession that we saw at Seastar and at South. In other cases, however, we saw two kinds of problems arise when the principal took his cues from outside sources. One kind comes when the principal views as the chief importance of his school its contribution to the objectives of some outside group—the district administration perhaps, a vocal community faction, or a special project to which the school belongs. Most of these principals appeared at Frontier and Peace Valley where the staffs were too fragmented to try much in the way of socializing the new principal anyway. The one example that seemed fairly clear occurred at Bell Street, where Peter M.'s concern about district constraints was at odds with the priorities that the staff put on internal school problems, with a resulting lack of coherence in the DDAE process.[4]

A second kind of problem occurred when a new principal was primarily interested in the school itself but was trying to build his role in the DDAE process according to criteria which differed from the staff's expectations for the role. The cases of Dewey Avenue and Shadyside are illustrations of the difficulties that teachers may then encounter as they try to socialize the new principal to their customary DDAE procedures. It is, of course, conceivable that a new principal may drastically change the staff's DDAE style. We think that something of this sort happened with Leonard B. at Woodacres and Arnold Z. at Independence, but we're dubious that such changes can occur as easily as is sometimes implied in strategies based upon leadership training. (We recognize as relevant here the whole area of leadership style and its possible relation to the socialization of new principals, but that is simply far more than we can deal with in this time and space.)[5]

Further Questions about DDAE

Three of the questions that are altogether farther down the path than we were able to go capture the chief concerns we were left with at the end of the League project. The first simply concerns the possibility of filling in further the sketch of receptivity to change that we presented on page 186. We could show only a few associations between a limited description of the DDAE process and certain other conditions of school staff life, and we have made guesses about what might be looked at next. Beyond such bits and pieces, however, is the possible emergence of broad patterns that characterize the interaction of staffs in schools more and less receptive to change. At the moment we have two strong hunches about those patterns, insofar as they may exist. We expect that the configurations of higher and lower receptivity do not, for the most part, constitute mirror images of one another, and we expect that there are more discernible variations of "high" patterns than of "low" patterns.

The question of patterns, of course, relates to our basic notion of the possibility of taking a reading on DDAE to indicate staff receptivity at a particular time. The next large question relates to the other way that we view the DDAE process—as a continual negotiation to sustain or to modify the current way of doing business. The question concerns the extent to which we might be able to predict stability or movement in a school's receptivity to change. All that we have to offer now in this respect are scraps of evidence that do substantiate some of our strong impressions at the end of the project about the future state of certain League schools.[6] The core of any formula for prediction would seem to involve an assessment of the comparative strength of internal school conditions and external pressures directed at the school. We admit, however, that our own interest is not primarily in developing a formula for accurate forecasts, which might conceivably direct certain emergency interventions, but in learning more about an array of conditions that could support staffs in maintaining their receptivity to change.

Finally, there remains the perfectly obvious question about relationships between what we have called staff receptivity to change and various kinds of changes that occur in school programs. As we said very early in this book, we recognize the ultimate need to address these relationships. We began with the belief that relationships exist, that the staff members are inevitably the doers or the undoers of school change. Nothing that we learned has altered that belief. We do not claim to have organized information about what happened to pupils in League schools; neither do we pretend to have been utterly oblivious to what was going on in classrooms during our hundreds of visits to those schools.[7] The altogether unscientific sum of that experience fits quite well with our notion of DDAE as the process by which a staff does whatever it finds necessary to do outside of the classroom in order to accomplish what it wants to accomplish in the classroom. The terms of that statement are open to interpretation and investigation from a number of value positions that might describe relationships between them.

A STRATEGY FOR INTERVENTION IN SCHOOLS

We'll not go back over the story of how we arrived at and then tried to stick to the magic feather principle, but we do want to emphasize one point about that story. It must be clear that just as our own predilections had a lot to do with finding the path of DDAE, so did they strongly influence our basic orientation to intervention in schools. An early decision was made to restrict our energies and resources to the school staff groups, and a little later we settled on the single strategy of building a peer group of schools.

Still, we could have come at that task in different ways. Looking back, we glimpse an underlying feeling, which we scarcely ever talked about explicitly, that a school should be a healthy and satisfying place of work for its staff as well as for its students. Surely, we would have uncovered disagreements if we had inquired too deeply about that idea, but, as it was, the interventions we devised were simply apt to take into account somehow the quality of professional life for a school staff.

The Effect of Our Strategy on the Schools

Those sometimes unspoken values made us sensitive, also, to changes in the quality of that life. Pehaps our earliest findings confirmed that being a teacher or a principal tends to be lonely, often dull, work, ringed about by fears of the unknown that might result from changes. Certainly we can't claim, whatever else came of it, that the League experience resulted all-round in more stimulating days for League school staffs, but we did become convinced of the power of increased interaction among schools to alleviate the loneliness, the dullness, the fear. It was clearest in the group of principals, and while it didn't happen for every League teacher, it happened for enough so that no staff was utterly untouched, if only by frustrated desires for more contacts. Descriptions of the excitement that the League brought fill our records—far too many from too diverse sources to be dismissed as ho-hum testimonials. League teachers have recounted these feelings in two publications,[8] and Adam S. of Mar Villa said it as well as anyone during an interview:

> "During the first year in the League I began to feel different. At first I thought it's going to give me an ulcer. Before the League I often didn't know what I was going to do when I got up in the morning. Now I have so much to read and exciting things going on that I can hardly wait. I wake up sometimes at 2:00 A.M. with new ideas; I can't wait to get going."

The value of the League excitement, however, was considerably more than the spice it added to lives that certainly needed it. The excitement was part of a broader moral support which League schools provided one another and which was, we think, an impetus in two major ways to increased receptivity to change. A League school staff was more likely to visualize the possibility of change in the first place, for in the League group that was considered neither daft nor especially daring. League meetings were places where a private dream could be let out of the bag, where it was safe to air foolish notions that had best be kept hidden in other proper professional assemblies.

Then, with an idea in mind, a League staff could more comfortably take the time it needed to acquire new skills and work out the bugs in new plans, since to try and fail a few times brought not censure but encouragement from the group. To allow members of other League staffs to see that things were going less than perfectly was all right because it was all in the family, a family that one could trust. The feeling is reflected in notes from an interview with one of the League principals, Mike D. of Peace Valley:

> "What one really needs, he says, is for someone to see the worst and still communicate trust in the midst of chaos. That opens the door so that you can solve your problems. Mike pointed out that it didn't do any good for somebody to come and tell him that he had a problem when he already knew he had a problem. What he wanted was a com-

munication of trust that said essentially, 'I know that you will figure out how to solve the problem.' Mike said that he didn't have too much faith in experts because they tend to be removed from the problem. He repeated several times that he would more than likely go to people who had the same problem, not necessarily to people who had any answers."

Nor was moral support the only kind of resource which the League schools had to give one another. We found that the League network could offer its members practical assistance as well. Teachers and principals could and did help each other to identify and solve problems; and we believe that we only tapped the surface of the full range of resources which actually existed. For example, we but glimpsed the possibilities for using the League network to disseminate specialized information made available to individual member schools through various research or development projects.

We had hoped that the League schools would identify themselves as a group and would come to hold certain expectations for the group and for themselves as League members. We think we can say that this came about—in a few ways that were apparent to us and, quite probably, in other ways on which we have no clear data. Our information does suggest that at least these things were "supposed to be" in League schools: League staffs were supposed to hold relatively non-traditional beliefs about schooling; League staffs were supposed to modify the roles of principal and teacher toward the creation of a work group which both respected and integrated the competencies of individual members; and League staffs were supposed to look critically at what they were doing. A statement volunteered by a League teacher on the subject of a disastrous attempt at team teaching may illustrate how some of these expectations appeared.

"That group of teachers is not unique, their failure will be repeated many times by other teams. There could have been, however, a deadlier failure—that is, if we thought we had found the truth and were so blinded that we would put down or seek to destroy anyone who looked at our achievement with objectivity. Far more deadly would have been blind allegiance to failure. We had no success in our program; neither did we become the blind leading the blind. We recognized our failure."

To say that we saw evidence of certain expectations for League schools is not to claim that all League schools met them. We do believe that to some extent they touched every League staff. For a few they brought little but discomfort. For a few others they pointed the way to fairly stable situations which demonstrated how attitudes favorable to inquiry could be implemented through flexible organization structures and could be bolstered by climates of mutual trust. For most they brought a professional life that was rarely peaceful, often satisfying, and never dull. Or, as one principal responded when asked about teachers who just didn't "give a damn," "On this staff there are very, very few people who don't give a damn."

THE EFFECT OF OUR STRATEGY ON THE INTERVENTIONIST ROLE

By far the most difficult part of an intervention limited to encouraging and facilitating contacts among schools is that almost everybody expects more. As hard as it is to change the expectations of the school staffs, it may be even harder to change the interventionists' notions of what they should and should not do. Still, such changes can be brought about. The trick is for the perceived "experts" to use their prestige not to tell schools what to do, but rather to legitimize a new, nonexpert role that they build for themselves.

The new role, however, is not to be thought of as putting oneself out of business. Maintaining effective contacts among schools requires a central organization which we think, at least at the moment, must be operated by outsiders. School staffs lack the time and other resources that are necessary to create that central organization or to make it quickly responsive to the information needs of the member schools. Though we do not believe that a very large staff is necessary, there must be people who know enough about what is going on in all the schools to coordinate a newsletter, to suggest and help set up interschool visits and meetings in order to bring together problems and potential solutions.

Finally, we must say that our experience indicates that in a peer group based, like the League, on a somewhat loose agreement with district administrations, a school's participation in the group can be severely curtailed or even halted if the district so chooses. We do not, however, view this as an extremely serious problem for interventionists for several reasons. First, when a district agrees to allow one school to deviate, it usually does allow it to do so even though the degree of permissible deviation did, in our project, vary a lot. (Perhaps this is so because the district finds one experimental school desirable or because one constitutes no great threat.) Second, if district interferences are minor, the appeal of the peer group activities leads school staffs to devise all sorts of ways to get around the road-blocks. And third, some districts may come to value the peer group approach when they understand what it can accomplish. Almost all our League districts made some use of information obtained through their member school's participation in our League.

A few League districts have been trying out the strategy within a single district. We see no reason why the peer group advantages should not come to pass within a district *if* the district were com-mitted to this kind of intervention, which, of course, implies a large degree of meaningful autonomy for the individual school. We do, however, recognize that such a setting might well bring certain prob-lems that were minimal in our League, chief of which is probably the built-in competition which could affect the schools' relationships with one another.[9]

Further Research Questions

We'll now indicate what we feel are four top-priority question areas that remain for next steps in developing the peer group strategy.

1. *The strategy must be tried with still other kinds of schools.* The most obvious omission in our League was a representative from a harsh inner-city environment. Nor can we say anything about what modifications might have to be made for a group of secondary schools. Also, more information is needed about how such a strategy would work within a single district.

One more exploration interests us. Our group of schools repre-sented a wide range of initial willingness to participate. We're curious as to what might be optimal mixes of volunteers, apathetic members, and recalcitrant schools. We do not like the idea of total lack of consultation with a school staff before it becomes a group member. That did happen in the case of Seastar, but just because we lucked out there, we do not recommend the practice.

2. *More and better data are needed to understand the growth of group ties and group expectations.* Group norms are not easy to study, but a better understanding of them would clearly be critical to the development of this strategy. We would also like to note in passing the paradox that occurs when the peer group strategy is successful. The more the schools take over the running of their own affairs, the more contacts and interactions they initiate on their own, the

more likely it is that relevant data will slip by those interventionists who may want to study the process of group growth.

3. *Problems of maintaining interschool contacts.* We were not as successful as we would have liked in encouraging activities that involved both principals and teachers. We would have liked to have seen a League which worked from the start to establish regular contacts between school groups composed of the principal and teacher representatives. Our limited experiences with this tactic suggest that such meetings could result in greater commitment of the school as a total group, a wider perspective on the possibilities of different role arrangements within a school, and more effective planning for additional meetings that involve teachers alone and principals alone.

The most troublesome problem in all interschool contacts, as we have now said often, is finding ways for teachers to have the time to meet. All we can offer at this point is that we saw too many ingenious solutions to believe that the problem is truly insurmountable.

Distance between schools poses another difficulty, though it is in turn bound up with a host of other factors. While face-to-face contacts are the most powerful builder of group ties, there seem to be possibilities for supplementary contacts. We were able to manage only a newsletter, but about the time that the project ended we were beginning to work on the exchange of audiotaped discussions among schools, slides, photographs, and other small packages of relevant materials. In one of the offshoot Leagues now in existence, plans are in process for communication through closed-circuit television, and we have heard of a few examples of an idea much desired by our League members—the exchange of teachers and of principals for brief periods of time.

4. *Problems for interventionists in starting a peer group of schools.* The interventionists must designate the schools as a potential group, then try to build truly functional relationships among the members. Must there be at the beginning some input of specific information on which the group is to work? In part this would depend upon the content objective of the intervention, about which we will say more in the next section. Our project began with a variety of inputs on new practices in schooling, but some of us wonder if a group might not start with wide sharing of problems, then move to searching out sources for potential solutions.

The major problem for interventionists is recognizing the magic feather that enables the group to grow and to realize its own capabilities, the token that keeps up their courage while they discover, practice, and strengthen what they can do for themselves. We think that the magic feather is the prestige of the interventionists, though we don't rule out other possibilities. The very prestige that has led schools to look to others for answers can be called upon to keep up their willingness to be part of the group while the interventionists are organizing the resources that exist in the group and allowing the bonds to develop which will hold the group together.

But the hardest part of the magic feather principle is that the interventionists must believe that out there in those school staffs are people who have innovative ideas, would like the chance to try them, and have valid knowledge and skills to make a good many work. After all, the mouse had to visualize that Dumbo's ears were potential wings. We are not impressed with the facile contention that "they've had the chance to do it—if they could," for schools have not had the chance to use their resources as we are suggesting. Schools have been commanded, cajoled, instructed, threatened, and bribed to change. They have been offered almost everything but trust. School staffs have been treated by interventionists with condescension, pity, scorn, and despair, but rarely with dignity. It may be harder to change interventionists than schools.

INTERVENTION IN SCHOOLS—A PROPOSAL

We return to our original question about intervention: can there be an intervention strategy which is effective in meeting the individual needs of schools and is feasible in its requirements for outside assistance to schools? We believe that the peer group strategy can satisfy those criteria and that the League of Cooperating Schools revealed, though it only partly demonstrated, how the strategy could work.

The rationale, as we see it, rests on a particular orientation toward intervention itself and on a belief that effective change in schooling requires socialization at two levels—the socialization of individuals within school staffs and the socialization of schools as organizations. We will try to describe our thinking so far.

Objectives and Kinds of Intervention

A number of times now we have said that the peer group strategy calls for interventionists to behave differently from traditional expert consultants. Since the statement has been presented in the context of our project, it might be taken to imply two things which we do not mean at all. First, we do not believe that the peer group strategy can be used only with our intervention objective of having schools become generally more receptive to change. Second, we do not believe that the peer group strategy is the only intervention strategy that should be used with schools.

There is no reason why the strategy of facilitating interschool exchange of information could not work for the dissemination of specific innovations. As a matter of fact, it should work very well. A group of school staffs who identified their jobs as figuring out how best to apply a particular new idea in schooling could conceivably go far toward instituting that idea. In this situation, after initial input of specific information, an effective peer group strategy simply mobilizes the pool of practical information which exists in the schools so that it is shared in ways that are meaningful to the staffs and in an atmosphere of mutual support. The focus of that information could be almost any proposed innovation in curriculum, instruction, or staff procedures.[10]

In one sense, then, the peer group strategy might be viewed as an extension of the field-testing and feedback components common in research and development strategies. We certainly agree that R&D activities can provide potentially valuable input for schools. We also agree that acting as a peer group facilitator is not and should not be every interventionist's cup of tea. There is no lack of need for full-time program developers, process consultants, and all sorts of educational researchers to offer specialized knowledge to school staffs through several kinds of intervention relationships. A peer group strategy could easily be one of a number of strategies in an overall design to maximize the impact of a limited supply of available experts by spreading the word, working out the bugs, and fitting to individual situations specific improvements that become available from research.

We believe, however, that the potential value of the strategy is greater than simply installing with wider success a series of changes recommended by the currently recognized producers of knowledge with school staffs from time to time requesting from the manufacturers replacement parts or new models. We still hope that somewhere along the line others will try what we could only begin with the League—to use the peer group strategy for the purpose of increasing each school staff's attention to its particular problems, its receptivity to new ideas about handling those problems, and its chances for developing the new information and skills that it will need in the process. That requires a picture of intervention in schools somewhat different from the one-way street implied (in spite of feedback loops) by the usual mental division of the world of education into outside knowledge producers at the sending end and school users of knowledge at the receiving end. Our picture is shown below:[11]

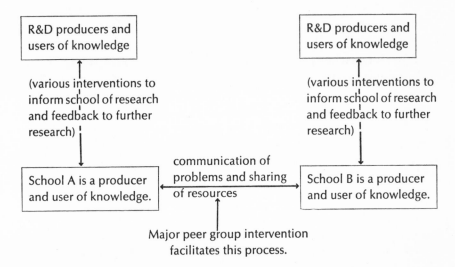

It is this view that we have in mind as we go on to describe the two levels of socialization which must occur to achieve schools which can maintain a continuing focus on their individual problems and search for more effective and satisfying ways of coping with them.

Socialization Inside the School

When we first described the genesis of the peer group strategy, we noted that the way we were thinking of League schools as peers interacting with one another was an extension of the well-known concept of peer groups of individuals. Since then we've referred also to the socialization that occurs within a school staff, and we want to be quite explicit that our proposed strategy does assume as one of its levels the socialization of individual staff members. Individuals learn what they are expected to do and how to do it, and they learn to want to do it that way.

We are talking about behavior in the conduct of staff business outside of classrooms, while usually the socialization of teachers has been treated from the standpoint of instructional procedures. Our focus dramatizes the importance of the immediate staff peer group, as compared with broad professional organizations of individuals, on at least three counts. First, the attention allotted to this area by professional teachers' organizations was traditionally insignificant (teachers taught in classrooms—period); principals' organizations finally discovered the territory of staff relationships after almost total immersion in budget management and building maintenance. When professional groups of teachers began to address questions of extrainstructional activities for teachers, they tended to emphasize confrontations of the worker-management sort. We're not at all saying that these conflicts are without value, but there may be more than two sides to any question in certain school situations.

Even though there is now some variety in the teachings offered by professional organizations on the conduct of school staff affairs, another limitation comes into play. As long as membership in those organizations is individually based, it would seem extremely difficult for a school staff, especially one with moderate turnover, to get together and keep together from such external influences a coherent orientation to its own work. In these respects, then, the learning for individuals that is available from broad professional organizations is skimpy or fragmented, and dependence upon individual membership in such organizations to socialize members of the kinds of staffs that we envision would therefore be a chancy business.

More obvious, though, is the simple power of that clump of daily colleagues compared to the distant, dispersed professional fraternity. Certainly principals and teachers vary in the extent to which they take cues for behavior from feelings of affiliation with a larger profession, but it seems likely that whatever those feelings it is primarily by and as a result of their own interaction that school staff members construct the sort of DDAE process which each learns to expect to use.

We are saying then that the most influential socialization in DDAE comes to an individual from the staff of which he is a member. And, of course, our proposed strategy is concerned with how to increase the number of school staffs who operate with a DDAE process that is responsibly receptive to change. We know, however, that most staffs learn and teach new members how to make it, if they make it at all, in the status quo, and we don't have much faith in the power of professional organizations of individuals or the inevitably small-scale overhaul of one school at a time by process consultants to change the situation very much. Therefore, we propose as the structure for a second level of socialization a peer group of individual schools.

Socialization of Schools as Organizations

Organizations as well as individuals respond to their environment. We discussed earlier some of the characteristics of typical school environments which make it difficult for one school at a time to institutionalize anything like an outlook that remains habitually open to new possibilities. It is true in a sense that a changing environment produces new demands with which a school must somehow cope, but it is also the case that certain characteristics of the immediate, familiar environment of the school tend to persist—in particular, difficulties in obtaining resources and a short supply of encouragement to strike out on a path of one's own finding. So we have suggested banding schools together to overcome, at least in part, those conditions inimical to open, inquiring procedures by school staffs.[12]

The intervention would occur at the level of treating school staffs as a *group of groups*—not, for reasons that we have just stated, a school staff as a group of individuals or a number of staffs together as a larger group of individuals. The intervention would attempt through tactics like those we have discussed to build the school units themselves into an environment within which each staff group would find both support to maintain open inquiry and the expectation that it would do so. Insofar as the strategy was successful—insofar, that is, as schools identified themselves as members of the group—each staff should attempt to socialize new members to behave in a manner befitting a school staff which had the institutional responsibility of membership in the group. There could, in this way, be created small environments in which schools receptive to change might develop and thrive.[13]

We have recounted in some detail the sorts of activities that might constitute a strategy to build such a group of schools. Here we will only underscore the fundamental guidelines of such a strategy. First, the individual characteristics of each member school staff would be of prime importance. Its problems, its resources, its interests would be treated as valuable in broadening the perspective of other staffs and increasing the available group resources. Second, and a corollary to the first, each school would find and follow its own path to receptivity to change. But third, while group resources and support would be available for individual school needs, so too would each school's efforts be under informal surveillance by the group. As a result, school staffs in such a group might learn and act upon beliefs like, "we can learn from failures, but not much from not trying anything" and "you may have to pretend for others but it's not helpful to try to fool yourself."

What sorts of expectations about the behavior of member school staffs have to be built up in a group that nourishes responsible receptivity to change as a way of staff life? These expectations are unlike the "norms" that we usually think of which call for all members of a group to conform to one pattern of behavior. Others have referred to the possibility of "meta-norms" in a group which would support each member's doing his own thing.[14] That's part of the idea that we have in mind—expectations among the schools in the group that staffs will and should differ in the ways that they try to handle their problems and resources—and shared resources within the group would support these efforts. But we also feel than an environment which would maintain receptivity to change as an organizational requirement for its member schools would also have the expectation that member schools would keep on their toes and not be too satisfied too soon; and interschool sharing of what happened and what was done about it should provide this sort of informal (but effective insofar as group membership is valued) nudging to think a little further.

As examples of what these expectations for school staffs might be, we summarize the major ones that we observed within the League.

1 Open communication by staff members within schools and among schools in order to share problems, personal suggestions, and references to other sources of information. This entails the recognition and willingness to use relevant knowledge, wherever it may be found.

2 Awareness of the DDAE process as it exists in a staff, whatever its characteristics, and understanding of how that process is bound up with receptivity to change.

3 Recognition of a variety of effective possibilities in the role relationships among principal and teachers on a staff.

4 Willingness to risk failure in trying out new ideas.

5 Commitment to ongoing staff evaluation of how tasks are being carried out.

Such an environment, we believe, would encourage schools to make more use of not only resources that reside in the persons of their own staffs but also information available from R&D activities. An organizational commitment to receptivity to change directs a staff to search widely for alternatives, and within such staffs we would expect wider impact of new information that might come through the involvement of only part of its members in particular special projects. Also, as we have said before, the peer group network of schools provides avenues for meaningful dissemination of knowledge from any one source. It is in this sense that we view a peer group strategy designed to develop expectations of receptivity to change among its member schools as an effective way to coordinate and spread specialized knowledge about improving school practices.[15]

In summary, then, we propose an intervention calculated to build and maintain group expectations for responsible receptivity to change which are seen to apply to schools as organizations. We believe that a school staff that is a "good" member of such a group will, in turn, press for appropriate behavior by its individual members. We know that it is not likely that every member school in such a group will live entirely up to group expectations, but our League experiences convince us that few are apt to be unaffected. Even the minimal changes that we saw strike us as important beginnings—acceptance of the idea that schools should not all be alike, some lessening of the boredom that leads to utter disinterest, a few challenges to old beliefs about education that somehow seep through, and the revelation of a staff to itself.

WORKING WITH SCHOOLS

Every now and then someone points out, that in any endeavor we don't know what really happened until we try to tell about it. Without getting into philosophical questions about reality, it is true that in the process of writing a report of a research project, as with any other sort of account of human interaction, certain things appear in a different light than they did at the time of the events. When we recall now John Goodlad's early admonition that the success of our efforts should be measured more in terms of how well we could explain why things had happened as they did rather than in some rating of successful change in the schools, we realize that we were thinking then of explaining what happened in the League schools. To explain that in retrospect we would draw upon Kurt Lewin's comment that if you want to find out how something works, just try to change it. At heart the peer group strategy attempts some basic changes in the way that intervention for change has proceeded. So we would say (as we have) that happenings in the League reflected a wrench away from strong traditions of dependence upon outside experts and learning to recognize and use new sources of support and knowledge.

But there is another big part of the "why it happened." Though we, like all interventionists, saw our task as trying to change the schools' behavior, in the process we had to dismantle the old role that would have been ours. We were stuck with having to change ourselves, and this was the critical incident, we believe, in the development of our working relationship with the schools. They knew that we were trying to change our ways, so neither of us felt in the position of being pressed to change by others who seemed quite sure of what they were doing. Our first truly common understanding was an admitted uncertainty about the roles that we should play.

Of course, it was easier for each group to suggest changes to others than to spot ones that it might make, and of course our various private work worlds never did become completely intelligible to one another. But we did understand that we had all ventured into alien territory. There grew up an atmosphere of trust. By that much-used term, we do not intend an image of peace and mutual approval. The League school staffs certainly did not all or always agree that we were on the right track as we grappled with new behaviors. Nor did we endorse all their innovations. But wrongheaded as we might at times appear to one another, we came to see the whole community of our project acting in good faith as it coped with problems of change which plagued us all.[16]

That condition must loom large in any explanation of what happened in the League.

We strongly urge all those who would change schools to disavow the role of onlooker in the process. The advantages of anticipating change in oneself are numerous and above all help avoid the trap of thinking that one has tidied up the world a bit when he has only hung on for dear life to orderliness in a particular conceptual scheme.

The recognition of ourselves on the inside of change has colored the account in this book of problems that schools face under pressure to change. More of our learnings will appear in another report from the League project.[17] And no doubt, we'll never quite finish looking into them further as we go on into other projects. Sometime during the last official week of the League project, the chief secretary of the SECSI staff sighed, "Oh dear, and I just got a great idea about how to re-organize the files!"

NOTES

1 We recognize that more sophisticated analyses of the scores on each item of the Basic DDAE Questionnaire might pick up some of these nuances, but we have at this point settled for a simple analysis of a simple instrument.

2 An interesting example of how this socialization procedure may continue to preserve a staff which is suffering a temporary decline in some aspects of DDAE was the behavior of the Dewey Avenue staff where newcomers continued to be brought into the daily action even when it was more or less a battlefield.

3 While it is easier to think of "overloading" as it applies to the more clear-cut socialization tactics which we associate with higher DDAE, we can imagine an analogous situation in which a drastic change in number or kind of newcomers might overload the checks which have customarily limited the DDAE process in a low DDAE school. We didn't observe such a case, but others have proposed, as an intervention tactic, sending in well-organized cadres of new teachers to overcome blocks to change within schools—sometimes perhaps by building a functional group where none existed before.

4 We can imagine, though we didn't see it, a situation in which the same outside orientation is held by the staff as well as the new principal and so causes little difficulty in socializing the new member. It is interesting, along this line, that Peter M. and his staff were from the start in accord in one area—a genuine concern for the minority group families in the school community. And what about the League as a special project that might have displaced his school as the prime focus for a new principal? For the moment we only remind the reader that the objectives of the League project required, first, attention to individual school problems.

5 The subject is touched in other contexts in two publications from this project: Ann Lieberman, "The Power of the Principal: Research Findings," in Carmen M. Culver and Gary J. Hoban (eds.), *The Power to Change: Issues for the Innovative Educator*, McGraw-Hill, New York, 1973, pp. 35–47; and Richard C. Williams, Charles C. Wall, W. Michael Martin, and Arthur Berchin, *Effecting Organizational Renewal in Schools: A Social Systems Perspective*, McGraw-Hill, New York, 1974.

6   Much of this evidence has come in the form of observations reported to us by persons who had later contacts with League schools. One organized body of data became available through a study conducted two years after the end of the League project. In that study the Basic DDAE Questionnaire was administered again in all eighteen League schools. The new information confirmed a number of the expectations stated or implied in Chapter 9: the severe decline of Hacienda, for example; the reversion of the upward swing at Mar Villa; and the recovery from the slump at Indian Flat. Elizabeth Frances Barry, "The Relationship between Propensity toward Self-directed Change in School Faculties and Selected Factors in the School's Subculture," unpublished doctoral dissertation, University of California at Los Angeles, 1974.

7   We do have some information about pupil attitudes, though the data must be considered as tentative since they are based on only a few classrooms and a few students. See Alice Z. Seeman and Melvin Seeman, "Staff Processes and Pupil Attitudes: A Study of Teacher Participation in Education Change," forthcoming.

8   Ann Lieberman (ed.), *Tell Us What to Do! But Don't Tell Me What to Do!* an |I|D|E|A| Monograph, Institute for Development of Educational Activities, Inc., Dayton, Ohio, 1971; and David A. Shiman, Carmen M. Culver, and Ann Lieberman (eds.), *Teachers on Individualization: The Way We Do It*, McGraw-Hill, New York, 1974.

9   Such potential district problems are treated indirectly in Richard C. Williams, "A Plan for an Accountable Elementary School District," in Culver and Hoban (eds.), op. cit., pp. 221–244.

10   An outgrowth of this study, for example, has been the development of a League-type strategy for the dissemination of the IGE program, in the |I|D|E|A| Change Program for Individually Guided Education now being used in over a thousand schools.

We should sound again, with respect to such a use of the peer group strategy with a specific input in mind, a warning that we've touched upon in our own story. The interventionists must walk a fine line between using competence within some group members to serve as a resource to other group members and inadvertently creating a "star" system in the group. If high-level performance of the new behavior in some schools is pointed out too much and too early by the interventionists, those schools tend to be viewed by other group members as teacher's pets, and the development of total group interdependence is discouraged. The hard lesson for interventionists to learn is that pushing the particular content of the desired innovation must be treated, in a true peer group strategy, as secondary to the development of the group as a vehicle for changing behavior. This is not to say that effective peer groups do not have members of higher and lower status. The point is that the status of a member school must come from judgment by its peers of the value of its performance, not from the premature approval of some schools by the interventionists.

11 This is a variation of a diagram presented with related discussion in Mary M. Bentzen and Kenneth A. Tye, "Effecting Change in Elementary Schools," in John I. Goodlad and Harold G. Shane (eds.), *The Elementary School in the United States*, the Seventy-second Yearbook of the National Society for the Study of Education, Part II, University of Chicago Press, Chicago, 1973, pp. 350–379.

12 This rationale is, of course, related to the often-used strategy of creating temporary groups of individuals who are thereby pulled out for a while from restrictions that normally inhibit new behaviors. We're simply saying in our League strategy that it could be organizations rather than individuals and it need not be a temporary system.

13 One interesting possibility, of which we caught only a glimmer in the League, is that such a group of schools, or a number of such groups, would be creating a pool of teachers socialized to these expectations—a kind of socialization that does not necessarily occur in the course of teacher training programs. One can speculate then about how these teachers might try to select other "group" schools if they had to move or how the schools might search out such experience in hiring new staff members.

14 For example, Matthew B. Miles, "The Development of Innovative Climates in Educational Organizations," Educational Policy Research Center, Research Note, EPRC-6747-10, April 1969.

15 An implication here is that such networks might in turn encourage greater flexibility on the part of R&D personnel in producing materials to meet specific school needs. This need is touched in James M. Bishop, "The Untidy World of Public Education: A Sociological Perspective and an Immodest Proposal," in Mary M. Bentzen, James M. Bishop, and Ann Lieberman, *Conducting Research in Schools: A Tidy Mind in an Untidy World*, McGraw-Hill, New York, in press.

16 Other comments on these phenomena are presented in Ann Lieberman, James Bishop, and Maxine Bentzen, "The League of Cooperating Schools: Us, Them, We," *Journal of Research and Development in Education*, vol. 6, no. 4, summer 1973, pp. 22–34.

17 Bentzen, Bishop, and Lieberman, op. cit.

APPENDIX A

DESCRIPTION OF LEAGUE SCHOOLS

Antigua School was situated in a commercial area in a medium-sized city. Its forty-year-old, two-story building was California Spanish in style and served about 400 pupils. Kindergarten and primary grades were downstairs; upper grades (through sixth) were upstairs. While most of the pupils were white, about 20 percent were black and Mexican-American, some of them bussed to the school in conformity with a district desegregation policy. The Antigua community consisted of middle- and lower-middle-class families.

Steve M., the principal, had been at Antigua for two years when the League began. A man of about forty, Steve had established a career in administration. When asked by the superintendent if he wanted to participate in the League project, he agreed although he knew little about it and was not much interested in research activities.

The staff of Antigua numbered just under twenty. Teachers had an average age of forty, and about a third of them were over fifty. Their average length of teaching experience was also high. These staff characteristics changed little during the project.

Steve reported all that he knew about the League study to his staff in the spring preceding the project. The primary teachers quickly decided to try a new program.

Bell Street School served an urban community in a long-established city within the Los Angeles area. The 450 pupils (K–6) were a broad representation of racial and ethnic groups; about a third were white, about a fourth were black, a fourth were of various Latin American backgrounds, and the rest were Oriental. The socioeconomic status of pupils' families ranged from welfare recipients to upper middle class. The school building, erected in 1950, consisted of several classroom wings and a library. There was little change in this general setting during the project.

213

Amanda Q., the principal of Bell Street in the first year of the League, was ending a long and successful career, about fifteen years of which she had spent at Bell Street. When she retired at the end of the first year of the project, Peter M. became principal. Peter was in his late forties and had some twenty years of experience in education, but he was rather new in this district. He had only a vague understanding of the League project.

The Bell Street staff was a fairly stable group, with a wide age range and an average age of thirty-five. The average teaching experience was rather high, about eleven years. The teachers were informed by the principal about the League project in the spring before the project began. In general, their reaction was favorable.

Country School belonged to a small but growing district in a suburban area near a medium-sized city. Although Country School had been selected as the League school by the district, it did not actually exist as a unit until the second year of the project. The principal and staff of the new school had already been selected, however, and while the new building was being completed in 1966–1967, they met regularly to plan an innovative program.

The principal, Andy S., felt he had been chosen because he had shown himself able to run a tight ship in his more than fifteen years of professional experience. Interested in the idea of innovation, he was nonetheless exceedingly modest about his ability to bring it off. The teachers who had been asked to form the staff of the new school came from several different schools in the district. Throughout the League study, the Country staff was fairly evenly split between teachers under thirty years old and teachers over thirty, although the change in personnel was moderately high. The average teaching experience of the staff fell in about the middle of the range found in League schools.

The new school plant consisted of four classroom pods, each with multipurpose areas, arranged around a central court. When the school opened, its approximately 700 pupils in kindergarten through sixth grade came from predominantly middle-class white families. In the second year of the project, however, Mexican-American children began to be bussed to Country School and made up one-fourth to one-third of the pupil population.

Dewey Avenue School belonged to a very large city school district and was situated in a rather stable, largely upper-middle-class urban residential area. Most of the 1,100 students were white and represented a number of different nationalities. The main building was some thirty-five years old; additional classroom space was provided by about a half-dozen World War II barracks.

Stan M. had been principal at Dewey Avenue for a year before the start of the League. With twenty years of experience, he was interested in innovation in education and welcomed the League as an opportunity to try nongrading and team teaching. In the spring of 1966, he discussed with the staff the coming League involvement and the kinds of changes that he anticipated.

The staff experienced a moderate rate of turnover but remained throughout the project a rather professionally mature group. Average teacher age was around thirty-seven, and teaching experience averaged more than eleven years with about a quarter of the staff having more than twenty years of experience. As they learned about the League project, the staff showed a mixture of apprehension and eagerness to try new ideas.

At the end of the second year of the League, Stan M. accepted a principalship in another school. He was replaced at Dewey Avenue by Edith B., who had a substantial administrative career in the district. She remained at the school for two years. In the final year of the project, Stan returned as principal of Dewey Avenue.

Fairfield School belonged to a district that covered a small rural town and served the low-income section of the town. Its 1,300 pupils in kindergarten through eighth grade were almost all Mexican-American with about 20 percent black and Filipino and a scant sprinkling of whites. Most of the parents were farm laborers, but as more and more acquired permanent jobs, the pupil population became increasingly stable. The school building was some ten years old in 1966 and was arranged in the conventional pattern of simply constructed finger units, each housing about six classrooms.

Ben U., principal of Fairfield, had been at the school for more than fifteen years, several as a teacher, when the League began. When he heard about the League project, he volunteered to participate and early indicated interest in changing from traditional administrative practices. He kept the staff informed of the League project as he learned about it in the spring before the first League year. As a whole, however, the forty-five teachers at Fairfield showed little interest in the League. The staff had little turnover, averaged about forty-five years old, and had substantial teaching experience (average over fifteen years).

Frontier School contained the seventh and eighth grades of a very small rural district. With an enrollment of 250 pupils, the school was housed in a relatively new plant of two conventionally constructed classroom wings. Most of the pupils were white; a few were Mexican-American. Most of the families were at the lower-middle income level; a few were at the upper-middle level.

Three men served as principal of Frontier during the League study. Jason R. had been at Frontier for a year when the project began. He had started a career in teaching, left it, and then returned to it. This was his first administrative position. Jason moved to another position at the end of the second year, and Tim M. became principal for the third year. He was succeeded in the fourth year by Carl C. Carl had been a teacher and vice-principal at Frontier for several years, and he remained as principal for the rest of the project.

More than half of the thirteen teachers were new to Frontier in 1966. The rate of teacher turnover remained relatively high. The majority of the staff were over thirty years old, and there were about equal proportions of those who had less than five years and those who had more than five years of teaching experience.

When Jason R. learned about the League project, he responded with enthusiasm and informed his staff of the school's involvement. Staff reactions were mixed. A few teachers seemed excited; a few were scornful of what they saw as an "ivory-tower" proposal; but most teachers remained noncommittal.

Hacienda School was only two years old when the League began. It belonged to a rapidly growing district in a complex of suburban communities about thirty-five miles from our office. The pupils came from middle-class families, and almost all were white. Other than increasing in size, the school community did not change much during this study.

The building at Hacienda was made up of six units surrounding an open court. A few units housed administration and special classroom facilities. Each of the classroom units had a central core room for use by the whole unit. Several kinds of grouping arrangements were used to organize pupils from kindergarten through eighth grade. Straight grades and self-contained classrooms characterized the older levels, while flexible groups and multilevel classes were seen with some of the younger pupils.

Jeff H., who was principal of Hacienda at the start of the League, was transferred to the district staff before the end of the first year. Chris M. then became the principal and remained there until the end of the project. A young man who had had only a few years in administration (as a vice-principal in another school in the district), Chris was excited about problems and prospects in his profession, and during the course of our project he earned a doctorate in education.

Like the building and the principal, the teachers at Hacienda belonged to a new look in schooling. Throughout the project they were the youngest staff in the League (average age under thirty), were new to teaching, had a high rate of turnover, and almost doubled their original staff size of fifteen.

Hacienda teachers, as well as the district and the principal, saw the League as a further means to facilitate changes that they had already planned to make.

Independence School was located in an urban residential neighborhood in a medium-sized city within the Los Angeles area. The newest part of the building was thirty-five years old, and early in the first year of the League the building was condemned. A hoped-for bond issue for new buildings failed to pass, and in the second year the teachers were spread into three other schools. Independence continued to exist formally as a unit, however, and in the fourth year of study, the staff came back together in portable classrooms on the original site. During the last year of the League, when the district complied with court-ordered integration, Independence was converted from a K–6 to a K–3 school.

The mobility rate among its 900 pupils was high, often over 50 percent turnover a year. Many pupils came from families associated with a nearby college and represented a great number of different nationalities. The community ranged from low income to high income. About 80 percent of the pupils were white in 1966, but in the last year the percentage dropped to about 40 percent as children were bussed in from other areas.

Duncan D., the principal of Independence in 1966, worked out plans for a new reading program in the spring of 1966, immediately upon learning that the school would participate in the League. He informed his staff of these plans, but the building crisis occurred before most of the planning was put into operation. The principal left the district at the end of the first year, and Arnold Z. became principal of Independence for the rest of the project. About forty years old, Arnold had some fifteen years of experience in education and showed at the start considerable enthusiasm for the League project.

The staff at Independence was a relatively mature group, with an average age of about thirty-seven and an average of about ten years of teaching experience. The rate of staff turnover was moderate until the last year, when it rose with the change of Independence to a K–3 school. Teachers' first reactions to the League project were generally favorable or neutral.

Indian Flat School was in a rapidly growing district in an outer suburban community of the Los Angeles area. With kindergarten-through-sixth-grade classrooms in a fairly new plant, which consisted of five finger units, the school served about 750 pupils from a large housing tract. The majority of the community were white, employed as skilled laborers and office personnel. There was little change in the pupil population of Indian Flat during the study.

The principal, Chet O., was new to the district and new to the job of principal in 1966, although he had some fifteen years of experience in education. He was, at the start, apprehensive about becoming a "League principal," but he remained at Indian Flat for the duration of the project.

The Indian Flat teachers were among the older staffs in the League, with an average age of about forty, and among the most experienced. The staff was also a relatively stable group. While they had some understanding that the League schools were to consider innovations, the Indian Flat staff originally found it very difficult to think about change in their own school.

James School, one of 153 schools in its district, is located somewhat away from the center, but not quite in the suburbs, of one of the larger cities in California. In September 1966, at the start of the League, James School had just been coverted from a kindergarten-through-sixth-grade school with an enrollment of about 1,000 to a third-through-sixth-grade school with 650 pupils. About 85 percent of the pupils were white; the rest, black, Oriental, and Mexican-American. The three-through-six grade range and the makeup of the pupil population did not change during the League project. The buildings in which James School was housed were World War II barracks, painted bright pink. At the beginning of the League, it was expected that the school would move to a new building within three years. At the end of the project the school was still in the same buildings.

James School was one of two League schools which served primarily the families of military personnel. More than 85 percent of the children in this school lived in housing units for Navy enlisted men stationed at a nearby base. Almost the first problem that the James staff mentioned was their concern about the attitudes toward school which developed in children and their families, who were accustomed to spending only a short time at any one school.

The principal of James School, Joe A., was new to the school in 1966 but had been a principal in the district for some years. A man about forty years old, Joe A. seemed to have a stable career in the district. He remained at James School throughout the project. The staff of James School consisted of seventeen teachers in 1966, had a moderate turnover, and grew by about 30 percent during our study. Although the staff was not particularly young (average age about thirty-five), they were one of the least experienced staffs at the start of the League.

James School was among the League schools farthest away from our office, and only one other League school (Peace Valley) was nearby. The principal was simply told by the district office that the school would participate in the League project because its pupil and teacher population were desirable for the study. Joe A. and his teachers showed moderate interest in the project. A district steering committee was set up to oversee the League activities of James School.

Mar Villa School was a kindergarten-through-sixth-grade school in a medium-sized city. In 1966 the neighborhood contained families whose incomes ranged from welfare payments to above average. Most of the pupils were white. The population was very transient, however, and during the League project its characteristics changed. The percentage of Mexican-American children increased greatly and the economic level of the neighborhood declined.

The school plant was a two-story California Spanish building, over forty years old in 1966. In the spring and summer before the last year of the League, the building was renovated; major changes in the layout of rooms provided for a variety of instructional groupings.

Adam S. had been at Mar Villa for nearly fifteen years, about half the time as a teacher and half the time as principal. Staff turnover was moderate; the average age of teachers was forty, and the average experience in teaching was fourteen years. When Adam was invited by the superintendent in the spring of 1966 to participate in the League, he accepted and very soon prepared and submitted to |I|D|E|A| a project for the school, as he believed was expected of him. He wanted to get reactions to this plan before making other moves. The teachers at Mar Villa had been given sketchy information about the League by a member of the district staff, and the district had also obtained each teacher's written consent to be involved in an innovative program. Nonetheless, the teachers at the start of the League seemed to have adopted a "wait and see" attitude.

Middleton School was in a rather small district in a suburban area of a medium-sized city. The majority of the pupils belonged to low-income families, but about a third of the pupils came from upper-middle-class homes. About 10 percent were Mexican-American, the rest white. The 700 pupils in grades K–5 were housed in a seven-year-old school plant, made up of four classroom wings, a kindergarten building, five portable classrooms, and a multi-use room.

The principal, Florence P., was new to Middleton when the League began but had a long career in educational administration. At the outset she seemed receptive to the League as an organization which would develop plans for change. The teachers had little information about the project and appeared, on the whole, rather neutral in reaction to it. The pattern of age and experience of staff members showed a normal curve type of distribution throughout the project. About a fourth to a third of the teachers were under thirty; another fourth to a third were over fifty. Around 40 percent had less than five years teaching experience, but around 25 percent had more than twenty years experience. This pattern was maintained even with a relatively high rate of turnover.

Peace Valley School was the only intermediate school (grades six through eight) in a small district which served an outlying rural area of a large city. The community was growing rapidly as a suburb, housing small-farm workers, city workers, and some military personnel from a nearby base. The number of pupils at Peace Valley increased from 800 to over 1,000 during the course of the project, although the grade range was reduced to seven–eight in the last year. Most of the pupils were white, from lower-middle- and middle-class homes. In 1966 the school plant at Peace Valley was only a year old. Designed for flexibility and versatility, it included large and small group instructional areas, some collapsible walls, a carpeted library, indoor and outdoor assembly areas, and individual counseling rooms.

Three different principals served at Peace Valley during the League project. Everett W. had just moved from vice-principal to principal in 1966. He welcomed the League as an opportunity to get consultant help for the school, but he remained at Peace Valley only through the second year of the project. He was followed by Mike D., a man of about thirty-five, who was working on a doctorate degree and who was interested in innovations in administration. A change in school-board and district-office personnel led to Mike's resignation at the end of the fourth year. Roy R., who had several years of administrative experience in another of the district's schools, became principal of Peace Valley during the last year of the project.

The staff did not learn about the League project until well into the first year but seemed reasonably interested in it when they were told about it. The size of the staff increased from thirty to about fifty during the project, but the age of teachers ranged only from mid-twenties to mid-forties and the average teaching experience of the Peace Valley staff was in the lower third of League schools.

Rainbow Hill School was one of thirteen elementary schools in a small and rather remote, semiagricultural community. Rainbow Hill was situated in a military housing area for master sergeants and officers, adjoining a base just outside of the main town. The pupil population (K–6) had a fairly high rate of turnover. The relatively new school plant consisted of several simply constructed classroom wings and supplementary units.

Gene G. was principal of Rainbow Hill during the study. He was about forty years old and had some fifteen years of experience in education, five at Rainbow Hill when the League began. The staff of twenty teachers was about evenly divided into those under thirty and those over thirty, and the average teaching experience was about five years. This picture of the staff remained much the same throughout the project.

Rainbow Hill was not initially chosen to be a League school. It was supposed to pinch-hit for a new school that was to be completed about a year and a half after the start of the project. Gene G. had been selected as principal of the new school, however, so he and his staff participated in the League. The principal seemed enthusiastic about having contacts with leaders in education, and the reactions of the staff were generally favorable. At the end of the second year of the project, the plans for the new school were abandoned and Rainbow Hill was officially designated as the League school.

Seastar School was one of nine elementary schools (K–6) in a district which covered a relatively small and long-established city within the metropolitan Los Angeles complex. About 20 percent of the approximately 800 pupils came from minority racial and ethnic groups, and the school community represented almost equal proportions of blue-collar occupations and a combination of clerical, business, and professional occupations. The fifteen-year-old school building consisted of several one-story units, each housing five or six classrooms.

Seastar was one of the most stable schools in the League. Teacher turnover was very low. The Seastar staff of twenty-five teachers was also considerably older (average age over forty) and had more teaching experience (average more than fifteen years) than most other League staffs. The principal for three years at Seastar, Dave W., entered the project with a substantial career of almost twenty years and an almost-completed doctorate in education. Both Dave and his staff were initially hostile to the League project. The staff learned from a newspaper story that they were to be in the League. They immediately voted not to join. As it turned out, however, Seastar remained in the project and Dave remained at Seastar until six months before the end of the project. At that point, he accepted an assistant superintendency in another district, and Paul S. became principal of Seastar.

Shadyside School was situated in the lowest-income community of a unified school district in an urban area. The original one-story, U-shaped building was typical of school architecture at the time it was built in 1925; not many years later an addition closed the open end of the U to form a central court.

In 1966 Shadyside had about 500 pupils, mostly white, in kindergarten through sixth grade. Very shortly before the opening of the last year of the League project, the district adopted new plans for racial integration, and Shadyside was converted to a K–3 school. The number of pupils remained about the same, but under the new plan the proportion of black and Mexican-American children was increased, and many of the pupils came from outside the immediate neighborhood.

Russ D., who was principal of Shadyside in 1966, was succeeded in the second year of the project by Lucy K., a woman with more than twenty years of professional experience. Lucy stayed at the school until close to the end of the third year, when she was transferred to a position on the district staff. The principal during the rest of the project was Brad C., a young man whose first experience as a principal was at Shadyside. He planned a career in educational administration and entered a doctoral program in that field.

The teachers at Shadyside numbered twenty, with moderate turnover until the last year when Shadyside became a K–3 school. The change then resulted in about 40 percent new teachers. Throughout the study the Shadyside staff were relatively young and were on the lower end of the scale among League schools as far as years of teaching experience was concerned. They were quite self-confident, however, and initially expressed interest in learning about desirable changes.

South School was in 1966 the second largest elementary school (670 pupils) of the fourteen schools in its district. The district covered a small city in the Los Angeles metropolitan area, about a half-hour's drive from our office. South School was opened in 1952 in newly built "finger units," each housing three or four classrooms, a building style that became common in California schools. The pupils were assigned to traditional self-contained classrooms, kindergarten through sixth grade. The school in 1966 served a community of average-income families. Over the years of the project the community changed somewhat to a higher percentage of blue-collar workers. The pupil population of the school, however, tended to be relatively stable. Stability also characterized the staff of South School.

Alex R. had been principal of South School for fourteen years. He was, however, somewhat disenchanted with his long experience in schooling and was considering leaving the education profession. When the superintendent asked the district principals to select a school for the League, Alex expressed his interest in the project. After his school was chosen, Alex remained at South School until poor health forced him to retire at the end of the fourth year of the project. In the last year of the study, Harry L. was the principal at South. Harry was a younger man who had only a few years of experience as an administrator.

The staff of South School, about twenty-five members, were, by and large, teachers with considerable professional experience who tended to remain at the school. The teachers at South were one of two League staffs who learned that their school would participate in the project by reading a newspaper story. They showed little understanding about the new group and considerable apprehension about their ability to carry out the innovations they felt were expected.

Woodacres School was in a very rapidly growing district in an outlying Los Angeles suburban area. The school was opened in a brand-new plant several months after the beginning of the 1966 school year. The plant consisted of five classroom pods, three of which had sliding panels rather than interior walls. The classroom space was carpeted and acoustically treated. Families in the neighborhood were middle and upper middle class, and almost all the pupils were white. Both the pupil population and staff size tripled in the course of the League study, ending with about 750 pupils and twenty-four teachers.

During the first year of the League, Jerry W., the assistant superintendent of the district, served as acting principal of Woodacres. He had been closely involved in planning the district's participation in the League, including the selection of teachers for the new school, and had decided on a team-teaching project for Woodacres. In the second year Leonard B., a young man who had been a teacher at Woodacres, became vice-principal, then principal. The teachers were relatively young (average age just over thirty) and averaged about six years of professional experience. The staff realized that they were in an innovative situation and seemed open to new ideas from the League project.

APPENDIX B

OUT-OF-STATE SCHOOLS

	Schools from Each State Represented			
	Colorado	Connecticut	Georgia	Maryland
No. of Schools	5	1	4	3

	Size of Town or City		
	< 10,000	10–99,000	100–500,000
No. of Schools	2	7	3

	Age of School Building			
	$\leq$ 5 years	6–10 years	11–19 years	$\geq$ 20 years
No. of Schools	3	4	4	2

	Size of Teaching Staff			
	< 20	20–29	$\geq$ 30	No data
No. of Schools	3	6	3	1

	Pupil Enrollment			
	< 500	500–749	750–999	$\geq$ 1,000
No. of Schools	4	5	3	1

	Age Range of Pupils		
	5–8 years	5–12 years	6–13 years
No. of Schools	1	8	4

	Number of Schools × Percentage Ethnic Population		
	< 25%	25–75%	> 75%
White	0	1	12
Black	12	1	0
Other	13	0	0
Language Other Than English	13	0	0

	Number of Schools × Percentage Parents Occupation			
	< 25%	25–75%	> 75%	No data
Professional	5	3	4	1
Business Owner or Executive	8	3	1	1
Clerical Worker	9	2	0	2
Skilled Laborer	10	1	0	2
Unskilled Laborer	9	2	0	2
Unemployed	11	0	0	2

APPENDIX C

INSTRUMENTS

This appendix contains the measurement instruments used to collect the data described and discussed in Chapters 5 to 8. Each questionnaire is identified by the symbol Q followed by an identifying number. For example, "Q3" is the third questionnaire listed in this appendix. At appropriate places within the text as well as in the tables in Appendix D, the reader is directed to the relevant questionnaire(s) using this numbering system.

Date_____

Q1: BASIC DDAE QUESTIONNAIRE

We would like you to describe *two* problems discussed in your school this
year:

1   In the first section, describe a problem which involved the *total
    school staff.*
2   In the second section, describe a problem involving a subgroup in
    which you participated (e.g. committee, team, pod, grade group, etc.).

Problem I: Total School Staff

In the space below please describe an important problem your school staff
has worked on this school year.

_____

_____

_____

Please answer the following questions in terms of *discussions* about the
problem:

1   Who actually participated in the discussion(s)?

open participation by entire group	most of the group participated	small subgroup dominated	dominated by an individual

2   How important would you say the problem was?

unimportant (e.g.) routine matter	of little importance	somewhat important	very important (e.g.) important issue or problem

3   To what extent was the problem related to your school program and
    philosophy?

very much (e.g.) basic to the school program	a good deal (e.g.) related to school objectives	little (e.g.) only in part related to the school program	not at all (e.g.) an isolated matter

4   How flexible and open-minded was the discussion of the problem?

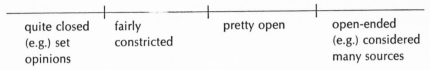

| quite closed (e.g.) set opinions | fairly constricted | pretty open | open-ended (e.g.) considered many sources |

The four questions below deal with the *decision* (or decisions) that were made:

1   Who participated in the decision making?

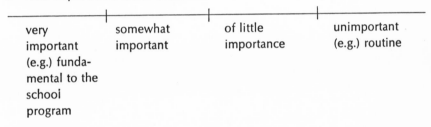

| decided by one individual (e.g.) by administra- tive decision | decided by small subgroup | most of the group | all members participated (e.g.) by vote or consensus |

2   How important was the decision?

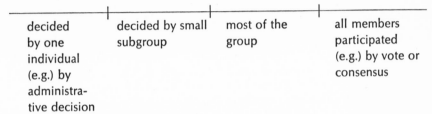

| very important (e.g.) funda- mental to the school program | somewhat important | of little importance | unimportant (e.g.) routine |

3   How did the decision fit into the total school program?

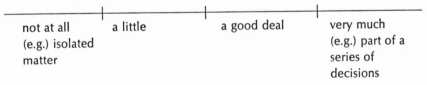

| not at all (e.g.) isolated matter | a little | a good deal | very much (e.g.) part of a series of decisions |

4   How flexible was the decision?

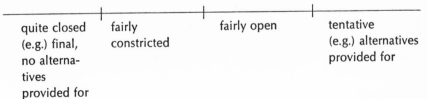

| quite closed (e.g.) final, no alterna- tives provided for | fairly constricted | fairly open | tentative (e.g.) alternatives provided for |

The five questions below concern the *action* (or actions) taken as a result of the discussion and decision(s).

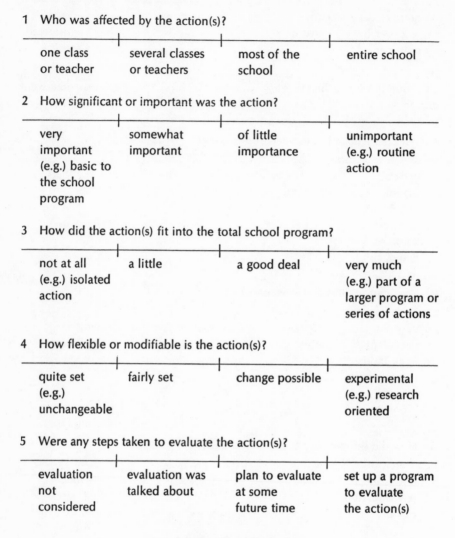

1 Who was affected by the action(s)?

| one class or teacher | several classes or teachers | most of the school | entire school |

2 How significant or important was the action?

| very important (e.g.) basic to the school program | somewhat important | of little importance | unimportant (e.g.) routine action |

3 How did the action(s) fit into the total school program?

| not at all (e.g.) isolated action | a little | a good deal | very much (e.g.) part of a larger program or series of actions |

4 How flexible or modifiable is the action(s)?

| quite set (e.g.) unchangeable | fairly set | change possible | experimental (e.g.) research oriented |

5 Were any steps taken to evaluate the action(s)?

| evaluation not considered | evaluation was talked about | plan to evaluate at some future time | set up a program to evaluate the action(s) |

Problem II: Subgroup

In the space below please describe an important problem your subgroup has worked on this school year.

_____

_____

_____

Please answer the following questions in terms of *discussions* about the problem:

1 Who actually participated in the discussion(s)?

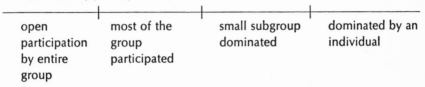

| open participation by entire group | most of the group participated | small subgroup dominated | dominated by an individual |

2 How important would you say the problem was?

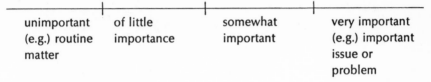

| unimportant (e.g.) routine matter | of little importance | somewhat important | very important (e.g.) important issue or problem |

3 To what extent was the problem related to your school program and philosophy?

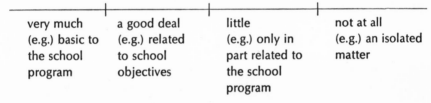

| very much (e.g.) basic to the school program | a good deal (e.g.) related to school objectives | little (e.g.) only in part related to the school program | not at all (e.g.) an isolated matter |

4 How flexible and open-minded was the discussion of the problem?

| quite closed (e.g.) set opinions | fairly constricted | pretty open | open-ended (e.g.) considered many sources |

The four questions below deal with the decision (or decisions) that were made:

1 Who participated in the decision making?

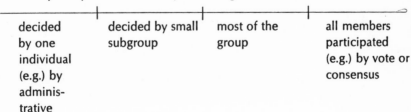

| decided by one individual (e.g.) by administrative decision | decided by small subgroup | most of the group | all members participated (e.g.) by vote or consensus |

2   How important was the decision?

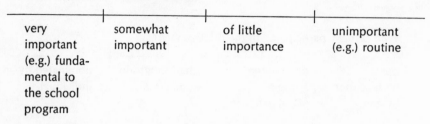

| very important (e.g.) fundamental to the school program | somewhat important | of little importance | unimportant (e.g.) routine |

3   How did the decision fit into the total school program?

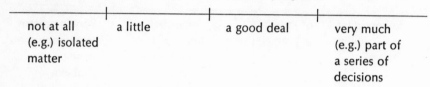

| not at all (e.g.) isolated matter | a little | a good deal | very much (e.g.) part of a series of decisions |

4   How flexible was the decision?

| quite closed (e.g.) final, no alternatives provided for | fairly constricted | fairly open | tentative (e.g.) alternatives provided for |

The five questions below concern the *action* (or actions) taken as a result of the discussion and decision(s).

1   Who was affected by the action(s)?

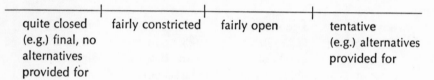

| one class or teacher | several classes or teachers within the group | most of the group | entire group or more |

2   How significant or important was the action?

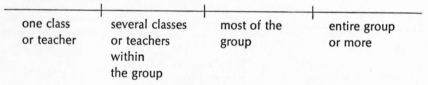

| very important (e.g.) basic to the school program | somewhat important | of little importance | unimportant (e.g.) routine action |

3   How did the action(s) fit into the total school program?

not at all (e.g.) isolated action	a little	a good deal	very much (e.g.) part of a larger program or series of actions

4   How flexible or modifiable is the action(s)?

quite set (e.g.) un- changeable	fairly set	change possible	experimental (e.g.) research oriented

5   Were any steps taken to evaluate the action(s)?

evaluation not considered	evaluation was talked about	plan to evaluate at some future time	set up a program to evaluate the action(s)

Q2: CRITERIA

This instrument contains a series of questions about various school practices. Read each statement and check the category ("Never, Seldom, Sometimes, Frequently, Usually, or Always") which best describes the existence of this practice in your school. Check only one response for each statement. Please answer all questions, being certain to indicate *what actually exists in your school* rather than what you believe ought to exist. Your responses will be kept confidential.

In my school:

	Never	Seldom	Sometimes	Frequently	Usually	Always
1 Discussions include contributions by most of the members present.						
2 Staff meetings are generally reserved for matters concerned with curriculum, instruction, and school organization—not administrivia.						
3 Decisions are clearly communicated to all persons who are affected by the decision.						
4 Meetings are on time.						
5 The staff engages in discussions aimed at defining school goals.						
6 When a decision is made, action is taken to implement it.						
7 Teachers make instructional decisions.						
8 The principal has the respect and good will of the students.						
9 Persons examine and/or experiment with several approaches before making a decision.						
10 Teachers visit other schools.						
11 Teachers read professional educational material.						
12 Anyone who is interested is encouraged to take the responsibility for implementing decisions.						

	Never	Seldom	Sometimes	Frequently	Usually	Always

In my school:

13 Teachers periodically visit other classrooms in the school.

14 The principal respects the teachers.

15 Meetings are such that members listen to each other.

16 Teachers can arrange to have their teaching critiqued by other teachers.

17 Meetings are followed by written memorandum that summarizes the proceedings of the meeting.

18 The principal knows his staff well.

19 Teachers attend conferences relative to their professional growth.

20 Many persons assume the leadership positions during group discussions, depending upon the function to be performed.

21 Both principal and teachers participate in making decisions which affect the school.

22 Meetings have an agenda composed of items that any member of the staff can suggest.

23 Teachers try to evaluate the extent to which school goals have been realized.

24 Issues and programs discussed by the staff are suggested by both teachers and principal.

25 Dialogue is appropriate to the problem confronted; e.g., brainstorming when seeking new and imaginative ideas and task-oriented when attempting to solve a particular problem.

	Never	Seldom	Sometimes	Frequently	Usually	Always
In my school:						

26 Persons become familiar with the experiences of other schools before making a decision.

27 The principal encourages others to provide leadership.

28 Meetings involve only persons who need to be involved.

29 The principal encourages and assists the staff in developing goals for the school.

30 Actions can be modified to handle unanticipated situations.

31 Issues and programs discussed by the staff can be suggested by parents.

32 The principal communicates effectively with students.

33 Teachers work to implement the goals of the school.

34 Group decisions are reached by consensus.

35 Dialogue has a purpose.

36 Teachers critique each other's teaching.

37 Dialogue allows for in-depth discussion of issues that are pertinent to the education of children.

38 Decisions are made on the basis of school goals.

39 The principal utilizes resource persons from the district to help teachers.

40 The principal builds the status of his staff.

41 Issues and programs discussed by the staff can be suggested by the students.

	Never	Seldom	Sometimes	Frequently	Usually	Always

In my school:

42 Teachers attend courses at colleges and universities.

43 The principal shows that he appreciates his staff.

44 Responsibilities for carrying out actions are assumed by many different people on the staff.

45 Meetings are such that persons can engage in an open and frank discussion of issues.

46 Decisions are carried out with enthusiasm and good will.

47 The principal communicates effectively with teachers.

48 Actions are carried out with a high degree of organization and efficiency.

49 When appropriate the advice of district personnel is sought before a decision is made.

50 Teachers experiment with new materials.

51 The principal encourages the staff to visit other classrooms.

52 The principal has the respect and good will of the teachers.

53 Before a decision is made, the implications of alternative actions are thoroughly explored.

54 There is a high degree of commitment on the part of people responsible for putting decisions into action.

55 Group decisions are reached by voting.

56 The principal respects the opinions and beliefs of teachers.

	Never	Seldom	Sometimes	Frequently	Usually	Always

In my school:

57 Appropriate actions are taken based on the decisions made.

58 Meetings are such that there is an interaction of teachers.

59 The principal communicates effectively with the community.

60 Persons read what scholars and informed practitioners have written on the subject and bring relevant ideas from their reading into the dialogue.

61 The principal provides fair and equitable treatment for all.

62 Teachers respect the opinions and beliefs of students.

63 The principal promotes openness in his staff.

64 Teachers evaluate their teaching in terms of achieving school goals.

65 After an action has been taken, it is evaluated.

66 Meetings can be called by both teachers and the principal.

67 The principal attends conferences relative to his professional growth.

68 Teachers respect the opinions and beliefs of other teachers.

Date_____

Q3: BIOGRAPHICAL INFORMATION

Please place a check mark to the right of the appropriate category.

Position	Principal	1._____
	Teacher	
	Full-time ⌠at this	2._____
	Part-time ⌡school	3._____
	Other	4._____
Sex	Male	1._____
	Female	2._____
Age		~_____
Highest degree received		1._____
In what subject was the degree obtained?		2._____
Years of experience in education		_____
Years at this school		_____
Ages of pupils presently teaching		From____to____
Ages of pupils taught before this year		From____to____

Do you teach in a self-contained classroom, or
are you part of a teaching team?

_____Teach in self-contained classroom
_____Part of a teaching team
_____Other arrangement (please explain)

Q4: SAMPLE ITEMS FROM THE ROKEACH DOGMATISM SCALE[1] AND THE ROTTER INTERNAL-EXTERNAL CONTROL SCALE[2]

Dogmatism Scale

8   Of all the different philosophies which have existed in this world, there is probably only one which is correct.

21   To compromise with our political opponents is dangerous because it usually leads to the betrayal of our own side.

26   There are two kinds of people in this world: those who are on the side of truth and those who are against it.

38   It is only natural for a person to be rather fearful of the future.

Internal-External Scale

1   _____A lasting peace can be achieved by those of us who work toward it.

_____There's very little we can do to bring about a permanent world peace.

7   _____Most people don't realize how much their lives are the result of accidental happenings.

_____There is really no such thing as "luck."

9   _____This world is run by the few people in power, and there is not much the little guy can do about it.

_____The average citizen can have an influence on government decisions.

[1] Milton Rokeach, *The Open and Closed Mind,* Basic Books, New York, 1960.
[2] Julian B. Rotter, "Generalized Expectancies for Internal vs. External Control of Reinforcements," *Psychological Monographs* vol. 80, 1966.

Q5: INFORMAL ORGANIZATION[1]

Please indicate here *your own* identification
number from the special list given to you
today by the school secretary. Do *not* write
your name.   #_____

In answering the first question, please use the special numbering system
given to you today by the secretary to indicate your answers. Please do *not*
use names in your answers.

1   Who are the two or three people with whom you *most often* discuss
    matters of classroom discipline?

    1_____   3_____

    2_____   4_____

2   How often would you say you have such discussions?

    _____Several times a week
    _____At least once a week.
    _____Less than once a week.
    _____Two or three times a month.
    _____Once a month or less.

3   How often would you say you request advice about matters of
    classroom discipline from the *first person* you have identified?

    _____Several times a week.
    _____At least once a week.
    _____Less than once a week.
    _____Two or three times a month.
    _____Once a month or less.
    _____Never.

Please indicate here your own identification
number from the special list given to you
today by the school secretary. Do *not* write
your name.   #_____

In answering the first question, please use the special numbering system
given to you today by the secretary to indicate your answers. Please do *not*
use names in your answers.

[1] James M. Bishop, "Organizational Work Context, Informal Organization, and the Development of Occupational Ideologies Among Elementary Teachers: A Comparative Study of Twenty-four Public Schools," unpublished doctoral dissertation, University of California, Los Angeles, 1972.

1 Please write down the numbers of your three best friends here in this school.

1_____

2_____

3_____

2 Are most of the friends you see socially *outside the school* members of the faculty here?

_____Yes.

_____No.

Please indicate here your own identification number from the special list given to you today by the school secretary. Do *not* write your name. #_____

In answering the first question, please use the special numbering system given to you today by the secretary to indicate your answers. Please do *not* use names in your answers.

1 Who are the two or three people in the school with whom you most often discuss instructional programs, curriculum, and other matters relating to instruction?

1_____ 3_____

2_____ 4_____

2 How often would you say you have such discussions?

_____Several times a week.

_____At least once a week.

_____Less than once a week.

_____Two or three times a month.

_____Less than once a month.

3 How often would you say you request *advice* about matters relating to instruction from the *first person* you have identified?

_____Several times a week.

_____At least once a week.

_____Less than once a week.

_____Two or three times a month.

_____Less than once a month.

_____Never.

Q6: TEACHER POWER QUESTIONNAIRE

The responsibilities that teachers have, outside of teaching in the classroom, vary from school to school. Sometimes these responsibilities are small in number, sometimes they are large in number. Below is a list of some of the things about which teachers may help to make decisions. Please check those items you believe apply generally to the teachers in your school. You may check all, some, or none of the items, whatever you think best describes your school.

The teachers in this school have a lot of influence in making decisions about

1 _____curriculum.
2 _____standards of pupil behavior in their own classrooms.
3 _____standards of pupil behavior in halls and on playground.
4 _____daily schedule in their own classrooms.
5 _____daily schedule in the whole school.
6 _____special discipline problems with pupils.
7 _____special all-school affairs, such as open house, assemblies, etc.
8 _____unusual problems that affect the whole school.
9 _____time of staff meetings.
10 _____content of staff meetings.
11 _____arrangements for parent conferences.
12 _____assignments for duties outside of classrooms (yard duty, etc.).
13 _____planning of social gatherings of school staff.
14 _____standards of dress.
15 _____assignment of pupils to classes.
16 _____assignment of teachers to classes.
17 _____ways of reporting pupil progress to parents.
18 _____preparation of the school budget.
19 _____selection of teachers to be hired in the school.
20 _____evaluation of each other's teaching performance.
21 _____selection of teachers to be dismissed from the school.

Q7: ORGANIZATIONAL CLIMATE DESCRIPTION QUESTIONNAIRE (OCDQ)[1]

Marking Instructions

Printed below is an example of a typical item found in this questionnaire:

1 Rarely occurs
2 Sometimes occurs
3 Often occurs
4 Very frequently occurs

Teachers call each other by their first names.   1   2   ③   4

In this example, the respondent marked alternative 3 to show that the interpersonal relationship described by this item "often occurs" at his school. Of course, any of the other alternatives could be selected, depending upon how often the behavior described by the item does, indeed, occur in your school.

Please mark your response clearly, as in the example. *Please be sure that you mark every item.*

1 Rarely occurs
2 Sometimes occurs
3 Often occurs
4 Very frequently occurs

		1	2	3	4
13	Teachers' closest friends are other faculty members at this school.	1	2	3	4
14	The mannerisms of teachers at this school are annoying.	1	2	3	4
15	Teachers spend time after school with students who have individual problems.	1	2	3	4
16	Instructions for the operation of teaching aids are available.	1	2	3	4
17	Teachers invite other faculty members to visit them at home.	1	2	3	4
18	There is a minority group of teachers who always oppose the majority.	1	2	3	4
19	Extra books are available for classroom use.	1	2	3	4

[1] Andrew W. Halpin and Don B. Croft, Midwest Administration Center, University of Chicago, 1963.

1   Rarely occurs
2   Sometimes occurs
3   Often occurs
4   Very frequently occurs

20	Sufficient time is given to prepare administrative reports.	1	2	3	4
21	Teachers know the family background of other faculty members.	1	2	3	4
22	Teachers exert group pressure on nonconforming faculty members.	1	2	3	4
23	In faculty meetings, there is a feeling of "let's get things done."	1	2	3	4
24	Administrative paper work is burdensome at this school.	1	2	3	4
25	Teachers talk about their personal life to other faculty members.	1	2	3	4
26	Teachers seek special favors from the principal.	1	2	3	4
27	School supplies are readily available for use in classwork.	1	2	3	4
28	Student progress reports require too much work.	1	2	3	4
29	Teachers have fun socializing together during school time.	1	2	3	4
30	Teachers interrupt other faculty members who are talking in staff meetings.	1	2	3	4
31	Most of the teachers here accept the faults of their colleagues.	1	2	3	4
32	Teachers have too many committee requirements.	1	2	3	4
33	There is considerable laughter when teachers gather informally.	1	2	3	4
34	Teachers ask nonsensical questions in faculty meetings.	1	2	3	4
35	Custodial service is available when needed.	1	2	3	4
36	Routine duties interfere with the job of teaching.	1	2	3	4

1 Rarely occurs
2 Sometimes occurs
3 Often occurs
4 Very frequently occurs

37	Teachers prepare administrative reports by themselves.	1	2	3	4
38	Teachers ramble when they talk in faculty meetings.	1	2	3	4
39	Teachers at this school show much school spirit.	1	2	3	4
40	The principal goes out of his way to help teachers.	1	2	3	4
41	The principal helps teachers solve personal problems.	1	2	3	4
42	Teachers at this school stay by themselves.	1	2	3	4
43	The teachers accomplish their work with great vim, vigor, and pleasure.	1	2	3	4
44	The principal sets an example by working hard himself.	1	2	3	4
45	The principal does personal favors for teachers.	1	2	3	4
46	Teachers eat lunch by themselves in their own classrooms.	1	2	3	4
47	The morale of the teachers is high.	1	2	3	4
48	The principal uses constructive criticism.	1	2	3	4
49	The principal stays after school to help teachers finish their work.	1	2	3	4
50	Teachers socialize together in small select groups.	1	2	3	4
51	The principal makes all class-scheduling decisions.	1	2	3	4
52	The teachers are contacted by the principal each day.	1	2	3	4
53	The principal is well prepared when he speaks at school functions.	1	2	3	4
54	The principal helps staff members settle minor differences.	1	2	3	4

1   Rarely occurs
2   Sometimes occurs
3   Often occurs
4   Very frequently occurs

55	The principal schedules the work for the teachers.	1	2	3	4
56	Teachers leave the grounds during the school day.	1	2	3	4
57	The principal criticizes a specific act rather than a staff member.	1	2	3	4
58	Teachers help select which courses will be taught.	1	2	3	4
59	The principal corrects teachers' mistakes.	1	2	3	4
60	The principal talks a great deal.	1	2	3	4
61	The principal explains his reasons for criticism to teachers.	1	2	3	4
62	The principal tries to get better salaries for teachers.	1	2	3	4
63	Extra duty for teachers is posted conspicuously.	1	2	3	4
64	The rules set by the principal are never questioned.	1	2	3	4
65	The principal looks out for the personal welfare of teachers.	1	2	3	4
66	School secretarial service is available for teachers' use.	1	2	3	4
67	The principal runs the faculty meeting like a business conference.	1	2	3	4
68	The principal is in the building before the teachers arrive.	1	2	3	4
69	Teachers work together preparing administrative reports.	1	2	3	4
70	Faculty meetings are organized according to a tight agenda.	1	2	3	4
71	Faculty meetings are mainly principal-report meetings	1	2	3	4
72	The principal tells teachers of new ideas he has run across.	1	2	3	4

1   Rarely occurs
2   Sometimes occurs
3   Often occurs
4   Very frequently occurs

73	Teachers talk about leaving the school system.	1	2	3	4
74	The principal checks the subject-matter ability of teachers.	1	2	3	4
75	The principal is easy to understand.	1	2	3	4
76	Teachers are informed of the results of a supervisor's visit.	1	2	3	4
77	Grading practices are standardized at this school.	1	2	3	4
78	Principal ensures that teachers work to their full capacity.	1	2	3	4
79	Teachers leave the building as soon as possible at day's end.	1	2	3	4
80	The principal clarifies wrong ideas a teacher may have.	1	2	3	4

Description of Teacher and Principal Sub-Scale OCDQ Scores

Teachers' Behavior

1   *Disengagement* refers to the teachers' tendency to be "not with it." This dimension describes a group which is "going through the motions," a group that is "not in gear" with respect to the task at hand.

2   *Hindrance* refers to the teachers' feeling that the principal burdens them with routine duties, committee demands, and other requirements which the teachers construe as unnecessary busywork. The teachers perceive that the principal is hindering rather than facilitating their work.

3   *Esprit* refers to "morale." The teachers feel that their social needs are being satisfied and that they are, at the same time, enjoying a sense of accomplishment in their job.

4   *Intimacy* refers to the teachers' enjoyment of friendly social relations with each other. This dimension describes a social-needs satisfaction which is not necessarily associated with task accomplishment.

Principal's Behavior

5 *Aloofness* refers to behavior by the principal which is characterized as formal and impersonal. He "goes by the book" and prefers to be guided by rules and policies rather than to deal with the teachers in an informal, face-to-face situation. To maintain this style, he keeps himself—at least "emotionally"—at a distance from his staff.

6 *Production Emphasis* refers to behavior by the principal which is characterized by close supervision of the staff. He is highly directive and plays the role of a "straw boss." His communication tends to go in only one direction, and he is not sensitive to feedback from the staff.

7 *Thrust* refers to behavior by the principal which is characterized by his evident effort in trying to "move the organization." "Thrust" behavior is marked not by close supervision, but by the principal's attempt to motivate the teachers through the example which he personally sets. Apparently, because he does not ask the teachers to give of themselves any more than he willingly gives of himself, his behavior, though starkly task-oriented, is nonetheless viewed favorably by the teachers.

8 *Consideration* refers to behavior by the principal which is characterized by an inclination to treat the teachers "humanly," to try to do a little something extra for them in human terms.

Q8: ADJECTIVE LIST

Below are some terms which have been used to describe school atmosphere. Please indicate how you would apply them to your school. (A check mark is all that is required.)

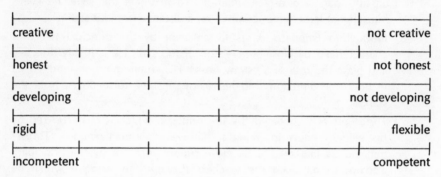

creative						not creative
honest						not honest
developing						not developing
rigid						flexible
incompetent						competent

Q9: BASES OF PRINCIPAL'S POWER[1]

Listed below are five reasons generally given by people when they are asked why they do the things their superiors suggest or want them to do. Please read all five carefully. Then number them according to their importance to you as reasons for doing the things your principal suggests or wants you to do. Give rank "1" to the most important factor, "2" to the next, etc.

I do the things my principal suggests or wants me to do because:

_____A   I admire him for his personal qualities and I want to act in a way that merits his respect and admiration;

_____B   I respect his competence and good judgment about things with which he is more experienced than I;

_____C   He can give special help and benefits to those who cooperate with him;

_____D   He can apply pressure or penalize those who do not cooperate;

_____E   He has a legitimate right, considering his position, to expect that his suggestions will be carried out.

[1] J. R. P. French and B. H. Raven, "The Bases of Social Power," in Dorwin Cartwright (ed.), *Studies in Social Power,* Institute for Social Research, Ann Arbor, Michigan, 1959, pp. 150–167.

Q10: SCHOOL PROBLEMS

In the spaces provided below, please list the five major problems *you* see facing your school today. After each problem you list, check the box which indicates what percentage of the staff *you* feel *would agree with you* that this *is* a major problem facing your school, even though they may disagree with you about how to handle it.

	Less than 25%	25%–50%	50%–75%	Over 75%
1				
2				
3				
4				
5				

If you can, please indicate which one of these problems you think is *most* important (circle the number).

Description of the Categories Used in Scoring Problems Listed by School Staffs

1   *Discipline*
    Mentions of "discipline" or "behavior" of students.

2   *Racial-Language*
    Specific reference to racial, ethnic, or language characteristics of students.

3   *Student Attitudes*
    Reference to attitude toward school, teachers, learning, lack of respect for property.

    Community
4   Reference to lack of community support or understanding or cooperation.

5   Reference to the need for the school to do a better job of community relations or interpretation of program.

    The difference between categories 4 and 5 was based on how the problem was stated. If the response was, for example, "We lack community support" or "Parents don't understand what we're trying to do," it was scored in 4. If the response was something like, "We need to do a better job of involving parents," or "Need to educate parents about nongrading," the response was scored in 5.

6   *Lack of Facilities and Resources*
Include all references to undesirable physical environment, need for resource persons and materials, need for release time.

7   *Constraints from Outside Groups*
Include references to school-board requirements, government requirements, disruptive union activities, burdens caused by research requirements, and undesirable attitudes in society in general.

8   *Administration*
Specific references to principal's behavior and references to schedules, meetings, and resource distribution controlled by the principal.

9   *Curriculum, Instruction, and School Organization*
All mentions of specific instructional programs, need for better instructional techniques, grouping of pupils, team arrangements, and evaluation procedures.

10   *Teacher Group Cohesiveness*
Specific references to need for more or better teacher-teacher communication, and mentions of staff morale.

11   *Goals*
Mentions of need to define objectives or list goals of the school.

12   *Orientation of Staff*
References to teacher attitude toward pupils or education, need for unification of individual philosophies, need for innovation, need to orient new teachers, need to follow through on decisions.

Q11: EDUCATIONAL BELIEFS[1]

The row of boxes opposite each item below represents a range of responses from strongly agree to strongly disagree. Please place an X in the box opposite each item that best indicates your degree of agreement or disagreement with the area represented. Check only *one* response opposite each item.

	Strongly Agree	Agree	No Opinion	Disagree	Strongly Disagree
1 Good teacher-pupil relations are enhanced when it is clear that the teacher, not the pupils, is in charge of classroom activities.	□	□	□	□	□
2 As long as they have control over teaching in their own classrooms, it is not necessary for teachers to have a voice in school administrative affairs.	□	□	□	□	□
3 The learning of basic facts in less important in schooling than acquiring the ability to synthesize facts and ideas into a broader perspective.	□	□	□	□	□
4 Learning is enhanced when teachers praise generously the accomplishments of individual pupils.	□	□	□	□	□
5 There is too great an emphasis on keeping order in most classrooms.	□	□	□	□	□
6 Learning in the elementary school is essentially a process of increasing one's store of information about the various basic fields of knowledge.	□	□	□	□	□
7 The best learning atmosphere is created when the teacher takes an					

[1] James M. Bishop, "Organizational Work Context, Informal Organization, and the Development of Occupational Ideologies Among Elementary Teachers: A Comparative Study of 24 Public Schools," unpublished doctoral dissertation, UCLA, 1972.

	Strongly Agree	Agree	No Opinion	Disagree	Strongly Disagree
active interest in the problems and affairs of students.	☐	☐	☐	☐	☐
8 An orderly classroom is the major prerequisite to effective learning.	☐	☐	☐	☐	☐
9 Effective learning depends primarily upon the use of adequate instructional techniques and resources.	☐	☐	☐	☐	☐
10 Pupil initiation and participation in planning classroom activities are essential to the maintenance of an effective classroom atmosphere.	☐	☐	☐	☐	☐
11 Pupils must be kept busy or they soon get into trouble.	☐	☐	☐	☐	☐
12 When pupils are allowed to participate in the choice of activities, discipline problems are generally averted.	☐	☐	☐	☐	☐
13 When given a choice of activities, most pupils select what is best for them.	☐	☐	☐	☐	☐
14 In planning their work, teachers should rely heavily on the knowledge and skills pupils have acquired outside the classroom.	☐	☐	☐	☐	☐
15 Pupil motivation is greatest when pupils can gauge their own progress rather than depending on regular evaluation by the teacher.	☐	☐	☐	☐	☐
16 Children need and should have more supervision than they usually get.	☐	☐	☐	☐	☐
17 Before pupils are encouraged to exercise independent thought they should be thoroughly grounded in facts and knowledge about basic subjects.	☐	☐	☐	☐	☐

	Strongly Agree	Agree	No Opinion	Disagree	Strongly Disagree
18 In the interest of good discipline, pupils who repeatedly disrupt the class must be firmly punished.	☐	☐	☐	☐	☐
19 Teaching of basic skills and subject matter is the most important function of the school.	☐	☐	☐	☐	☐
20 Proper control of a class is amply demonstrated when the pupils work quietly while the teacher is out of the room.	☐	☐	☐	☐	☐
21 Pupils are motivated to do better work when they feel free to move around the room while class is in session.	☐	☐	☐	☐	☐

APPENDIX D

DATA TABLES

This appendix contains the tabular results of the data analyses performed to investigate the relationships described and discussed in Chapters 5 through 8. Each table is identified by a pair of numbers, "X.Y." X refers to the chapter to which the table is relevant and Y is the number of the table within the chapter. For example, Table 6.3 refers to Chapter 6, third table. These table numbers are also cross-referenced at the appropriate places within the text of each chapter.

It should be emphasized that the tables presented here represent only some of the relatively large number of data analyses performed over the course of the SECSI project. The tables were selected in an attempt to highlight the most important analyses and concepts which best described the League experience. In coordinating the material in this appendix with that presented in the relevant chapters, the reader should be advised of several methodological considerations:

1. *Measurement Instruments.* The data presented in each of the subsequent tables are always based on teacher and/or principal responses to one or more *questionnaires,* developed (or adopted) for use in the SECSI project. Appendix C contains these instruments; defining the variables or measures used in each table, then, is easily accomplished by referring to the instruments in Appendix C.

2. *Units of Analysis.* The primary units of *response* were the individual teachers and principals of the schools. Each individual responded to each questionnaire and received one (or more) scores on the concept (or subconcepts) represented by the questionnaire. Secondarily, however, each school could receive "teacher scores" equal to summary statistics computed over all its teachers' scores for any given measure or "principal scores" equal, simply, to its principal's score on any given measure. In effect, the school "responds" (via its teachers) to a set of items and receives a "score" (e.g. the *mean* of the

teacher scores). Depending upon the purpose of the analysis, the *unit* of analysis could be either the individual scores or the school scores. In other words, a set of school scores (e.g. means) does not necessarily possess the same characteristics (or do the same job) as the set of individual scores. For our purposes here, it will generally be the case that differences among *teacher* scores on any given measure (teacher score *variance*)—and how this variability *correlates* with variability on other measures—will be of primary concern when we analyze the internal structure of our questionnaires. On the other hand, variation in *school* scores will be of primary concern when we analyze the outcomes of our intervention strategy and investigate the interrelationships most important to describing the concept of receptivity to change. Thus, Tables 5.1 through 5.4, dealing with the reliability and validity of the Basic DDAE Questionnaire, are based upon the teacher as the unit of analysis. The tables thereafter are generally based upon the school as the unit of analysis.

3. *Groups of Analysis.* Three distinct groups of schools were assessed at one or more times throughout the course of the project: (1) the original 18 League schools, surveyed beginning in 1967; (2) the 18 Comparison schools, one other school in each of the 18 League districts, surveyed beginning in 1970; and (3) the 13 Out-of-State schools selected nationally and surveyed once in 1971. Depending upon the purpose of our analysis and the completeness of our data, one or more of these groups would serve as an appropriate data base. In general, the tables summarize the data analyses *across* all 49 schools when questions regarding general relationships between constructs (and their measures) are being investigated. When the investigations are additionally concerned with obtaining a handle on the effects of the SECSI intervention process, the data are usually presented separately for the 18 League and 31 non-League schools.

4. *Tests of Statistical Significance.* The reader will note that nowhere in the text or in the tables to follow does there appear an X^2, t value, F value, asterisk next to an r signifying $p < .05$ or $.01$, or any other type of index associated with tests of statistical inference. This is not because they are particularly difficult to compute—in fact, many have been computed as a matter of course in analyzing the data using statistical computer packages. However, we strongly feel that the study reported here was hypothesis *generating*, not hypothesis *testing*. In a very real sense, the project as a whole should be regarded as a case study. Accordingly, our analysis of the data is wholly descrip-

tive, and resultant interpretations are offered more with heuristic rather than generalizable purposes in mind. Inferential analyses, therefore, were not particularly relevant—we were just as willing to interpret a "statistically insignificant" but interesting difference or relationship as we were unwilling to interpret a "statistically significant" but uninteresting difference or relationship. This is not to say, however, that the reader could not use the results of significance tests applied to our data in an "extra-statistical" inferential fashion. This would be appropriate if the reader were willing to assume that our sample of teachers and schools are representative of similar teachers and schools for a particular population of interest. Therefore, most of the tables that follow are sufficiently detailed so as to allow the obvious inferential statistic to be computed.

DATA TABLES—CHAPTER 5

TABLE 5.1 INTERNAL CONSISTENCY INDICES (COEFFICIENT ALPHAS*)
FOR TOTAL SCHOOL, SUBGROUP, AND COMPOSITE SCORES
OBTAINED ON THE BASIC DDAE QUESTIONNAIRE (Q1) FOR LEAGUE
SCHOOL TEACHERS (N=460) AND COMPARISON SCHOOL TEACHERS
(N=409)

| | Number of Items | Coefficient Alpha | |
Basic DDAE Scores		League	Comparison
Total School	12	.81	.82
Subgroup	12	.83	.84
Composite	24	.85	.85

* L. J. Cronbach, "Coefficient Alpha and the Internal Structure of Tests," *Psychometrika*, 1951, 16, pp. 297–334.

Coefficient alpha measures the degree to which a total score is positively correlated with the item scores of which it is comprised. The coefficient ranges from 0 to 1 such that the larger its value, the more internal consistency, i.e., the greater the tendency for items to "hang together" or to be correlated with one another.

TABLE 5.2 INTERCORRELATIONS BETWEEN DIALOGUE, DECISION MAKING, ACTION, AND EVALUATION FOR TOTAL SCHOOL AND SUBGROUP ON THE BASIC DDAE QUESTIONNAIRE (Q1) FOR BOTH LEAGUE AND COMPARISON TEACHERS

		Dialogue	Decision Making	Action	Evaluation
League:					
Total School	Dialogue	–	.64	.54	.31
	Decision Making		–	.67	.38
	Action			–	.34
	Evaluation				–
Subgroup	Dialogue	–	.71	.59	.30
	Decision Making		–	.67	.36
	Action			–	.35
	Evaluation				–
Comparison:					
Total School	Dialogue	–	.57	.52	.36
	Decision Making		–	.67	.40
	Action			–	.37
	Evaluation				–
Subgroup	Dialogue	–	.69	.59	.24
	Decision Making		–	.74	.35
	Action			–	.30
	Evaluation				–

The expectation that the DDAE process is a "cumulative" one—that is, that there exists a *taxonomical* or *hierarchical* structure such that there can be little "evaluation" without "action"; little "action" without "decision"; and little "decision" without "dialogue"—leads to the expectation that intercorrelations among these form DDAE subscores which approximate a Guttman simplex. This pattern of correlations exists when the variables are ordered in their postulated hierarchical order and adjacent variables are more highly correlated than nonadjacent variables.

This pattern of correlations is evidenced above insofar as dialogue is more correlated with decision than with action or evaluation, and decision is more correlated with action than with evaluation.

TABLE 5.3   INTERCORRELATIONS BETWEEN BASIC DDAE SCORE AND TEACHER CHARACTERISTICS* FOR LEAGUE AND COMPARISON TEACHERS

		Correlations of DDAE with			
Group	Age	Years Experience	School Experience	Dogmatism	Internal-External
League	.00	.08	.05	−.10	−.07
Comparison	.07	.11	.00	−.12	.02

* Teacher characteristics consist of: (1) chronological age (Q3); (2) years of teaching experience (Q3); (3) years of teaching experience in their present school (Q3); (4) Rokeach's Dogmatism scale score (Q4); (5) Rotter's Internal-External Control Scale score (Q4).

TABLE 5.4   LEAGUE AND COMPARISON TEACHER FACTOR ANALYSES OF BASIC DDAE TOTAL SCHOOL AND SUBGROUP ITEMS (TWO FACTOR SOLUTION*)

	League Teachers				Comparison Teachers			
	Total School		Subgroup		Total School		Subgroup	
Basic DDAE Items	I	II	I	II	I	II	I	II
Dialogue								
Scope	.29	.42†	.25	.59	.07	.58	.19	.52
Importance	.73	.08	.69	.14	.65	.03	.74	.12
Relationship	.70	.13	.76	.11	.68	.19	.72	.13
Flexibility	.31	.67	.19	.76	.26	.61	.14	.73
Decision								
Scope	.10	.71	.24	.74	.14	.66	.18	.70
Importance	.82	.08	.76	.18	.84	.09	.84	.09
Relationship	.75	.24	.75	.09	.73	.31	.79	.26
Flexibility	.06	.75	.03	.79	.05	.73	.11	.81
Action								
Scope	.32	.13	.30	.31	.28	.12	.22	.31
Importance	.84	.09	.74	.23	.88	.02	.86	.10
Relationship	.78	.14	.72	.11	.73	.24	.72	.29
Flexibility	.00	.76	.01	.73	.15	.67	−.01	.76

* Between 50% and 55% of the total variance is accounted for by these two-factor solutions; results are presented for principal components (one in the diagonal of correlation matrix) analyses with Kaiser Varimex rotations. Parallel analyses were performed using (1) oblique rotations and (2) iterated communalities, but substantive conclusions as well as general factor patterns remained unchanged.
† Loadings greater than .40 are underlined.

Factor analysis is essentially a tool for statistically analyzing a correlation matrix to see whether or not clusters of variables exist such that (1) variables *within* a cluster are relatively highly correlated and (2) variables *between* clusters are relatively uncorrelated. The output of a factor analysis is a set of indices (loadings) for each variable, indicating the degree of association that variable has with each factor. (The indices can be interpreted in exactly the same manner as one interprets a correlation coefficient.)

TABLE 5.5 DESCRIPTIVE STATISTICS FOR THE DISTRIBUTIONS OF BASIC DDAE QUESTIONNAIRE SCHOOL SCORES* FOR 1971 LEAGUE ($N=18$), NON-LEAGUE ($N=31$), AND COMBINED ($N=49$) DATA BASES

Statistics	League	Non-League	Combined
Mean	3.31	3.27	3.29
33rd Percentile	3.25	3.21	3.22
Median	3.30	3.30	3.29
67th Percentile	3.40	3.36	3.38
Standard Deviation	0.16	0.17	0.17
Range	2.99–3.57	2.93–3.57	2.93–3.57

* Score for each school is equal to the mean of the individual teacher scores at that school. The Basic DDAE Questionnaire consists of 24 items (Q1). Total scores over these items are divided by 24 so that the above data reflect the average scale position of the schools as defined by the 4-point item scales of the questionnaire.

Clearly, relatively little variance among Basic DDAE score was evidenced, with the schools generally falling in the upper end (3–4) of the DDAE scale. The data within schools (not tabled here) also indicate little variance suggesting that school staffs are not generally willing to use the lower half of the 4-point item scales. In other words, given the nature of school staffs and the DDAE questionnaire, we suspected that the upper end of the scale was really providing dichotomous information—a basically favorable or basically unfavorable opinion of the DDAE "climate." Stretching the variance and trichotomizing the distribution, however, proved to be reasonable insofar as the resultant League school distribution of high, middle and low DDAE schools conformed with other available measures and assessments of their DDAE standing. Additionally, the relationships uncovered between high-low DDAE levels and other variables were more clearly in evidence when the "middle" group was accounted for in the data analyses.

TABLE 5.6   RELATIONSHIP BETWEEN FORMAL TEACHING ARRANGEMENT AND DDAE LEVEL OVER SCHOOLS (N=49)

Dominant Type of Teaching Arrangement	High	Middle	Low	Total	Percent
Cooperative	9 (69%)*	6 (26%)	0 (0%)	15	31
Mixed	2 (15%)	4 (17%)	2 (15%)	8	16
Self-Contained	2 (15%)	13 (57%)	11 (85%)	26	53
Total	13	23	13	49	
Percent	26.5	46.9	26.5		100

* Cell "entries" are the number of schools and the percentage that number constitutes of the column total. This format is used in all subsequent cross-tabulation tables.

TABLE 5.7   RELATIONSHIP (SPEARMAN RANK-ORDER CORRELATION) BETWEEN EXTENT OF INFORMAL ASSOCIATION (Q5) AMONG TEACHERS AND TOTAL SCHOOL AND SUBGROUP BASIC DDAE SCORES OVER SCHOOLS (N=25)

	Basic DDAE Scores	
Type of Informal Association*	Total School	Subgroup
Mutual Friendship	.30	.34
Mutual Discussion on:		
Classroom Discipline	.06	.50
Curriculum and Instruction	.05	.40

* School scores for these three measures were based upon a sociogram analysis of mutual choices in the three areas of informal association; each school score was essentially the number of mutual choices divided by the total number of teachers in the school.

TABLE 5.8 RELATIONSHIP BETWEEN INFORMAL ASSOCIATION AMONG TEACHERS AND FORMAL TEACHING ARRANGEMENTS OVER SCHOOLS (N=25)

Median Splits on Measures of Informal Associations*	Dominant Type of Teaching Arrangement				
	Cooperative	Mixed	Self-Contained	Total	Percent
Mutual Friendship:					
High	6 (67%)	4 (80%)	2 (18%)	12	48
Low	3 (33%)	1 (20%)	9 (82%)	13	52
Mutual Discussion on Classroom Discipline:					
High	7 (78%)	4 (80%)	2 (18%)	13	52
Low	2 (22%)	1 (20%)	9 (82%)	12	48
Mutual Discussion on Curriculum and Instruction:					
High	6 (67%)	4 (80%)	3 (27%)	13	52
Low	3 (33%)	1 (20%)	8 (73%)	12	48
Total	9	5	11	25	
Percent	36	20	44		100

* School scores for these three measures were based upon a sociogram analysis of mutual choices in the three areas of informal association; each school score was essentially the number of mutual choices divided by the total number of teachers in the school.

TABLE 5.9 RELATIONSHIP BETWEEN TEACHER POWER (Q6) AND DDAE LEVEL OVER SCHOOLS (N=49)

Median Split on Teacher Power	DDAE				
	High	Middle	Low	Total	Percent
High	11 (85%)	11 (48%)	3 (23%)	25	51
Low	2 (15%)	12 (52%)	10 (77%)	24	49
Total	13	23	13	49	
Percent	26.5	46.9	26.5		100

TABLE 5.10   ITEM-BY-ITEM ASSESSMENT OF LOW-LEVEL ($N=13$)
AND HIGH-LEVEL ($N=13$) DDAE SCHOOLS ON TEACHER POWER (Q6)

"The teachers in this school have a lot of influence in making decisions about":	Mean Percentage of Affirmative Responses		
	Low DDAE	High DDAE	Difference
*1 Selecting teachers to be dismissed from the school	1.54	3.69	2.15
2 Daily schedules in their own classrooms	92.69	97.15	4.46
3 Standards of pupil behavior in their own classrooms	92.23	97.62	5.39
4 Parent conferences	84.08	78.38	−5.70
5 Assignments for duties outside of the classroom (yard duty, etc.)	38.54	45.54	7.00
*6 Preparing the school budget	8.00	17.92	9.92
7 Content of staff meetings	33.77	44.23	10.46
*8 Evaluating each other's teaching performance	2.69	14.69	12.00
9 Daily schedule in the whole school	20.38	34.31	13.93
10 Time of staff meetings	19.69	34.31	14.62
11 Standards of dress	49.77	64.85	15.08
12 Planning social gatherings of school staff	68.54	84.23	15.69
13 Special all-school affairs, such as open house, assemblies, etc.	45.54	61.46	15.92
14 Standards of pupil behavior in halls and on playground	65.00	81.15	16.15
15 Special discipline problems with pupils	61.31	78.15	16.84
*16 Curriculum	56.54	76.15	19.61
17 Ways of reporting pupil progress to parents	48.69	69.54	20.85
*18 Assigning teachers to classes	10.15	31.62	21.47
*19 Selecting teachers to be hired in the school	2.38	24.00	21.62
*20 Assigning pupils to classes	31.54	53.92	22.38
*21 Unusual problems that affect the whole school	36.46	70.77	34.31

* Describes areas in which teachers have not traditionally participated in the decision making.

TABLE 5.11   RELATIONSHIP BETWEEN GENERAL TEACHER MORALE AND DDAE LEVEL OVER SCHOOL (N=36)

Median Split on General Morale*	DDAE			Total	Percent
	High	**Middle**	**Low**	**Total**	**Percent**
High	5 (63%)	11 (58%)	2 (22%)	18	50
Low	3 (38%)	8 (42%)	7 (78%)	18	50
Total	8	19	9	36	
Percent	22	53	25		100

* Each school received a general morale score equal to the composite of mean OCDQ (Q7) profiles on those scales dealing with general feeling tone variables: Esprit + Intimacy − Disengagement − Hindrance.

TABLE 5.12   RELATIONSHIP BETWEEN SCHOOL CLIMATE ADJECTIVE LIST (Q8) AND DDAE LEVEL OVER SCHOOLS (N=49)

Median Split on Climate Score	DDAE Level			Total	Percent
	High	**Middle**	**Low**	**Total**	**Percent**
High	13 (100%)	11 (48%)	1 (8%)	25	51
Low	0	12 (52%)	12 (92%)	24	49
Total	13	23	13	49	
Percent	27	47	27		100

TABLE 5.13   RELATIONSHIP BETWEEN AGREEMENT AMONG
TEACHERS WITHIN SCHOOLS IN DESCRIBING SELECTED FEATURES
OF SCHOOL ORGANIZATION AND LEVEL OF DDAE

Median Split on Agreement Scores for Selected Measures*	Level of DDAE		
	High	Middle	Low
OCDQ (Q7): Disengagement			
High	3 (38%)	7 (37%)	8 (89%)
Low	5 (62%)	12 (63%)	1 (11%)
OCDQ: Hindrance			
High	2 (25%)	10 (53%)	6 (67%)
Low	6 (75%)	9 (47%)	3 (33%)
OCDQ: Esprit			
High	1 (12%)	11 (58%)	6 (67%)
Low	7 (88%)	8 (42%)	3 (33%)
OCDQ: Intimacy			
High	5 (62%)	8 (42%)	5 (56%)
Low	3 (38%)	11 (58%)	4 (44%)
OCDQ: Aloofness			
High	5 (62%)	9 (47%)	4 (44%)
Low	3 (38%)	10 (53%)	5 (56%)
OCDQ: Production Emphasis			
High	1 (12%)	9 (47%)	8 (89%)
Low	7 (88%)	10 (53%)	1 (11%)
OCDQ: Thrust			
High	4 (50%)	10 (53%)	4 (44%)
Low	4 (50%)	9 (47%)	5 (56%)
OCDQ: Consideration			
High	6 (75%)	8 (42%)	4 (44%)
Low	2 (25%)	11 (58%)	5 (56%)
CRITERIA (Q2): Meetings			
High	2 (15%)	13 (59%)	9 (69%)
Low	11 (85%)	9 (41%)	4 (31%)
CRITERIA: Principal			
High	2 (15%)	14 (61%)	8 (62%)
Low	11 (85%)	9 (39%)	5 (38%)
CRITERIA: Teachers			
High	5 (38%)	12 (52%)	7 (62%)
Low	8 (62%)	11 (48%)	6 (38%)
Teacher Power (Q6)			
High	9 (69%)	11 (48%)	4 (31%)
Low	4 (31%)	12 (52%)	9 (69%)
Climate Adjectives (Q8)			
High	1 (8%)	14 (61%)	9 (69%)
Low	12 (92%)	9 (39%)	4 (31%)

* Teacher agreement scores for each school were defined as the variance (or standard deviation) of the teacher scores for each selected variable. Low variance indicates a greater degree of agreement among teachers.

TABLE 5.14   INTERCORRELATIONS (RANK-ORDER) OF SELECTED TEACHER BEHAVIORS FOR HIGH (N=13) AND LOW (N=13) DDAE LEVEL SCHOOLS

Selected Behaviors*	2	3	4	5
High DDAE				
1 Disengagement	.58	−.40	.23	−.22
2 Hindrance	–	−.89	−.13	−.23
3 Esprit			.41	.10
4 Intimacy			–	.05
5 Teachers				–
Low DDAE				
1 Disengagement	.19	−.92	−.39	−.72
2 Hindrance	–	−.44	−.82	−.45
3 Esprit			.57	.65
4 Intimacy			–	.73
5 Teachers				–

* OCDQ subscales: Disengagement, Hindrance, Esprit, Intimacy (Q7), and CRITERIA: Teachers (Q2).

Note that the magnitude of correlations between traditionally desirable attributes is generally higher for low DDAE schools. For example, opportunity for professional growth (measured on the "teacher" dimension) correlates high and negatively with undesirable attributes "disengagement" and "hindrance" and correlates high and positively with desirable attributes "esprit" and "intimacy." These correlations are low and/or near zero for the high DDAE schools. This type of correlation comparison will be used often in later tables.

TABLE 5.15   RANK-ORDER INTERCORRELATIONS OF THE ADJECTIVE LIST (SCHOOL CLIMATE) SCORE (Q8) WITH OCDQ (Q7) AND CRITERIA (Q2) SCALE SCORES FOR HIGH (N=13) AND LOW (N=13) DDAE LEVEL SCORES

OCDQ	DDAE Level	
	High	Low
Teacher Scales:		
Disengagement	.34	−.75
Hindrance	.15	−.39
Esprit	.15	.73
Intimacy	.90	.78
Principal Scales:		
Aloofness	−.31	.86
Production Emphasis	−.82	−.43
Thrust	.05	.81
Consideration	−.46	.40
CRITERIA:		
Teachers	.58	.77
Principal	.27	.40
Meetings	.25	.72

TABLE 5.16   RANK-ORDER CORRELATIONS BETWEEN PRINCIPAL'S
SCORE AND TEACHERS' MEAN SCORE FOR SELECTED SCHOOL
DESCRIPTION VARIABLES FOR HIGH (N=13) AND LOW (N=13)
DDAE LEVEL SCHOOLS

Selected Schools Description Variables	Correlations by DDAE Level	
	High	Low
OCDQ (Q7)		
Principal Scales:		
Aloofness	.25	.39
Production Emphasis	−.34	.22
Thrust	.71	.02
Consideration	.30	.14
CRITERIA (Q2)		
Principal	.68	−.09
Meetings	.24	−.05
Adjective List (Q8)	.53	−.26
Teacher Power (Q6)	.86	−.36

TABLE 5.17   RELATIONSHIP BETWEEN PRINCIPAL INFLUENCE
MEASURES (Q9) AND DDAE LEVEL OVER SCHOOLS

Median Splits on Measures of Principal Influence	DDAE			Total	Percent
	High	Middle	Low		
Personal					
High	9 (70%)	10 (43%)	5 (39%)	24	49
Low	4 (31%)	13 (57%)	8 (61%)	25	51
Competent					
High	10 (77%)	10 (43%)	5 (39%)	25	51
Low	3 (23%)	13 (57%)	8 (61%)	24	49
Reward					
High	3 (23%)	15 (65%)	7 (54%)	25	51
Low	10 (77%)	8 (35%)	6 (46%)	24	49
Punishment					
High	2 (15%)	13 (57%)	9 (69%)	24	49
Low	11 (85%)	10 (43%)	4 (31%)	25	51
Legitimate Right					
High	4 (31%)	14 (61%)	7 (54%)	25	51
Low	9 (69%)	9 (39%)	6 (46%)	24	49
Total	13	23	13	49	
Percent	26.5	46.9	26.5		100

TABLE 5.18   RELATIONSHIP BETWEEN PRINCIPAL'S PERCEPTION OF TEACHER POWER (Q6) AND DDAE LEVEL OVER SCHOOLS ($N=39$)

Median Split on Teacher Power	DDAE			Total	Percent
	High	Middle	Low		
High	5 (63%)	12 (60%)	2 (18%)	19	49
Low	3 (37%)	8 (40%)	9 (82%)	20	51
Total	8	20	11	39	
Percent	20	51	28		100

TABLE 5.19   CORRELATION BETWEEN PRINCIPAL'S PERCEPTION OF TEACHER POWER (Q6) AND PRINCIPAL'S PERCEPTION OF SCHOOL CLIMATE (Q8), PRINCIPAL LEADERSHIP BEHAVIOR (Q2) AND TEACHER BEHAVIOR (Q2) FOR HIGH AND LOW DDAE SCHOOLS

	High DDAE Schools	Low DDAE Schools
School Climate	.42	−.34
CRITERIA: Principal	.63	−.10
CRITERIA: Teachers	.51	−.07

TABLE 5.20   INTERCORRELATION (RANK-ORDER) OF TEACHERS' PERCEPTIONS OF SELECTED PRINCIPAL BEHAVIORS FOR HIGH ($N=13$) AND LOW ($N=13$) DDAE LEVEL SCHOOLS

Selected Behaviors*	2	3	4	5	6
High DDAE					
1 Aloofness	.26	−.02	−.02	−.33	−.08
2 Production Emphasis	−	−.35	.20	.06	−.05
3 Thrust		−	.17	.52	.11
4 Consideration			−	.14	.22
5 CRITERIA: Principals				−	.23
6 CRITERIA: Meetings					−
Low DDAE					
1 Aloofness	−.60	.80	.22	.69	.89
2 Production Emphasis	−	−.48	−.39	−.27	−.75
3 Thrust		−	.52	.87	.71
4 Consideration			−	.57	.38
5 CRITERIA: Principals				−	.60
6 CRITERIA: Meetings					−

* Selected behaviors include principal scales of OCDQ (Q7) and CRITERIA (Q2).

TABLE 5.21 INTERCORRELATIONS (RANK-ORDER) BETWEEN
SELECTED PRINCIPAL AND TEACHER BEHAVIORS FOR HIGH
(N=13) AND LOW (N=13) DDAE LEVEL SCHOOLS

Principal Behaviors*	Teacher Behaviors†				
	Disengage-ment	Hindrance	Esprit	Intimacy	CRITERIA: Teachers
High DDAE:					
1 Aloofness	−.52	−.02	−.21	−.16	−.01
2 Production Emphasis	.11	.20	−.49	−.79	.13
3 Thrust	−.26	.21	.02	.05	−.11
4 Consideration	−.26	−.60	.50	−.17	.33
5 CRITERIA: Principals	.02	.17	.05	−.10	.30
6 CRITERIA: Meetings	−.01	−.23	.29	−.15	.05
Low DDAE:					
1 Aloofness	−.68	−.30	.64	.70	.85
2 Production Emphasis	.27	.34	−.15	−.42	−.62
3 Thrust	−.58	−.36	.62	.68	.69
4 Consideration	.11	−.25	−.10	.45	.41
5 CRITERIA: Principals	−.47	−.58	.50	.73	.55
6 CRITERIA: Meetings	−.40	−.42	.34	.73	.72

* Selected behaviors include principal scales of OCDQ (Q7) and CRITERIA (Q2).
† Selected behaviors include teacher scales of OCDQ (Q7) and CRITERIA (Q2).

DATA TABLES—CHAPTER 6

TABLE 6.1 RELATIONSHIP BETWEEN TEACHER POWER (Q6) AND
LEAGUE MEMBERSHIP OVER SCHOOLS (N=49)

Median Split on Teacher Power	League Membership		Total
	League	Non-League	
High	13 (72%)	12 (39%)	25
Low	5 (28%)	19 (61%)	24
Total	18	31	49

TABLE 6.2   ITEM-BY-ITEM ASSESSMENT OF LEAGUE (N=18) AND NON-LEAGUE (N=31) SCHOOLS ON TEACHER POWER (Q6)

"The teachers in this school have a lot of influence in making decisions about":	Mean Percentage of Affirmative Responses		
	League	Non-League	Difference
1 Parent conferences	82.11	82.68	.57
2 Daily schedules in their own classrooms	95.56	95.52	.04
3 Standards of pupil behavior in their own classrooms	95.89	95.58	.31
4 Standards of pupil behavior in halls and on playground	77.39	75.81	1.58
5 Assignments for duties outside of classroom (yard duty, etc.)	37.78	35.26	2.52
6 Selecting teachers to be dismissed from the school	4.83	1.52	3.31
7 Evaluating each other's teaching performance	9.67	5.90	3.77
8 Standards of dress	62.72	57.97	4.75
9 Special all-school affairs, such as open houses, assemblies, etc.	62.33	57.33	5.00
10 Special discipline problems with pupils	76.22	69.13	7.09
11 Planning social gatherings of school staff	82.56	74.26	8.30
12 Preparing the school budget	23.72	14.58	9.14
13 Selecting teachers to be hired in the school	23.61	11.74	11.87
14 Daily schedule in the whole school	36.61	24.52	12.09
15 Time of staff meetings	36.33	22.29	14.04
16 Unusual problems that affect the whole school	65.00	49.65	15.35
17 Assigning teachers to classes	31.67	14.39	17.28
18 Ways of reporting pupil progress to parents	75.06	55.77	19.29
19 Assigning pupils to classes	59.39	36.39	23.00
20 Curriculum	81.67	57.00	24.67
21 Content of staff meetings	51.78	27.10	24.68

TABLE 6.3   RELATIONSHIP BETWEEN PRINCIPAL INFLUENCE
MEASURES (Q9) AND LEAGUE MEMBERSHIP OVER SCHOOLS (N=49)

Median Splits on Measures of Principal Influence	League Membership		Total
	League	Non-League	
Personal			
High	11 (61%)	13 (42%)	24
Low	7 (39%)	18 (58%)	25
Competent			
High	11 (61%)	14 (45%)	25
Low	7 (39%)	17 (55%)	24
Reward			
High	11 (61%)	14 (45%)	25
Low	7 (39%)	17 (55%)	24
Punishment			
High	7 (39%)	17 (55%)	24
Low	11 (61%)	14 (45%)	25
Legitimate Right			
High	9 (50%)	16 (52%)	25
Low	9 (50%)	15 (48%)	24
Total	18	31	49

TABLE 6.4   INTERCORRELATIONS (RANK-ORDER) OF SELECTED
TEACHER BEHAVIORS* FOR LEAGUE (N=18) AND NON-LEAGUE
(N=31) SCHOOLS, BASED ON TEACHER MEAN SCORES

Selected Behaviors	2	3	4	5
League				
1 Disengagement	.18	−.47	−.03	−.46
2 Hindrance	−	−.38	.12	.17
3 Esprit		−	.51	.69
4 Intimacy			−	.29
5 CRITERIA: Teachers				−
Non-League				
1 Disengagement	.27	−.89	−.60	−.36
2 Hindrance	−	−.32	−.60	−.39
3 Esprit		−	.74	.42
4 Intimacy			−	.55
5 CRITERIA: Teachers				−

* Selected behaviors include OCDQ Teacher Scales (Q7) and CRITERIA Teacher Scale (Q2).

TABLE 6.5 INTERCORRELATIONS (RANK-ORDER) BETWEEN SELECTED PRINCIPAL AND TEACHER BEHAVIORS FOR LEAGUE (N=18) AND NON-LEAGUE (N=31) SCHOOLS, BASED ON TEACHER MEAN SCORES

	Teacher Behaviors†				
Principal Behaviors*	Disengage-ment	Hindrance	Esprit	Intimacy	CRITERIA: Teachers
League:					
1 Aloofness	−.23	−.13	.00	.02	.03
2 Production Emphasis	.21	−.14	−.20	−.22	−.19
3 Thrust	−.26	−.06	.29	.24	.54
4 Confidence	−.18	−.40	.23	.15	.48
5 CRITERIA: Principal	−.23	−.10	.41	.24	.76
6 CRITERIA: Meetings	−.43	−.36	.60	.42	.52
Non-League:					
1 Aloofness	−.48	−.24	.59	.56	.52
2 Production Emphasis	.12	.42	.00	−.17	−.26
3 Thrust	−.26	−.19	.40	.42	.32
4 Confidence	−.05	−.30	.29	.41	.45
5 CRITERIA: Principal	−.30	−.56	.55	.67	.59
6 CRITERIA: Meetings	−.24	−.35	.31	.35	.67

* Selected principal behaviors include principal scales of OCDQ (Q7) and CRITERIA (Q2).
† Selected teacher behaviors include teacher scales of OCDQ (Q7) and CRITERIA (Q2).

TABLE 6.6   RANK-ORDER INTERCORRELATIONS AMONG OCDQ
(Q7) SCALE SCORES OVER THE LEAGUE SCHOOLS (N=18)
FOR THE YEARS 1967, 1969, AND 1971

OCDQ Scales	1	2	3	4	5	6	7	8
1967								
1 Disengagement	−							
2 Hindrance	.52	−						
3 Esprit	−.81	−.57	−					
4 Intimacy	−.42	−.38	.40	−				
5 Aloofness	−.34	−.56	.38	.08	−			
6 Production								
Emphasis	.42	.29	−.55	−.32	.02	−		
7 Thrust	−.49	−.43	.71	.27	.30	.70	−	
8 Consideration	−.31	−.62	.59	.39	.42	−.50	.80	−
1969								
1 Disengagement	−							
2 Hindrance	.41	−						
3 Esprit	−.49	−.42	−					
4 Intimacy	.11	−.04	.52	−				
5 Aloofness	−.39	−.44	.02	−.31	−			
6 Production								
Emphasis	.30	.21	−.55	−.40	.28	−		
7 Thrust	−.28	−.28	.27	−.10	.20	−.32	−	
8 Consideration	−.28	−.45	.47	.29	.01	−.26	.65	−
1971								
1 Disengagement	−							
2 Hindrance	.18	−						
3 Esprit	−.47	−.38	−					
4 Intimacy	−.03	.12	.51	−				
5 Aloofness	−.23	−.13	.00	.02	−			
6 Production								
Emphasis	.21	−.14	−.20	−.22	.34	−		
7 Thrust	−.26	−.06	.29	.24	.32	−.11	−	
8 Consideration	−.18	−.40	.23	.15	.22	−.01	.76	−

DATA TABLES—CHAPTER 7

TABLE 7.1   INTERCORRELATIONS (OVER SCHOOLS) BETWEEN BASIC DDAE SCORE AND OTHER INDICES OF THE DDAE PROCESS (Q1) FOR THE LEAGUE (N=18) AND COMPARISON (N=18) SCHOOLS

	CRITERIA (Q2)	Teacher Interview DDAE Rating	Staff Meeting DDAE Rating	Observation, Percent Participation
League	.26	.02	.10	.28
Comparison	.70	.34	Data Not Collected	

TABLE 7.2   INTERCORRELATIONS (OVER SCHOOLS) BETWEEN BASIC DDAE SCORE (Q1) AND SELECTED TEACHER CHARACTERISTICS (Q3) FOR THE LEAGUE (N=18) AND COMPARISON (N=18) SCHOOLS

	Age	Years of Teaching Experience: Total	Years of Teaching Experience: Present School
League	−.08	−.09	−.07
Comparison	−.42	−.24	−.45

TABLE 7.3   RELATIONSHIP BETWEEN FORMAL TEACHING ARRANGEMENT AND LEAGUE MEMBERSHIP

Dominant Formal Teaching Arrangement	League Membership		Total	Percent
	League	Non-League		
Cooperative	6 (33%)	9 (29%)	15	31
Mixed	5 (28%)	3 (10%)	8	16
Self-Contained	7 (39%)	19 (61%)	26	53
Total	18	31	49	
Percent	37	63		100

TABLE 7.4   RELATIONSHIP BETWEEN FORMAL TEACHING
ARRANGEMENT FOR THE LEAGUE (N=18) SCHOOLS
IN 1967 AND 1971

	Dominant Formal Teaching Arrangement				
	1971				
1967	Cooperative	Mixed	Self-Contained	Total	Percent
Cooperative	1 (17%)	1 (20%)	0 (0%)	2	11
Mixed	0 (0%)	0 (0%)	0 (0%)	0	0
Self-Contained	5 (83%)	4 (80%)	7 (100%)	16	89
Total	6	5	7	18	
Percent	33	28	39		100

TABLE 7.5   RELATIONSHIP BETWEEN LEAGUE MEMBERSHIP, FORMAL
TEACHING ARRANGEMENT, AND TEACHER POWER (Q6)

Dominant Formal Teaching Arrangement	League	Non-League
Cooperative	12.2 (N=6)	10.2 (N=9)
Mixed	12.2 (N=5)	9.6 (N=3)
Self-Contained	11.0 (N=7)	8.7 (N=19)

(Cell entries are the means of school mean Teacher Power Scores.)

TABLE 7.6   RELATIONSHIP OF SCHOOL CLIMATE ADJECTIVE LIST
(Q8) AND LEAGUE MEMBERSHIP

Median Split on Climate Score	League Membership		Total	Percent
	League	Non-League		
High	13 (72%)	12 (39%)	25	51
Low	5 (28%)	19 (61%)	24	49
Total	18	31	49	
Percent	37	63		100

TABLE 7.7   DIFFERENCES BETWEEN LEAGUE (N=18) AND NON-LEAGUE (N=31) ON STAFF PERCEPTION OF MAJOR PROBLEM AREAS (Q10)

Problem Categories*	Mean Percentage of Teachers Indicating Given Problem Areas		Difference
	League	Non-League	
Student Characteristics:			
1 Discipline	26.1	40.1	14.0
2 Ethnicity/Language†	8.7	3.9	4.8
3 Attitudes	14.4	16.5	2.1
External Problems:			
4 Community	9.1	13.5	4.4
6 Facilities/Resources	57.6	66.5	8.9
7 Outside Constraints	46.3	33.6	12.7
Internal Problems:			
5 Community Public Relations	10.0	8.1	1.9
8 Administration	25.8	19.0	6.8
9 Curriculum/Instruction/ Organization	55.4	52.4	3.0
10 Teacher Cohesiveness	28.5	25.5	3.0
11 Goals	9.6	3.1	6.5
12 Staff Orientation	26.0	23.0	3.0

* See Q10 for detailed description of these twelve problem areas.
† Several of the schools which indicated problems in this category were in districts with new bussing policies.

TABLE 7.8 RELATIONSHIP BETWEEN AGREEMENT AMONG TEACHERS WITHIN SCHOOLS IN DESCRIBING SELECTED FEATURES OF SCHOOL ORGANIZATION AND LEAGUE MEMBERSHIP

Median Split on Agreement Scores* for Selected Measures	League Membership	
	League	Non-League
OCDQ (Q7): Disengagement		
High	6 (33%)	12 (67%)
Low	12 (67%)	6 (33%)
OCDQ: Hindrance		
High	8 (44%)	10 (56%)
Low	10 (56%)	8 (44%)
OCDQ: Esprit		
High	6 (33%)	12 (67%)
Low	12 (67%)	6 (33%)
OCDQ: Intimacy		
High	6 (33%)	12 (67%)
Low	12 (67%)	6 (33%)
OCDQ: Aloofness		
High	10 (56%)	8 (44%)
Low	8 (44%)	10 (56%)
OCDQ: Production Emphasis		
High	7 (39%)	11 (61%)
Low	11 (61%)	7 (39%)
OCDQ: Thrust		
High	7 (39%)	11 (61%)
Low	11 (61%)	7 (39%)
OCDQ: Consideration		
High	7 (39%)	11 (61%)
Low	11 (61%)	7 (39%)
Teacher Power (Q6)		
High	9 (50%)	15 (48%)
Low	9 (50%)	16 (52%)
CRITERIA (Q2): Meetings		
High	6 (33%)	18 (60%)
Low	12 (67%)	12 (40%)
CRITERIA: Principal		
High	4 (22%)	20 (64%)
Low	14 (78%)	11 (36%)
CRITERIA: Teachers		
High	6 (33%)	18 (58%)
Low	12 (67%)	13 (42%)
Climate Adjectives (Q8)		
High	7 (39%)	17 (55%)
Low	11 (61%)	14 (45%)

* Teacher agreement scores for each school were defined as the variance (or standard deviation) of the teacher scores for each selected variable. Low variance indicates a greater degree of agreement among teachers.

TABLE 7.9   CORRELATIONS OF SCHOOL CLIMATE ADJECTIVE LIST (Q8) WITH TEACHER AGREEMENT ON SELECTED SCHOOL ORGANIZATION CHARACTERISTICS FOR LEAGUE (N=18) AND NON-LEAGUE (N=31) SCHOOLS*

Selected Measures	League	Non-League
OCDQ:		
Disengagement	−.01	−.62
Hindrance	.19	−.33
Esprit	.05	−.61
Intimacy	.67	.21
Aloofness	.68	−.49
Production Emphasis	−.40	−.12
Thrust	.20	−.23
Consideration	.58	−.29
Teacher Power	−.07	−.25
CRITERIA:		
Meetings	−.43	−.67
Principal	−.31	−.49
Teachers	.20	−.31
Climate	−.30	−.53

* For each organizational characteristic, the correlation is between school *means* on Adjective List and school *variances* on the selected measure.

DATA TABLES—CHAPTER 8

TABLE 8.1   RELATIONSHIP BETWEEN EDUCATIONAL BELIEFS (Q11) AND LEAGUE MEMBERSHIP

Median Split on Educational Beliefs	League Membership	
	League	Non-League
Pupil Participation		
High (Traditional)	4 (22%)	20 (65%)
Low (Nontraditional)	14 (78%)	11 (35%)
Discipline and Control		
High (Traditional)	5 (28%)	20 (65%)
Low (Nontraditional)	13 (72%)	11 (35%)
Instruction Goals		
High (Traditional)	7 (39%)	18 (58%)
Low (Nontraditional)	11 (61%)	13 (42%)

TABLE 8.2   RELATIONSHIP BETWEEN LEAGUE MEMBERSHIP AND
AGE, TEACHING EXPERIENCE, AND TENURE IN PRESENT
SCHOOL FOR TEACHERS

Category Splits on Teacher Characteristics	League Membership	
	League	Non-League
Age		
40 years	177 (41%)	236 (39%)
30–39 years	120 (28%)	140 (23%)
29 years	131 (31%)	237 (39%)
Teaching Experience: Total		
15 years	113 (25%)	177 (27%)
5–14 years	201 (45%)	260 (39%)
4 years	138 (31%)	224 (34%)
Teaching Experience: Present School		
6 years	122 (27%)	187 (28%)
2–5 years	232 (51%)	306 (46%)
1 year	98 (22%)	169 (26%)

TABLE 8.3   RELATIONSHIP BETWEEN LEAGUE MEMBERSHIP IN
HIGH-LEVEL DDAE SCHOOL AND AGE, TEACHING
EXPERIENCE, AND TENURE IN PRESENT SCHOOL
FOR TEACHERS

Category Splits on Teacher Characteristics	League Membership	
	High DDAE League	High DDAE Non-League
Age		
40 years	44 (36%)	48 (32%)
30–39 years	34 (27%)	29 (20%)
29 years	46 (37%)	71 (48%)
Teaching Experience: Total		
15 years	32 (24%)	37 (23%)
5–14 years	52 (40%)	60 (37%)
4 years	47 (36%)	65 (40%)
Teaching Experience: Present School		
6 years	21 (16%)	32 (20%)
2–5 years	90 (69%)	66 (41%)
1 year	20 (15%)	64 (40%)

TABLE 8.4   RELATIONSHIP BETWEEN LEAGUE MEMBERSHIP,
LENGTH OF TENURE IN PRESENT SCHOOL, AND EDUCATIONAL
BELIEFS (Q11) FOR TEACHERS FROM HIGH AND LOW
DDAE LEVEL SCHOOLS

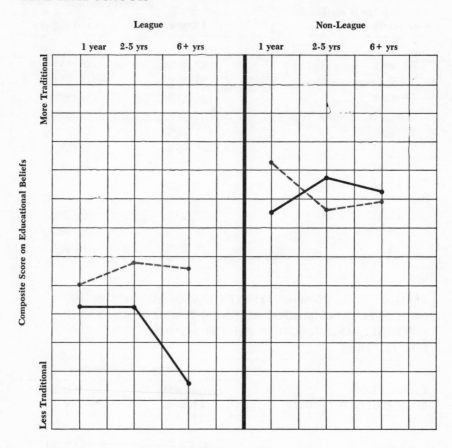

High DDAE ▬▬▬▬▬▬

Low DDAE ▬ ▬ ▬ ▬ ▬ ▬

TABLE 8.5 RELATIONSHIP BETWEEN LEAGUE MEMBERSHIP, LENGTH OF TENURE IN PRESENT SCHOOL, AND TEACHER POWER AS PERCEIVED BY TEACHERS FROM HIGH AND LOW DDAE LEVEL SCHOOLS

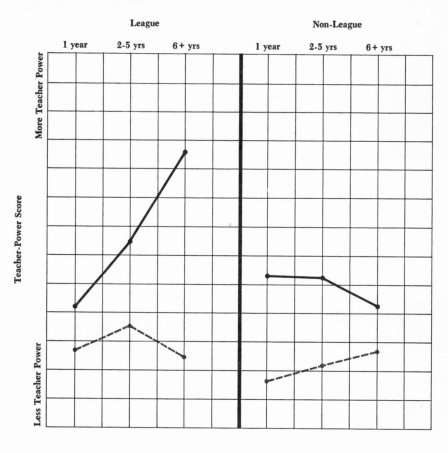

High DDAE ━━━━━━━

Low DDAE ━ ━ ━ ━ ━ ━ ━

INDEX